SIXTY PLUS IN CALIFORNIA

Making the Most of Benefits and Services for Seniors

Portions of this book are based on a 1979 publication, *Rights of the Elderly & Retired. Sixty Plus in California* is an expansion and thorough update of the original book and also contains new, detailed information on many state, community, and privately sponsored benefits and services for California seniors.

Dedicated to
the late Margaret Reynolds Colman
— who never knew what being old means.

SIXTY PLUS IN CALIFORNIA

Making the Most of Benefits and Services for Seniors

William R. Wishard, LL.B.

and

Laurie Wishard, M.S.W.

cp

cragmont publications

SIXTY PLUS IN CALIFORNIA

Published by
Cragmont Publications
P.O. Box 77072
San Francisco, California 94107

Manufactured in the United States of America
First printing April, 1981

Editor: Diane Sipes
Research associate: Betty Wishard
Proofreader: Kathleen Hartley
Design consultant: Carolyn Bean
Associate publisher: Pauline McGuire
Publisher: Fred E. Felder
Typesetting: Medallion Graphics
Printing & binding: George Banta Company, Inc.

Library of Congress Cataloging in Publication Data

Wishard, William R., 1930-
Sixty plus in California.

Includes index.
1. Aged—Services for—California. 2. Social security—California. 3. Medicare—California.
I. Wishard, Laurie, 1948- II. Title.
HV1468.C2W58 362.6'09794 81-2823
ISBN 0-89666-013-3 AACR2
ISBN 0-89666-014-1 (pbk.)

A Note to Readers

This publication is designed to provide accurate and authoritative information in regard to the subject matter covered. It is sold or given with the understanding that the publisher and those who distribute the book are not engaged in rendering legal or other professional service. If legal advice or other expert assistance is required, the services of a competent professional person should be sought.

— Based on a Declaration of Principles jointly adopted by a Committee of the American Bar Association and a Committee of Publishers and Associations

The authors have researched and written this book with great care in order to provide useful and accurate information on benefits and services for California seniors. Readers should be aware, however, that laws change from time to time and are subject to various interpretations. Accordingly, *Sixty Plus in California* is to be used with the understanding that the authors, the publisher, and those who distribute the book make no guarantees concerning its content and the use to which it is put.

Keeping Up to Date

Laws and regulations, by their very nature, change from time to time. Keeping track of these changes is a difficult and time-consuming task, even for attorneys and other professionals.

In order to keep readers informed about changes in the benefits and services available to seniors, the publisher will periodically issue update supplements at a nominal charge. See page 287 at the back of this book for more details.

Acknowledgments

We are indebted to the numerous local, state, and federal agencies for their assistance in providing resource material and answering our many questions.

Volunteers and employees of the local agencies that provide direct services to seniors deserve special acknowledgment. Their dedication and enthusiasm was a breath of fresh air. Almost without exception, they were conscientious, knowledgeable, and willingly provided us with much of the practical information we needed to write this book.

Contents

Introduction

As late as 1941, hot dogs were a nickel, movies were a quarter, and apartments rented for $50 a month. James Hilton's new best-selling novel, *Lost Horizons,* was available for 25 cents.

Today's seniors remember those times. They also remember — and lived through — the Great Depression. Fifteen million of them were jobless, and some killed themselves over the shame of accepting federal "relief" to keep their families alive. Most listened with hope and skepticism in 1937 to the promise that the new Social Security system would assure them of "a comfortable old age" if they participated.

After World War II, they raised families and built schools, started new industries, paid taxes, and saved for a rainy day. Self-sufficiency, independence, and productivity were still esteemed as virtues.

And today? The lives of every Californian — including the seniors — are inextricably intertwined with the bureaucracies in Washington and Sacramento. Self-sufficiency, under the impact of inflation, is a luxury very few people on a fixed income can afford. The great majority of our seniors depend on Social Security benefits as their primary source of income, and few can afford adequate health care or decent housing without federal or state help.

For better or for worse, then, most of our seniors are dependent for their survival on legislators, administrators, and the complex laws and regulations they issue.

In 1981, a new administration took office, announcing that inflation must be reversed if we are to survive economically. Public benefit programs are and will continue to be under severe scrutiny.

To survive, every program must prove its basic worth and effectiveness to our society as a whole. Along with other special interest groups, seniors will undoubtedly defend their programs and benefit as best they can. To do this, you must understand how the system works. This book is intended to help you understand that.

Who Is a Senior?

Nobody really knows. Some of us are young at 70; others are old at 30. A student of human nature once noted that anybody's definition of old age is "my age plus 20 years." In any event, for the purposes of this book seniors are persons who are entitled to *additional* benefits because of their age.

Additional — because whether you are 21 or 81 you are still entitled to your full rights as a person. Two examples: regardless of your age, you are protected against discrimination based on age in housing, employment, and credit. And, if you meet the requirements, you are entitled to be admitted to a university and to compete with other students for loans.

When Do You Become a Senior? For some purposes, the answer is around age 55, when a few retirement and job benefits become available to you. At age 60 you have achieved "junior" status as a senior, and you can share in the benefits provided by the Older Americans' Act.

You become a provisional senior at age 62, when you become eligible for Social Security retirement benefits. And at age 65 you are a full-fledged, Medicare-card-carrying senior. You then meet the criteria for almost every senior benefit provided by federal, state, and county law.

Are Seniors Different? Do birds fly and fish swim? Seriously, when a person is classified by age, he or she is often expected to fit the stereotype of others of that age.

We all know that this is not true. Our president is a senior. So is the alcoholic you perhaps have seen in your neighborhood who is a danger to himself and his family. Golda Meier and Senator Margaret Chase Smith were seniors when they were at the height of their careers. So are the senile, quarrelsome people some of us know who make life impossible for themselves and their loved ones.

Even within the age group we call seniors, there are persons of 65 and persons of 95, a difference of 30 years. Small wonder that seniors have very different needs, interests, and capabilities.

Kinds of Major Benefits

There are three kinds of major benefits available to California seniors. They are based on:

- age
- age plus need
- age plus working record

The first kind, based on age, is available to you solely because you are a given age. These benefits include access to senior centers and nutrition programs, certain tax deductions, and, to some extent, Medicare.

The second kind, based on age plus need, is available to you at a certain age only if you are needy. These include SSI payments and Medi-Cal.

The third kind, based on age plus a working record, is your Social Security benefits, which are "earned." These benefits are available to a worker of a certain age (or his or her dependents or survivors) because he or she has worked for a given period of time and contributed to the Social Security system.

If you are eligible for earned or "entitlement" benefits, your financial worth does not affect your eligibility for the benefits. For example:

Mrs. Libby is wealthy and receives a monthly income of $5,000 from stock and bond dividends. She is still entitled to her monthly Social Security retirement check of $417.

Mr. Thompson has no income at all from any outside source other than Social Security. He too receives a monthly retirement check of $417.

Of course, Mr. Thompson might be eligible for need benefits such as SSI and Medi-Cal, whereas Mrs. Libby would not. Both, however, are eligible for Medicare provided they are 65 or older.

You might wonder why it is important to understand the differences between the major senior benefits. The answer is that the federal and state governments have the power to reduce or eliminate taxpayer-supported need benefits at will, provided the legislative bodies agree, whereas an earned benefit, such as Social Security retirement, cannot be eliminated, because you have paid into it. (Even these benefits, however, may be changed with regard to the amount payable.)

Making the Benefit System Work for You

The seniors who receive the most benefits are those who work the hardest at understanding their rights and benefits as seniors. They understand the basic senior benefits and programs, and they make sure they are aware of new ones that become available. They persevere, pay attention to detail, and know how to best present their individual situation to receive the largest benefits.

Fortunately for senior Californians, the benefit system has and is being simplified. That may be a lot to ask you to believe, but it's true. Social Security offices are now equipped with computers and can readily produce your entire working record upon request. Their telephone service is also efficient and informed.

An effort is being made to centralize information about all the senior benefits and programs available in senior centers in each area of the state. And each area has — or will soon have — an Information and Referral Service where you can get answers to any question you may have.

To keep abreast of the benefits to which you are entitled, you must educate yourself about the system and keep current with the changes in it. Senior newsletters and similar publications can help you to do this. For example, many low-income seniors were eligible for a one-time-only utility rebate in January 1981. Although this benefit was not highly publicized, it was noted in many newsletters for seniors.

Subscribe to state as well as local newsletters. A good example of the former is ERA, published by the

California State Department on Aging
918 J Street
Sacramento, CA 95814

It is available on request, free of charge. Why not subscribe today? Local senior newsletters are available at your nearest senior center or local Area Agency on Aging (see Appendix).

If you are Spanish-speaking, you can get publications for seniors, written in Spanish, by writing to the State Department of Aging at the address given above.

Dealing with Public Agencies

Whenever you have any contact with an agency that receives public funding, you have many legal rights. These rights include the right not to be discriminated against on the basis of your race, religion, national origin, sex, or *age*. Furthermore, you must be treated with respect; programs must be explained to you, and, if you are denied benefits, you must be given a reason. Most agencies have standardized procedures that they are required to follow.

When dealing with any agency, you should be aware of the following:

- Don't assume the agency employees will be competent. Call back to check on the status of your situation.
- Always ask for names. Write down important names, dates, and facts.
- Don't assume the regulations are fair or based on common sense. They are often just "the rules of the game."
- Try to pin down responsibility. Ask a specific person to identify himself or herself before giving you an answer or solving your problem.
- Don't be afraid to exercise your legal rights. Your future benefits are unlikely to be affected by the fact that you complained, appealed, or sought legal assistance.

A state law called the Information Practices Act of 1977 established the Office of Information Practices to assure that state agencies and departments comply with the law. The personnel at this office will help you identify what records may contain relevant information about you, and they will also help you obtain these records, as well as amend the records when they are wrong.

This office also protects you against unauthorized disclosure of certain information under your right to privacy. For further information on protection or disclosure of such information, contact the

Office of Information Practices
801 Capitol Mall
Sacramento, CA 95814

Telephone toll-free, (800) 952-5562.

Whatever Else — Stay in Touch

Isolation and loneliness are among the most severe problems facing seniors. When anyone is cut off from the warmth and stimulation of human contact, problems that otherwise might easily be solved become nightmares. Physical and mental health decline, as does one's general interest in life.

It is true that our society generally tends to isolate and ignore its older citizens. Probably many seniors were guilty of the same thing when they were younger. Still, you *can* stay in touch with friends and family, other seniors, and the community, even though this may be difficult and require extra energy on your part. But it is worth the effort. The problems of seniors are part of the national consciousness, and there is much more help available now than there was years ago.

Remember, it took a lot of effort by a lot of seniors to get this far. And you are one of the survivors! Surviving isn't easy, but worrying about it need not consume your whole life. We hope that this book will help you make the most of senior benefits and services so that you can better enjoy your years ahead as a senior in California.

PART I
SOCIAL SECURITY BENEFITS

1
Eligibility and General Procedures

Almost all people over age 62 are entitled to Social Security, either from their own earnings as employees or self-employed persons, or as dependents of other people who were employed. Included in the latter group are wives who worked only as homemakers, divorced wives who were married for ten years or longer, and parents who were dependent on a son or daughter prior to their retirement.

Aside from private income, Social Security benefits are by far the major source of income for seniors. One out of every seven persons in the United States receives a Social Security check each month. In addition, there are various federal and state programs available when Social Security and private income fail to meet the basic needs of food, housing, clothing and medical care.

You can obtain information regarding Social Security and other available resources from the federal and state agencies administering the various programs. Securing this information, however, involves correspondence, which many people find time-consuming, difficult, and sometimes frustrating.

This introductory chapter is intended to give you a broad overview of the various benefits available from the Social Security system, who is entitled to receive these benefits and in what amounts, and how to apply for and obtain one or more of them. In the rest of Part I, each of these benefits is explained in detail so that you can find specific answers to specific problems.

Social Security: What Is It?

"Social Security" refers to a variety of federal income programs that are administered by the Social Security Administration under the Department of Health and Human Services. Most commonly, Social Security refers to those federal programs which provide retirement, dependents' and survivors', and disability benefits to eligible persons. The money for these programs comes from employer-employee Social Security taxes, which employed people have had deducted from their wages each pay period.

Other benefit programs are administered by the Social Security Administration but are not Social Security programs. Among these are Supplemental Security Income — commonly called SSI — and Medicare and (indirectly) Medi-Cal.

Recently the Social Security laws have been "de-sexed." That is, any laws that gave particular benefits to men or women on the basis of sex, as in the case of widows and widowers, have been changed to extend these benefits or rights to the other sex also.

Social Security and SSI: The Differences Seniors who are eligible have a *right* to Social Security benefits such as retirement, dependents' or survivors', or disability payments. That is, eligible people will have earned those benefits. No one in Washington or anywhere else has the right to decide whether anyone deserves them. If you are eligible, you are entitled to retirement benefits, for example, even though you may have a large income from savings accounts and investments. Earnings from a job, however, can reduce the amount of your Social Security retirement check. (See Chapter Two.)

SSI benefits are paid to the same kinds of people — seniors, the disabled, and the blind — but only if they are needy and have little or no other income or resources. As the name of these benefits implies, SSI monthly checks are *supplementary* income to such persons. Unlike Social Security benefits, which are earned, SSI benefits are unearned in the sense that they are not based on the person's contributions to the Social Security system.

SSI benefits are the modern version of the former Old Age Assistance benefit program, which was administered by each state. Now SSI payments come to eligible persons in the form of a "gold check" from the federal government each month, and they include money provided by the state. These benefits, and how to obtain them, are discussed in detail in Chapter Five.

Obtaining More Than One Benefit It is quite common for older people to qualify for more than one benefit under the federal income programs. For example, seniors who are receiving retirement benefits at age 66 may become disabled at age 67. In such cases, they may be eligible for both retirement and disability benefits. But unfortunately they can't collect both. The general rule is that a person who is eligible for more than one Social Security benefit will be paid the higher of the two — but not both.

But, as stated previously, SSI payments are supplemental; that is, they are almost always paid in addition to other basic Social Security benefits, depending on the person's need. For example, in California your SSI payment can be $402 or more a month if you are disabled or age 65 or above, and over $450 if you are a senior and blind.

Recent Changes in the Social Security Laws There are many important changes in the Social Security laws, some of which will be effective in 1981. In the following chapters, each change that affects your rights as a senior Californian is discussed.

In addition, the Reagan administration is studying a number of proposals aimed at reducing the cost of Social Security coverage. One proposal is to bring federal employees into the system, and another is to change the formula for calculating benefits. Some of these suggestions will no doubt be opposed by many seniors' lobbies, both in Sacramento and Washington.

Miscellaneous Programs Two other programs administered by the Social Security Administration that may be of interest to you are the Aid to Families with Dependent Children (AFDC), which is administered by the state and counties, and the Indo-Chinese Refugee Assistance Program, which provides benefits to refugees until they become self-sufficient. This second program is administered jointly by the state and the federal government. If you are a senior who wants further information about either of these programs, contact your county welfare office or Social Security office for assistance.

Applying for Benefits

The Social Security Administration maintains a district office in every large city in the state and in each county. In the largest cities, such as Los Angeles and San Francisco, the district offices have several branch offices conveniently located in various neighborhoods. If you have a question or are seeking general information about Social Security or SSI benefits, you should start at the office nearest your home. The telephone numbers of the offices, together with the addresses, are listed in the white pages of the telephone directory under "United States Government, Social Security." The large offices also list a general information telephone number.

If you prefer, you may write to the main Social Security office at:

Social Security Administration
Office of Public Inquiries
6401 Security Boulevard
Baltimore, Maryland 21235

When to Contact the Social Security Office You should get in touch with your nearest Social Security office when:

- you are unable to work because of an illness or injury that will probably last one year or longer
- you are 62 years or older and plan to retire
- you are within two or three months of 65 even if you don't plan to retire
- someone in your family dies or is disabled

Be sure to call, visit, or write your Social Security office *before* you reach 65, not only to establish your eligibility for benefits like retirement payments, but also to apply for Medicare, which is available whether or not you retire at 65.

Warning: A long delay in applying for monthly benefits may cause you to lose some benefits, since back payments can be made for no more than twelve months.

Papers to Have with You When you apply for any Social Security benefit, you should have with you:

- your own Social Security card or a record of your Social Security number — if you are claiming benefits on another person's working record, such as on that of your wife or husband, you will need that person's card or number

- a birth or baptismal certificate to prove your age — if you have neither, a census record will be accepted. You can get census records by writing the U.S. Commerce Dept., Bureau of Census, and requesting an "Application for Search of Census Records" (the fee is $8.00)
- if you have neither a birth or baptismal certificate nor a census record, you may submit at least three of the following four papers: school records, marriage certificate, family Bible, or a life insurance policy
- your marriage certificate, if applying for dependents or survivors benefits (see below)
- your children's birth certificates, if you are applying on their behalf
- your W-2 form (withholding statement) if you worked in the previous year
- a copy of your federal income tax return for the prior year if you were self-employed

If you are applying for Social Security benefits as a dependent parent whose major support came from a son or daughter who has died, you will need proof that you were dependent for your support on the deceased person. This might include:

- copies of the deceased person's federal and state income tax returns showing such dependent status
- copies of receipts, checks, paid bills, etc., showing expenditures by the deceased person
- other papers requested by the Social Security employee

Ordinarily, you must prove to the Social Security office that you are a dependent parent within *two years* after your son or daughter dies or two years after he or she applied for Social Security benefits. The same is true if you are applying for a lump sum death payment. If you can't remember when your son or daughter applied for cash benefits, if he or she did, call or write the Social Security office nearest you. If the deceased person did apply, they'll give you the date.

Note: If a worker in your family dies, don't delay in obtaining this information — whether the deceased worker lived with you or not.

The papers you will need if you are claiming Social Security benefits as a disabled person are discussed in Chapter Three.

Depending on the type of claim you are making, you may not have all of the necessary papers readily available. If not, don't delay in making your claim. Processing these claims takes time anyway, and the people in the Social Security office will go ahead and start the necessary paperwork while you collect the rest of the required papers.

Going to the Office It is preferable to file your Social Security claims in person. If you cannot get to the nearest Social Security office on your own, have someone drive you or take public transportation — as difficult as that might be.

You *can* call in your claim but it takes several more weeks to process it. You can also call for and receive the necessary papers by mail and fill them out at home. However, the chances are that you will not completely understand some of the questions, give incorrect answers, and have to do it all over again anyway.

Unfortunately, you cannot make an appointment but must take your chances as to how crowded the office will be. Most Social Security offices open at 9:00 a.m. and are open until 4:00 p.m. The best time of the day to go, if you can, is as close to opening time as you can make it. Also, avoid the early parts of each month, if possible. Toward the end of the month, the offices will be less crowded.

Save a Trip — Telephone Social Security has a special telephone number that you can call with any questions about your benefits or eligibility. This service is called "Teleservice," and the number is listed in your telephone directory under "Social Security Administration."

You can use Teleservice to:

- apply for Social Security or SSI benefits
- apply for Medicare or get help in filling out Medicare forms
- find out if a particular physician or hospital participates in Medicare
- change your name, address, or marital status
- make reports that may change your benefits (such as starting or stopping work)
- report a lost or stolen check

- get help in arranging for direct deposit of your check
- get an estimate of your monthly benefits
- get a statement of your earnings record
- get help in requesting a review (appeal) of a decision made on your claim

When you call Social Security about any of these matters, you will be asked to give the Social Security number that appears on your Social Security check or, where necessary, your Medicare number.

The best time to make Teleservice inquiries is after the middle of the month. This is because benefit checks are delivered during the first week of each month and the phone lines are usually tied up at that time. All Social Security offices offer this Teleservice Monday through Friday, and some also have the service in operation evenings and Saturday.

If you are calling on behalf of a senior who cannot visit the office in person to apply for benefits, you will need at least the following information:

- the senior's Social Security number
- his or her date of birth
- his or her residence address and phone number
- your relationship to the person
- some facts as to why he or she cannot personally appear and make the claim

Further information, as needed, will be requested by the person you contact at the Social Security office.

Your Claim At the Social Security office you will be assigned a service worker who will handle your claim, give you the proper forms, and start processing the information. You will be given a claim number. After your first visit, always use this claim number when you contact the office for any reason.

The service worker assigned to you will process your papers and send them in to the payment center. Generally, you should receive your first check about six to eight weeks after you make your claim.

Even though it may be difficult, be patient when making your claim. The people at Social Security offices throughout the country are generally courteous, helpful, and do their best under trying conditions. There is no need to be servile — but there also is no need to treat the office personnel as your enemies. In short, relax and keep your sense of humor.

Substitute or Representative Payee

In the case of seniors or disabled persons who are unable to care for themselves, family members who provide care for them may ask to be substituted as the payee for their Social Security checks.

If you make this request, the Social Security employee will require you to sign an affidavit, which is a legally binding form signed under oath. The affidavit states that you, the family member, are willing and able to care for the senior or disabled person and will use the monthly check(s) for his or her benefit. The family member must also produce some medical proof that the person is unable to manage his or her own affairs — usually statements from family doctors or the physician who has been providing treatment.

The Social Security office checks these affidavits and medical documents carefully — as they should. Furthermore, they will require the substitute payee to account now and then for the benefits. "Account" means simply to offer some financial statements to them, on occasion, showing how and where the money was spent.

A substitute or representative payee is not authorized to use another person's income payments to pay old bills — that is, bills incurred before the substitution. On the other hand, the substitute payee may use this income to make mortgage payments on the senior's house or to pay taxes and insurance premiums. If you are a substitute payee and have some doubts about your obligations, call Teleservice and inquire or, if you wish, ask at your nearest Social Security office for the pamphlet entitled "Your Duties as a Representative Payee."

Alternatively, some family member may have already gone to court and had himself or herself appointed as guardian or conservator of the senior. If that has been done, then the guardian or conservator makes application for Social Security benefits in that capacity and the Social Security people accept that fact without further question.

Receiving Your Monthly Check

Your Social Security and/or SSI payment should arrive in the mail from the federal government on about the same date near the beginning of each month. SSI checks are gold colored. If your check does not arrive on the usual date, wait a few days before you call your Social Security office.

Cashing Checks You cannot make out your monthly Social Security or SSI check to someone else, by endorsement, to pay a bill. You must cash it yourself, and you should wait until you are in the presence of the person who will cash it before you endorse it. If you sign your check and lose it, it may be cashed by anyone who finds it.

Automatic Bank Deposit If you desire, your monthly check can be deposited directly in your checking or savings account in a bank or savings and loan, a credit association, or some similar financial institution. This saves many people an immense amount of trouble and bookkeeping and also eliminates the possibility of losing or misplacing the check.

If you have no such account at present, you should consider opening one. In addition to the safeguards, you will generally receive credit for interest on the amount of the check when it is credited to your deposit.

The form used for automatic bank deposits of federal benefits that are paid regularly is called Form "SF 1199." You obtain this form at the bank where the deposits are to be made, and personnel at the bank will help you fill out the form. It is then mailed by the bank to the Social Security office or other offices that issue the benefits.

Note: Automatic deposits are not limited to Social Security benefits. You may also deposit, through this method, other federal benefits that are paid on a regular basis, such as pension, retirement, and disability checks.

Completion of this form only authorizes deposits into your account. Only you or your designated substitute can make withdrawals.

Returning Checks Sent in Error If you should receive a Social Security check or SSI check that is not due you, return it to the U.S. Treasury Department, Division of Disbursement. The return address of the Department is on the envelope it came in. You might also take it with you to the nearest Social Security office where they will give you a receipt for it.

Note: Social Security or SSI overpayments may be forgiven by the government, rather than recovered. If your local Social Security office notifies you that your Social Security benefits or SSI payments will be reduced because of overpayments, you have a right to apply for a waiver of recovery, as long as you did not cause the overpayment. Ask at the office for the proper form to request such a waiver.

Changing Your Name If you are receiving Social Security benefits or are eligible to receive them and will be changing your name (because of marriage, divorce, etc.), be sure to notify your Social Security office. You will also be required to show proof of your identity under both your old name and your new name. You can find out exactly what documents you will need by calling the Social Security Teleservice.

Appeals

If You Disagree with a Decision If your application for Social Security benefits or Supplemental Security Income (SSI) is denied or if a benefit you are already receiving is reduced or stopped, you have the right to appeal. For example, you may disagree with the Social Security office as to how many work credits you have earned when making a retirement benefit claim. Or, when making a claim for disability benefits, there may be a dispute about whether or not you are disabled and, if so, to what extent. Similarly, there may be differences of opinion about your need for SSI benefits in light of your circumstances.

Recommendation: If you think you are eligible for any Social Security benefit, always insist on filling out a written application and being given a written decision about your eligibility. Without something in writing, you have no basis for appeal.

Request for Reconsideration There are several steps to the procedure for appealing Social Security decisions. The first thing you must do is to ask the Social Security Administration to reconsider their decision. Obtain the necessary form, called a "Request for Reconsideration," at your local Social Security office, and fill it out.

As indicated on the form, state your reasons why you feel the original decision was not correct and attach to the form any additional evidence that may help you — copies of papers, doctor's reports, income statements, etc., that you did not file with your application. When the form is completed and signed, mail or take it in to the local Social Security office. (Keep a copy.)

Your claim is completely reviewed at the local Social Security office by someone who did not take part in the original decision, and you are then notified of the decision.

Next Steps If you disagree with the decision on your Request for Reconsideration, your next step is to ask for a hearing on your case by an administrative law judge of the Bureau of Hearings and Appeals. This must be done within 30 days after the decision on your Request for Reconsideration. Your Social Security office has the necessary forms for this procedure and will advise you of the steps to take, but you should seek a lawyer's help at this stage.

Assuming you are not satisfied with the hearing decision, you may request further review by the Appeals Council. This step requires a personal appearance by you, however, which may be difficult or impossible, since the Appeals Council hears cases in only five cities throughout the country.

Finally, you have the right to appeal the decision to a federal court. Again, these steps should not be taken without legal representation.

How Long Does an Appeal Take? The Social Security Administration must make a decision within ninety days after a blind person has requested a hearing. Other than that, there are no time limits within which they must decide an appeal. For a variety of reasons — primarily understaffing — there is a large backlog of hearing requests causing delays of six months or more before a hearing is actually held and another three to six months before a written decision is issued.

Is an Appeal a Waste of Time? *No.* Results of various studies show that at least *one half* of the cases that have hearings are decided in favor of the claimant. If you are truly dissatisfied with the disposition of your claim, go ahead and appeal it, but do it with the understanding that it may take a lot of time. Remember, though, that if the final decision *is* in your favor you will probably be awarded the correct amount as of the time you were entitled to it — you may receive a large check that makes your patience worthwhile.

Legal Representation A Social Security claimant has the *right* to be represented on his appeal by a person of his choice — a friend, a senior citizens' organization, or a lawyer. (For a discussion of how to find legal help, see Chapter Fourteen.)

The person or lawyer representing you on the appeal may charge a fee that will be paid by the Social Security Administration — up to a maximum. There are many skilled lawyers who are familiar with Social Security procedures and know how the "system" works. Contact one of them if you are involved in appealing a Social Security decision. Don't take a chance on appealing your own case!

2
Retirement Benefits

Nine out of ten workers in the United States contribute to Social Security. Under the present law, retirement benefit coverage includes most self-employed persons, the majority of state and local governmental employees, household and agricultural workers, members of the armed forces, and members of the clergy.

You will have earned Social Security retirement benefits if you have worked the required amount of time in your life and had Social Security retirement taxes deducted from your paycheck. Self-employed persons are also entitled to Social Security benefits if they meet the eligibility requirements. Important changes have been made recently in the laws governing your right to Social Security retirement benefits.

As noted in Chapter One, your right to retirement benefits does not depend on how wealthy you are (in contrast, for example, to Supplementary Security Income benefts [SSI]). But the amount of your retirement check may be reduced by what you earn each year after you start receiving these checks.

Monthly Social Security checks are also paid to certain dependents of workers who have earned retirement benefits. The rights of these persons are discussed in detail in Chapter Four. And if your monthly retirement check is insufficient to meet your basic needs, you may, in addition to that payment, receive a monthly SSI check.

Who Is Eligible?

Before you or your family can receive monthly cash benefits from the Social Security retirement fund, you must have been credited for a certain amount of work that was covered by Social Security. The exact amount of credit depends on your age.

Quarters of Coverage To be eligible for retirement benefits a person must have worked:

- forty quarters ("quarters" refers to quarters of years — forty quarters is ten years)

OR

- one quarter every calendar year after 1950

OR

- one quarter each year since the person's twenty-first birthday if that birthday was after 1950

OR

- when dependents or survivors benefits apply, the insured worker must have at least six quarters during the thirteen quarter period ending with the quarter in which he or she died or became entitled to retirement benefits (see Chapter Three).

Starting in 1978, employees and self-employed persons are credited with one quarter of coverage for each $250 of yearly earnings that are under Social Security. In other words, to be credited with one quarter you must have made at least $250 of covered yearly earnings. However, no more than four quarters a year can be credited to your retirement benefits.

All this means is that you cannot earn a lot of money in one or two years, for example, and ensure your retirement benefits. You still must be credited with forty quarters or one of the other alternative work records listed earlier.

Don't worry too much about figuring out the extent of your coverage — the Social Security people take the necessary figures from your work record and simply make a mathematical calculation, which is usually correct. Still, it doesn't hurt to know how it is done.

Reminder: Even though only $250, four times a year, can be credited to your retirement account, the *amount* of your check depends on your average earnings over a period of years.

Unfortunately, if you stopped working under Social Security before you earned enough quarters to become eligible for retirement benefits, you can't receive benefits. But, if you return to work covered by Social Security, your former work will be credited to make up the necessary quarters.

Veterans' Credits Veterans and their dependents are entitled to all the same Social Security benefits as other workers, provided they have the necessary work credits. Active duty or training for active duty counts for such credits. Service personnel and veterans also receive an extra $300 credit for each quarter in which they received any basic pay for active duty or training for active duty since 1956. In addition, Social Security credits of $160 a month may be granted to veterans who served after September 1, 1940, and before 1957 (even though deductions were not withheld from their paychecks).

Retirement at 65 or 62? You can retire at 65 years of age and be eligible for full retirement benefits, based on your earnings record, if you have fulfilled the necessary number of quarters. *Or,* you have the option of retiring at 62. If you retire at 62, however, your monthly cash benefits are reduced.

Table 2-1 shows you how the necessary credits are figured — in this case for a person who is retiring at 62 and is working right up to the time benefits are claimed (see the last item in "Quarters of Coverage"):

Table 2-1

If you reach 62 in	You need this many covered years
1981	7½
1982	7¾
1983	8
1987	9
1991 or later	10

Occupations Covered by Special Rules Special rules apply to some jobs and occupations. These are too numerous to discuss in detail here, but anyone affected by them can get the necessary information from the nearest Social Security office, which publishes, free of charge, leaflets containing the important rules that cover these occupations. The occupations include:

- housecleaners, gardeners, or babysitters
- students who are employed by their schools
- owners, operators, or workers on farms

- members of religious orders
- work from which cash tips are received
- employees of state or local government, non-profit organizations, or international organizations

Amount of Monthly Checks

For workers who reach 62, become disabled, or die *after 1978*, a new way of figuring benefits is in effect. The old method, used for workers who reached 62, became disabled, or died before 1979, used the actual dollar value of the worker's past earnings.

Under the new method, actual earnings for past years will be adjusted to reflect changes in average wages since 1951. These adjusted earnings will be averaged together and a formula applied to determine the benefit amount. To protect workers nearing retirement now, the law contains a guarantee for workers who reach 62 after 1978 and before 1984. Under this guarantee, both the old and new methods of figuring benefits will be used, and the worker will be paid the higher of the two calculations.

Taxability of Checks Social Security checks are not subject to federal or state income tax.

Where Husband and Wife Are Both Eligible When husband and wife are both eligible in their own right to receive checks, they do not receive two checks based on their individual earnings records. Instead, they receive a family benefit check, payable to both of them, which is the maximum they can receive. Unfortunately, this maximum amount is always smaller than the total they would be entitled to individually. Message? Marriage after retirement age can cost you money!

When You Qualify for Two Checks Seniors often qualify for retirement benefit checks on the basis of their own work record and earnings, and on the work record of someone else, generally a spouse. As stated previously, if you qualify for more than one Social Security check, your monthly check will be the larger of the two amounts.

When You Receive a Pension If you qualify for Social Security retirement benefits as a husband, wife, widow, or widower and, in addition, receive a pension based on your work in public employment not covered by Social Security, your monthly cash retirement Social Security benefits will be reduced. This rule, and exceptions to it, are discussed in detail in Chapter Four.

Lump Sum Death Payments In addition to monthly retirement benefits, there is a lump-sum payment of $255 made at a worker's death and on the death of a veteran. This is also discussed in Chapter Four.

Maximum Earnings Creditable The Social Security Administration has worked out maximum earnings per year that may be credited to your retirement account. They are:

1951-1954 — $ 3,600	1974 — $13,200	1980 — $25,900
1955-1958 — $ 4,200	1975 — $14,100	1981 — $29,700
1959-1965 — $ 4,800	1976 — $15,300	1982 — $32,100
1966-1967 — $ 6,600	1977 — $16,500	1983 — $34,500
1968-1971 — $ 7,800	1978 — $17,700	1984 — $36,900
1972 — $ 9,000	1979 — $22,900	1985 — $39,600
1973 — $10,800		

Many people think that if they've always earned the maximum amount covered they will get the highest benefits, but this isn't so, because the years when the limits were lower are counted in with the ones when the limits were higher to figure the yearly average earnings — which determines the amount of the monthly cash benefit.

Estimating Retirement Checks

The Social Security system has been largely computerized, so that your earnings record and the amount of your estimated retirement check can be obtained in minutes by Social Security personnel.

If you cannot get the estimate by telephone, simply ask the nearest Social Security office to send you a postcard form OAR-7004 (3-74), called "Request for Statement of Earnings." You should fill out the form and mail it in to the office from which you received it. This can save a lot of wear and tear on you.

The SSA started a pilot project in 1980 of sending out notices to workers spelling out how much they (or their survivors) would receive if they should become disabled, die, or retire.

Currently, the Social Security Adminstration is evaluating the project and deciding whether to adopt the program on a wider scale. If adopted, annual notices would be sent to workers informing them of their potential Social Security benefits.

Errors in Your Earnings Record On occasion, an employer supplies incorrect information to the government about Social Security deductions. This may substantially affect the employee's benefits. If you suspect this may have happened in your case, write your local Social Security office or the Social Security Administration, Baltimore, Maryland 21235 and request the form referred to earlier (Statement for Request of Earnings).

Check this statement against your records. If there is a discrepancy, request another form, called "Request for Correction of Earnings Record" (OAR-7008). Document the errors with your own earnings record (W-2 Forms, etc.), and submit the form together with your documentation to the Social Security office. You may be required to pay a $3 certification fee to correct the records, but it will be well worth it in most cases. It may be a good idea, if you are still working, to repeat this checking procedure every three or years to avoid the necessity of going way back into lost or misplaced records.

Some seniors may prefer making their own estimates of retirement checks, even though the procedure is very difficult. If you want to test your mathematical powers rather than trust the computer, the Social Security people issue a pamphlet called "Estimating Your Social Security Retirement Check" (SSA Pub. No. 10047). Upon your request, they will mail this pamphlet to you free of charge and you can wrestle with the formulae involved. Good luck!

Reduced Benefits for Retirement at 62 You are entitled to elect to retire and receive monthly retirement checks at the age of 62. However, if you do your monthly benefits will be reduced permanently. The same is true if you are a survivor or dependent of a worker and receive payments before you are 62.

How much your monthly check will be reduced depends on the

number of checks you receive before you are 65. The result is that if you claim retirement benefits at 62, you will receive about the same value in total benefits over the years as you would have had you retired at 65. The monthly amounts will be smaller because you'll be receiving them longer.

Mr. Anthony is caretaker for an apartment house. At age 62 he is considering retirement. His yearly earnings are $7200 ($600 per month). He is fully insured and can receive retirement benefits of $356.80 per month. His wife is entitled to an additional $167.30 per month making a family income of $524.10. He will pay no income tax on his benefits nor will he have the deductions for retirement benefits he presently has. If Mr. Anthony waits until age 65 to retire, he and his wife will receive approximately $669 per month – a difference of $144.90 per month over his Social Security income at age 62. And at 65 he will be covered by Medicare. However, between ages 62 to 65 he will have lost substantial Social Security payments.

Your Social Security office will compute for you the amount you will receive at age 62 as contrasted with the amount you will receive at age 65.

Retirement After 65 If you do not apply for and receive retirement benefits before 65 and delay your retirement past 65, you are entitled to a special credit that means a larger cash benefit when you do retire. For each year you delay your retirement after age 65, through age 72, you will receive an added 1% per year to your retirement benefit.

Should Mr. Anthony, an apartment caretaker, decide to continue work past age 65 and retire at age 72, he and his wife will receive $672 per month in retirement benefits — an increase of 7% over his expected payments at age 65. However, he would have lost almost $53,000 in Social Security retirement benefits over these seven years.

This special credit has been increased to 3% for each year, or 4% for each month, if you reached 65 after 1981. Starting in June, 1978, a worker's credit for late retirement also applies to widow's and widower's benefits.

Minimum Benefits If you are eligible for any Social Security retirement benefits, the least to which you are entitled is about $121 a month. Although this amount was "frozen" as of January 1979, after you or your family start receiving these minimum benefits your monthly checks will actually go up, since there is a cost-of-living increase automatically built in to these minimum benefits.

Some people worked under the Social Security system many years ago when wages were very low, and have not worked since. If the amount of their monthly check were figured on their average wages of years ago, they would receive very little through no fault of their own.

Such persons are entitled to special minimum retirement benefits, provided they worked under Social Security more than twenty years. The amount of their minimum benefits depends on the number of years they worked under the Social Security system.

The years of coverage are figured as follows: from 1937 to 1950, their total wages are divided by $900 — with a maximum of fourteen years of coverage counted during that period. After 1950, they receive one year of coverage for each year they have earned at least 25% of the maximum covered by Social Security.

Mr. Clark worked from 1937 to 1957 — the necessary 20 years — under Social Security. From 1937 to 1950, he earned $52,000. For this period, he is credited with about 5.7 years of coverage ($52,000 divided by $900). From 1951 to 1957, he earned at least 25% of the maximum, and is credited with 7 more years of coverage, for a total of about 12.5 years covered. This is more than enough to qualify him for special minimum benefits.

How Much Are the Monthly Checks? The amount of your monthly special minimum check will depend, of course, on the number of years you worked under the system. A worker retiring before 1979, for example, with thirty years of coverage, was entitled to $180 a month. Starting in January 1979, however, the minimum amount increased to $230 a month. Furthermore, starting in 1979, the automatic cost-of-living benefit increases (about 6%) apply to these special minimum benefits (except for special midyear increases).

Back Benefits Before January 1978, workers could elect to receive, in a lump sum, retirement benefits for as much as twelve months before they applied for benefits, provided they were eligible during those twelve months. As of January 1978, however, such benefits will not be paid to workers since they would reduce their future benefits. A disabled widow or widower or a dependent, however, can still claim these back benefits.

Working After Payments Start

If you are under 72, are receiving monthly retirement checks, and go back to work, your earnings may reduce the amount of your monthly benefits. This is a bitter pill for many seniors to swallow, since they can make up to only $5,500 (in 1981) per year without having their benefits reduced. Using the average payment, then, a person can receive only $7,200 per year without being penalized — an amount below the federal poverty level. That's how it is, though, and how it probably will stay unless Congress hears loud and clear from enough people. One bright side of this, however, is that your later earnings will usually bring you higher cash benefits when you stop working and apply again for retirement benefits.

What Counts as Earnings? All earnings are counted, whether from wages or self-employment, and whether the work is covered by Social Security or not.

Counted
All earnings:
- from job or self-employment
- jobs with tips of more than $20 per month with one employer
- most pensions from civil service jobs
- from employment outside the U.S.

Not Counted
Income from:
- savings
- insurance
- investments
- royalties
- private pensions

Don't try to make much sense out of the above rules — it is fairly apparent that the government doesn't want you to work. Disability benefits, for example, are not reduced by earnings, although your status as a disabled person may be affected.

Annual Exempt Amount In 1981, you can earn the following without having your benefits reduced: $3,480 for persons under age 65, $5,500 for persons age 65 - 71, and any amount for persons age 72 and above. Starting in 1982, persons between ages 65 and 69 can earn $6,000 a year, and persons 70 and above can earn any amount without having their retirement benefits reduced.

Remember, in figuring your annual earnings, you must count your total wages or net self-employment earnings, not just your take-home pay. If you earn wages and are self-employed, you must add this income together.

You may need to find out whether retirement benefits are payable to you for any month in which you earned 1/12 or less of the annual exempt amount. You can use this "monthly" test only in the first year you have a month in which your earnings are not more than 1/12 of the annual exempt amount (or in which you do not perform substantial services in self-employment), even though you earned more than the annual exempt amount in that year.

Reporting Earnings You are under no obligation to report your earnings after you start receiving benefits, unless and until you exceed the maximum amount. At that time you must report your earnings. You may do this by letter or, in some instances, by telephone.

How Much Is Deducted? If you earn more than the annual exempt amount, your monthly retirement benefit check will be reduced $1 for every $2 you earn over the exempt amount.

Living Outside the U.S. If you leave the country for more than thirty days while you are receiving benefits, your monthly checks may be affected. Your nearest Social Security office will give you, free of charge, a booklet entitled "Your Social Security Check While You're Outside the United States," which explains the rules that apply.

Making Your Claim

The general procedure for making a Social Security claim is outlined in Chapter One. When making your claim for retirement benefits, be sure and start the necessary processing a few months before you will be eligible. This is particularly important when making a retirement benefit claim, since the Social Security office must obtain your entire work record, calculate your average earnings, and so on.

3
Disability Benefits

The constant risk of disability hangs over us all. But for our seniors — often struggling to sustain themselves financially — a disabling accident or injury can be a disaster. Such disabilities often affect seniors' families as well as seniors themselves, thus compounding the problem.

Disability Insurance and Benefits

The Social Security program provides disability protection in different situations and to persons of different ages and in different relationships to a covered worker — all of which are explained in this Chapter. Some of this protection benefits seniors themselves; some protects certain members of their families or their survivors. But most of the protection is based on the work and earnings record of the disabled senior. (See Chapter One for basic Social Security eligibility.) You may also be entitled to disability benefits if you work for a federally assisted employer.

Disability and Medicare

A senior who is eligible for Social Security benefits is entitled to Medicare coverage if he or she is *65 or older.* Medicare coverage is also available to persons under 65 who have been entitled to disability checks for two or more consecutive years, and to persons with permanent kidney failure who need dialysis or kidney transplant. (See Chapter Six for an outline of your rights under Medicare.)

Work Credits

What "work credits" are and how they are figured are explained in detail in Chapter Two.

All workers disabled at age 31 or over, other than the blind, need credit for at least five years of work out of the ten years ending when they became disabled. The years need not be continuous years, however, or even in units of full years — that is, the necessary five years of work can be figured in quarters of years, or halves, and so on.

For a senior disabled by blindness, the above requirement of recently covered work does not apply. But blind people do need credit for one-quarter year of work for each year since 1950 up to the year they became blind. A minimum of one and one-half years of work credit is needed.

Remember: If a disabled or blind person does not meet these work credit requirements, he or she still may qualify as a needy or aged person. (See Chapter Five, Supplemental Security Income [SSI].)

Who Is "Disabled"?

"Disabled," under the Social Security laws, means that you have a physical or mental condition that prevents you from doing any real amount of gainful work, that has lasted or is expected to last for at least twelve months, or that is expected to result in death. An exception is disability through blindness.

Seniors applying for disability benefits, when making their claims, should have doctors' reports ready showing their condition and how it prevents them from working. The Social Security people also consider such matters as age, education, training, and work experience in deciding whether an applicant can work.

Examples of Disabling Conditions Many times, the question of whether or not a person is disabled is arguable under the definitions set forth above. However, there are certain physical or mental conditions that are usually considered without much argument to be severe enough to be disabling under the law.

The Social Security regulations list these conditions. A copy of the regulations is available to you on request free of charge, at your Social Security office. Or you may write for a copy to:

Social Security Administration
Office of Public Inquiries
6401 Security Boulevard
Baltimore, Maryland 21235

Although the list of conditions is too long to cover in detail, here are some examples:

- loss of major function of both arms, both legs, or a leg and an arm
- progressive diseases that have resulted in the loss of a leg or have caused it to become useless
- severe arthritis that causes recurrent inflammation, pain, swelling, and deformity in major joints, so that the ability to get about or use the hands has been severely limited
- diseases of heart, lung, or blood vessels that have resulted in serious loss of heart or lung reserve as shown by X-ray, electrocardiogram, or other tests; and, in spite of medical treatment, there is breathlessness, pain, or fatigue
- diseases of the digestive system that result in severe malnutrition, weakness, and anemia
- serious loss of function of the kidneys
- cancer that is progressive and has not been controlled or cured
- damage to the brain or brain abnormality that has resulted in severe loss of judgment, intellect, orientation, or memory
- mental illness resulting in marked constriction of activities and interests, deterioration in personal habits, and seriously impaired ability to get along with other people
- total inability to speak

Note: In the case of people disabled before age 22, conditions less severe than those listed in the regulations can be considered disabling. This is because age, education, training, and work experience can also be taken into account for these applicants.

Blindness For the purposes of Social Security disability benefits, "blind" is defined as vision that is no better than 20/200 even with corrective lenses or a limited vision field of 20 degrees or less.

A person 55 to 65, blind under this definition, who has worked long enough under Social Security, can apply for and receive monthly cash benefits. However, that person must be unable to perform work requiring skills or ability that are about the same as those required by the regular work he or she performed before the age of

55 or the onset of blindness, whichever is latest.

Note: Disability benefits will not be paid for any month in which any real amount of gainful work was performed.

Mr. Carter (age 55) is blind by definition. He can no longer perform his work as an accountant. He has a wife and two teenage children, both in school. He is fully insured under Social Security. Since he is disabled, he is eligible now for the same benefits he would be at age 65 for himself, his wife, and two children. He had earnings on which the maximum Social Security deductions were withheld throughout his working career. Therefore, the family's income under Social Security equals $935.70 per month. He is also eligible for Medicare.

There are a number of federal and state agencies and organizations, public and private, that assist blind persons with their rights and rehabilitation. California, for example, has a vocational rehabilitation agency for disabled persons that particularly will advise the blind. This agency is listed in the white pages of the telephone directory under "California, State of."

Making Your Claim

The general procedure for making Social Security claims is outlined in Chapter Two. Should you make a disability claim you must, of course, produce proof of your disability in addition to the other papers specified in Chapter Two.

How the Decision on Disability Is Made

When you apply for Social Security disability benefits at your local Social Security Administration office, your claim is sent to a disability determination office in California. This office is usually part of, or associated with, the state's vocational rehabilitation agency. The people in the disability determination office — a physician and a disability evaluation specialist — decide whether you are disabled under the law.

Medical Information All the facts in your file are supposed to be considered by the doctor and specialist in disability. They will request medical evidence from your doctor or the institution where you have been treated. If a fee is involved, they will pay it, as well as for medical reports. Also, in many cases, additional medical information may be needed by them to decide whether you are disabled. Frequently they will seek such information from your family doctor. And you may be asked to undergo further medical examinations and tests, at the government's expense.

Note: Your doctor or medical institution is asked to give your medical history or a report of your condition — the extent of the disability, what treatment you have received, etc. They are *not* asked to make a decision on whether or not you are disabled under Social Security law. If they do, request the disability specialist to remove that report from your records — it is improper.

Although the rules for determining Social Security disability are not necessarily the same as those used, for example, by a private insurance company, the reports that others might make on your medical condition may be considered by the Social Security people.

Notification of Decision After you have filled out the necessary claim papers and submitted all the medical information required, you need do nothing more. The Social Security office at which you made the claim will notify you of the decision reached on your claim.

If Your Claim Is Denied If your disability claim is denied, you will receive a letter from the Social Security office informing you of the denial and stating why. The physician and disability evaluation specialist may conclude, on the medical evidence they have, that your condition is not serious enough to be considered a disability under the law. Or the evidence may show, in their opinion, that your condition probably won't last twelve months. And, of course, your claim may have been denied because you hadn't earned enough work credits.

Note: The fact that your claim for disability benefits has been denied does *not* mean that you are not eligible for other types of Social Security benefits.

If your disability benefit application is denied, you may furnish the Social Security office with additional, new evidence about your disability. For example, you may have received a new physical examination or undergone new laboratory tests and want to present these results to the Social Security office.

If you furnish new evidence of your disability, the Social Security people will send it on to the physician and evaluation specialist for reconsideration.

Even if you have no new evidence concerning your disability, you can request a reconsideration of your claim. The procedure for doing that is outlined in Chapter Two, as are the other steps in appealing a Social Security decision.

Remember: There are provisions for paying an attorney or other person you may want to appeal the decision.

Who Can Obtain Benefits

Monthly Social Security disability benefits can be paid to:

- disabled workers under 65 and their families
- dependent persons who were disabled before age 22 and are still disabled
- disabled surviving spouses of workers who were covered at their deaths
- under certain conditions, disabled, surviving divorced spouses of a worker who was insured at his or her death
- veterans (or their family members) in one of the above categories

If you are age 55 to 65 and receiving disability benefits, certain members of your family are also entitled to monthly checks as the list above indicates. These family members are:

- your unmarried children under 18
- your children 18 to 22 if they are single and attend school full time
- your unmarried children 18 or older who were disabled before 22 and are still disabled
- your spouse, regardless of age, if he or she cares for your child under 18 or disabled child
- your spouse 62 or older
- in some circumstances, stepchildren, adopted children, and grandchildren if the parents are dead and you care for them

Disabled Widows and Widowers If you are disabled and are the widow, widower, or surviving, divorced wife or husband of a worker who was eligible for Social Security payments, you are entitled to monthly benefits as early as age fifty. You do not need any work credits of your own — your benefits are based on the earnings of your deceased spouse or your prior spouse. These benefits, however, will be reduced, depending on the age at which you start receiving them.

Generally, the test as to whether you are eligible for such payments is the same as the test for a disabled worker. But there are some differences. For example, your disability must have started before your spouse died or within seven months thereafter. Exception: If you receive benefits as a widow with children, you may be eligible if you became disabled before those payments end or within seven years after they end.

Note: A disabled surviving divorced wife or husband is entitled to disability benefits based on the earnings of his or her former spouse only if the marriage lasted ten years or longer.

Mrs. Dodge, a widow, has a diagnosis of multiple sclerosis. The symptoms began a year after her husband's death but were only recently diagnosed. She does not have sufficient coverage under Social Security to be eligible in her own right, but her late husband, at his death, was fully covered. She presents medical evidence of her diagnosis, the onset of the disease prior to her husband's death, her prognosis and inability to work, and the fact that she was married 29 years. Evidence makes clear her husband's eligibility to disability and other benefits and her relationship to him. She is granted monthly disability benefits.

Amount of Benefits

Just like other Social Security benefits, you cannot figure exactly what your monthly disability benefits will be, since the amount is based on your earnings record. The Social Security Administration will figure your exact monthly benefits and is very dependable in this respect.

Benefits to workers disabled after 1978 and their dependents are based on earnings adjusted for wage increases. The benefits for workers disabled in 1979, for example, range from $122 to $502.60 per month. (In 1981, add about 12% for adjusted cost of living increases.)

What About Other Income? You are not entitled to disability benefits *and* other Social Security benefits. If you are eligible for more than one Social Security benefit at the same time, you will generally receive only the larger of the two payments. Recommendation: If you have been receiving other Social Security benefits and become disabled, it may be to your advantage to switch over to disability benefits. For example, if you are receiving reduced retirement benefits because you exercised the age 62 option and are disabled at age 63, your disability benefits will be higher than your retirement benefits. Ask the personnel at the Social Security office where you live to work out the various amounts for you in this situation.

Unlike the rules on retirement benefits discussed in Chapter Two, if you are entitled to and receive disability benefits as a disabled widow or widower, you are not subject to the rule under which benefits are lost or reduced if you have some meaningful earnings. Work may, of course, affect your status as a "disabled" person. The benefits your dependents receive, however, may be reduced if they earn more than $5,500 (1981) — generally by $1 for each $2 over that amount they earn in a given year.

Payments from worker's compensation may reduce disability benefits, but few older persons encounter this problem. If you do, however, the general rule is that the total monthly payments to you and your family (disability payments and worker's compensation payments) may not exceed 80% of your average monthly earnings before you became disabled. If the total is more than this, your Social Security payments will be reduced proportionately.

When Benefits Are Payable

First, you must wait five full months before any amount is paid; the first payment you receive will be for the sixth full month. But, if you were disabled more than six months before you applied, you are entitled to back benefits up to twelve months. Remember, though, you will not even receive these back benefits before the sixth month after you apply. And if you wait too long to apply for these benefits — more than fourteen months after you recover from the disability — you are not entitled to any back benefits. Try not to make any sense out of this rule — just apply for your disability benefits promptly!

Suppose your spouse is disabled and dies without filing for disability benefits. You are entitled to benefits if you file an application within three months after his or her death. Furthermore, survivors' benefits may be payable beginning with the month the worker died.

Ordinarily, if you are receiving disability benefits as a disabled widow or widower and remarry, the benefits will stop. In some instances (which are too complicated to explain here), they can be continued. Ask about this at your Social Security office if you happen to fall into this category.

Federally Assisted Employment Disability Benefits

In addition to disability benefits under Social Security, you may be entitled to disability benefits if you are an employee of an employer who is assisted by the federal government. "Assisted" means the employer receives federal money, services, or property.

This program is referred to as "Title V, section 504" of the Federal Rehabilitation Act and applies, for example, when you are employed by:

- a school
- a college
- a hospital
- any other employer receiving federal help

If you are not sure whether your employer comes within this program, ask your supervisor if the employer receives federal assistance in any form. If the answer is yes, inquire as to your eligibility at the nearest Social Security office that administers the 504 program.

Note: The 504 program also ensures your right to employment as a disabled or handicapped person without discrimination. See Chapter Sixteen.

Health Care As a disabled person under section 504, you are entitled to all medical services and medically related instruction available to the public generally. Hospitals receiving federal assistance, including those receiving Medicare payments, must accommodate you. Among other things, such hospitals must:

- provide an emergency room interpreter or make other effective provisions for deaf patients
- treat the physical injury of a person under the influence of alcohol or drugs

- admit disabled persons to natural childbirth, anti-smoking, and other public-service programs of instruction

Federally assisted long-term health care facilities may operate separate programs for different physical disabilities and mental disorders.

Example: A sanitarium for patients with lung disease is not required to have a mental health program for a patient with lung disease and an emotional disorder. On the other hand, the institution may not exclude a person with lung disease who also has other handicaps.

If your disabled child is in a long-term health care facility, the facility and the local public school district are jointly responsible for providing a free appropriate education for your child.

If you are a Medi-Cal patient, your private physician must:

- have an office physically accessible to you
- treat you in a hospital or your home, or, if this is not possible
- refer you to another physician whose office is accessible, after conferring with you

Services provided to you as a Medicare patient in a federally assisted hospital are covered under section 504, but services provided by a private physician are not.

Eligibility What constitutes a disability under Social Security generally was discussed above. Under the 504 program, you are eligible for benefits if you have a physical or mental disability that substantially impairs or restricts one of your major life activities, such as:

- walking
- speaking
- hearing
- working
- learning

You are disabled, under 504, if you have a history of one of the above disabilities or are believed by others to have such a disability, whether or not the disability or handicap is specifically recognized by the federal regulations.

Disabilities, or handicaps, include:

- alcoholism (if it limits a major life activity)
- cancer
- cerebral palsy

- deafness or hearing impairment
- diabetes
- drug addiction
- epilepsy
- heart disease
- mental or emotional illness
- mental retardation
- multiple sclerosis
- muscular dystrophy
- orthopedic, speech, or visual impairment
- perceptual handicaps such as dyslexia, minimal brain dysfunction, developmental aphasia

Other Benefits As a disabled person under section 504, you are entitled to participate in vocational rehabilitation, senior citizens' programs, and other social service programs receiving federal assistance.

You may not be excluded from vocational training because you are blind, mentally retarded, or paralyzed.

Where to Write In addition to your local Social Security office, if you are interested in more information about programs like the above, write:

Public Health Service
Department of Health and Human Services
Washington, D.C. 20852
or
Handicapped
Department of Health and Human Services
Washington, D.C. 20201

Rehabilitation Act of 1973

If you do not qualify for disability benefits under Social Security, you may be eligible for disability benefits under another law called the Rehabilitation Act of 1973 (Title V.) This law also covers disabled employees of schools, colleges, hospitals, etc. who receive federal assistance in any form. Check with your local Health and Human Services office (listed under "United States Government" in the white pages of your telephone directory) for further information on these benefits.

Disability from Occupational Hazards

Recently there has been considerable pressure for disability benefits based on special occupational hazards, such as those suffered in the steel, asbestos, and talc industries. Up to now, Congress has refused to act in this field.

One such disability that has been accepted, however, is black-lung disease. Disabled miners and their dependents and survivors have received disability benefits under federal assistance programs since 1969. For interested seniors in California, the U.S. Labor Department has responsibility for new claims resulting from this disability since 1973. If the condition resulted in a claim prior to 1973, the Social Security Administration remains responsible.

You will find the Labor Department in the white pages of the telephone directory under "United States Government."

Family Benefits

If you are a disabled senior with a work record and have one or more family dependents who are eligible for benefits, you receive the lower of two figures: either 85% of your average earnings before becoming disabled, or 150% of your disability benefit. If you were entitled to disability benefits before July 1980, your benefits are figured on a more generous basis.

In figuring your average earnings before July 1980, you were able to exclude 5 years of low or no earnings. But if you became entitled to disability benefits after July 1980, the years of low or no earnings are excluded as follows:

Worker's Age	Number of Dropout Years
Under 27	0
27 – 31	1
32 – 36	2
37 – 41	3
42 – 46	4
47 and over	5

Returning to Work

Most disabled seniors probably won't be returning to work. Many will, however, especially since mandatory retirement is illegal. (See Chapter Sixteen.)

Under the old law, many disabled seniors who otherwise might have tried to return to work chose not to, since they risked losing their disability benefits as well as Medicare and Medi-Cal protection. Those who did try and could not continue because of their disability were forced to reapply for all of these benefits and undergo waiting periods.

In December 1980 the laws were changed as follows:

- If you are disabled, return to work (within one year), and must stop working again, your benefits can be re-started automatically without a new application.
- Your Medicare coverage can now continue up to 3 years after you return to work.
- If you start receiving Social Security disability benefits again within 5 years after they ended and you were formerly entitled to Medicare, that protection will start again immediately.
- Starting in January 1981, for three years, SSI, Medi-Cal, and Social Security benefits may be paid to you even though you return to work and earn more than the "substantial gainful" activity amount (over $300 a month). As your earnings increase over this amount, your other payments will be scaled down.
- Starting in December 1980, any expenses you incur for daily living that relate to your disability (medical costs and equipment, drugs, and the like) can be deducted when figuring your earnings.
- Starting in December 1980, disabled widows and widowers are entitled to a trial period while testing their ability to work (and still collect benefits).

Vocational Rehabilitation by the State

When you apply for disability benefits, the State of California may offer you assistance in improving your physical condition and in finding employment. This assistance is administered by the State Vocational Rehabilitation Agency and is offered primarily to those seniors whose handicap is not severely disabling. The address to write in this connection is:

State Dept. of Rehabilitation
Attn. Public Affairs Office
830 K Street
Sacramento, CA 95814
Tel: (916) 445-8638

A senior who is disabled may also seek assistance from the State Employment Service, which offers some job counseling and special placement services. You will find this agency listed in the white pages of the telephone directory under "California, State of."

A note of caution: If you are entitled to disability benefits, are offered counseling and job training and refuse them, your disability benefits may be refused or terminated.

Periodic Review of Claims

As of December 1980, more and more disability claims will be examined periodically (at least once every three years), to make sure that only those persons eligible for disability benefits are receiving them.

You can expect that in most cases new medical evidence will be requested by the Social Security people and that you may be asked to undergo medical tests from time to time.

4
Dependents' and Survivors' Benefits

Monthly Social Security checks are paid to certain dependents of a worker who has retired or has become disabled, provided the worker is entitled to benefits. And when this person dies, certain survivors are entitled to Social Security benefits. Furthermore, a divorced wife or husband of a covered worker may receive such benefits. This chapter explains all of these rights.

Keep in mind, when reading this chapter, that the rights discussed are based on the work and earnings record of the *worker* — not those of the person making the claim. Of course, it may be that the person making the claim is entitled to or is receiving Social Security benefits in his or her own right. If that is your situation, you will receive an amount that is equal to the larger of the two amounts.

Keep in mind also that if you are a qualified dependent or survivor of an insured worker, your right to receive monthly benefits does not depend on your eligibility for Social Security benefits from your own earnings. Nor do survivorship benefits depend on your being of retirement age — that is, 62 or older.

Work Credits Needed

To be entitled to benefits as a dependent or survivor of a covered worker, the worker must have earned a certain number of work credits — just as he or she must when claiming retirement benefits. For dependents or survivors, though, the worker's credits are figured somewhat differently.

Tables 4.1 and 4.2 show how much work credit (years worked) is needed to obtain dependents' and survivors' benefits. Reminder:

These are work credits of the covered worker — not of the dependent or survivor making the claim.

Table 4.1. Work credit for dependents' benefits

If the worker reached 62 in	He or she needed
1975	6
1976	6¼
1977	6½
1978	6¾
1979	7
1980	7¼
1981	7½
1983	8
1987	9
1991 or later	10

Table 4.2. Work credit for survivors' benefits

If worker born after 1929, died at age	Years needed
28 or younger	1½
30	2
32	2½
34	3
36	3½
38	4
40	4½
42	5
44	5½
46	6
47	6¼
48	6½
50	7
52	7½
54	8
56	8½
58	9
60	9½
62 or older	10

Under a special rule, cash payments may be made to a worker's children and their mother or father even though the worker died with less work credits than is shown on the above table — provided he or she worked under Social Security 1½ years in the three years before his or her death.

Who Receives Monthly Checks

The following persons are entitled to monthly Social Security payments when a covered worker is retired or disabled: his or her

- unmarried children under 18 (or under 22 if they are full-time students)
- unmarried children 18 or over who were severely disabled before 22 and who still are
- spouse who is 62 or older
- spouse under 62 if caring for a child who is under 18 or is disabled and already receiving benefits based on the worker's earnings
- divorced spouse 62 or over if the marriage lasted 10 years

The following persons are entitled to receive monthly benefits when they survive a covered worker who has died: his or her

- unmarried children under 18 or under 22 if they are full-time students
- unmarried child 18 or older who was severely disabled before 22 and still is disabled
- widow or widower who is 60 or older
- widow, widower, or surviving divorced wife or husband if caring for the worker's child under 18 or who is disabled and already receiving benefits based on the worker's earnings
- widow or widower 50 or older who becomes disabled within seven years of the worker's death
- dependent parents 62 or older
- divorced spouse 60 or over or, if disabled, 50 or older if the marriage lasted 10 years or more (starting January, 1979 — 20 years required before that)

Grandchildren There are special rules governing the right of children to claim Social Security benefits based on a grandparent's earnings. Your Social Security office will gladly inform you of these rules.

Length of Marriage Generally, a marriage must have lasted one year before you are entitled to benefits as a dependent of a retired or disabled worker. If you are claiming as a survivor of such person, the requirement is usually nine months. Do not confuse these time requirements with those above relating to claims as a divorced wife or husband.

Amount of Checks

Monthly benefits paid to dependents or survivors of a covered worker are based on the worker's employment and earnings record. (For how this is figured, see Chapter Two.) There are basically the same restrictions on how much the dependents or survivors can earn annually without having their benefits reduced and the same rules governing what counts as earnings apply. There are some differences, however, which are explained below.

If You Receive a Public Pension Suppose you are a widow or widower receiving the retirement benefits of your deceased husband or wife, but you also receive a pension from your work in public employment that is not covered by Social Security. Unfortunately, your benefits as a dependent or survivor will be reduced by the amount of the pension.

Fortunately, however, your own governmental pension will not affect your dependent's or survivor's benefits if you were eligible for the pension before December 1982, and at the time you applied for the Social Security benefits you could have qualified for the benefits had the law in effect in January 1977 remained the same. At that time (January 1977), men had to prove they were dependent on their wives for support to be eligible for dependents' or survivors' benefits. This is no longer true, of course, but it means that a male applicant can only use this legal exception if he produces such proof.

Lump-Sum Death Payments In addition to the monthly benefits explained above, a lump-sum payment may be made to a covered worker's dependents or survivor, as those dependents and survivors are defined above. The amount of the payment is $255.

The Veterans Administration can provide from $450 to $1,100 for the burial expenses of a veteran, depending on whether the veteran is buried in a national cemetery and whether the death resulted from a service-connected condition. Call the VA under "United States Government" in the white pages of your telephone directory.

Effect of Remarriage Before January 1979, if you were a widow or widower and received survivor's benefits, your benefits were stopped or reduced if you remarried at age 60 or later. As of January 1979, this is no longer true. Furthermore, previously reduced benefits to widows or widowers have been increased.

Eligibility for Other Benefits You may be eligible for more than one Social Security benefit, in addition to dependents' or survivors' benefits. For example, you may be a disabled widow or widower of a disabled dependent of a covered worker. Or, even with the dependents' or survivors' checks you receive, you may still be needy and qualify for Supplemental Security Income (SSI). (SSI benefits are explained in Chapter Five.)

Remember the general rule that if you are entitled to more than one Social Security benefit, you will usually receive only the larger amount to which you are entitled.

Making Your Claim

The procedure for making Social Security claims generally is explained in Chapter Two. When making a dependents' or survivors' claim, proof of your relationship with the covered worker is particularly important.

If you are claiming benefits as a dependent, the worker's income tax returns — showing his or her allowed deductions — is important. If you claim as the survivor, your proof will include the fact of death (death certificate) and papers showing you as the survivor (marriage certificate, etc.).

5
Supplemental Security Income (SSI)

The Supplemental Security Income program, known as SSI, is a federal and state income maintenance program that provides monthly checks to needy persons aged 65 or older and to needy persons under 65 who are disabled and have little or no income or resources. These checks are often called "gold checks." SSI benefits are *not* Social Security retirement and survivors' benefits ("green checks"), even though the Social Security Administration does administer the program.

SSI is a public assistance program. Unlike Social Security, SSI benefits are not earned by a person's contributions as a worker. Seniors receive SSI simply because they are financially needy. As a result, this program is vulnerable to state and federal budget cuts. In fact, recently, California's legislators lowered the basic monthly SSI amount by about $20 a month.

If you become eligible for SSI, you also become eligible for other benefits, such as Medi-Cal, which can be much more important to you than the actual check you will receive. For this reason, apply for SSI even if you expect to receive only a token amount.

Mr. Robinson, aged 65, lives in his own home with his daughter and her family. A recent stroke victim, he requires the almost constant care of his daughter in order to stay at home. His Social Security retirement benefits are $388.20 a month, and his SSI comes to only an additional $35.80 a month. However, because of his SSI eligibility he receives Medi-Cal and other lesser benefits, and his daughter is paid $500 a month to provide for his personal care.

Amount of SSI Cash Benefits

Following is a list of the maximum monthly SSI payments for individuals and couples in various living arrangements as of January 1, 1981 (Source: California Rural Legal Assistance Legislative Office, Senior Citizens Component):

- for a single person 65 or over or a single disabled person — $402
- for a single blind person — $451
- for a couple where both members are aged or disabled — $746
- for a couple where one person is aged or disabled and the other is blind — $828
- for a couple where both members are blind — $877
- for a disabled person under 18 — $319

(If you are living in the household of another person and receiving room and board in kind, your benefits will be lower than the above by about $80 for a single person.)

As discussed later in this chapter, the maximum amounts may be reduced if you receive other income or if you own property above a certain amount.

You are entitled to a restaurant allowance of $43 a month, in addition to your basic benefits, if you are a senior or disabled person and don't live in a place where you can prepare or store food.

You may also be entitled to a special allowance for one-time needs, such as loss of property by fire, necessary moving expenses, housing repair and changes (provided they are necessary), and help to prevent mortgage foreclosure. If you are receiving SSI payments now and have any of these special needs, contact your county welfare office or Department of Social Services and present your case.

In the event that you are a senior who is blind and receive SSI payments, you are entitled to a special allowance for the purchase and care of a guide dog. And if you have a child in your care who is blind, disabled, or mentally retarded and you are receiving Aid to Families with Dependent Children (AFDC), you may be eligible for higher SSI benefits. For either of the above, contact your county welfare office or Department of Social Services.

The basic benefit is $465 per month if you are living in a non-medical out-of-home care facility. You are entitled to receive at least $54 for your personal needs out of this amount.

You are not eligible for Food Stamps, if you receive SSI. However, members of your family who do not receive SSI can apply for Food Stamps.

Social Services Even though the federal government has taken over the SSI program, the counties of this state still give services to needy aged, blind, or disabled persons who are on SSI. Inquire about them at your local welfare or public assistance office (sometimes listed in the telephone book under "Social Services"). Such services include:

- in-home care, such as housework and shopping services
- out-of-home care supportive services
- educational and improvement counseling
- housing improvement services
- physical and mental rehabilitation services

Who Receives SSI Checks: Amount

The SSI program is intended to supplement other sources of income. If your income from all sources that count is less than $422.00 a month or if you are a couple with an income of less than $746.00 a month, you are eligible for some benefits. How your income is figured and the effect of income on your monthly SSI check are discussed in the following sections. Remember that you may receive Social Security checks such as retirement, disability, or dependents' and survivors' benefits and still be entitled to SSI checks if you are eligible. On the other hand, you need not be eligible for Social Security benefits to receive SSI checks.

First, in order to qualify for SSI benefits you must be a United States citizen or a lawfully admitted immigrant; you must reside in the United States; and, if you are claiming SSI benefits as a disabled person, you must accept vocational rehabilitation if it is offered to you. Also, disabled drug addicts and alcoholics must accept treatment if it is offered.

Second, you must be 65 or older, or disabled. What "disabled" means is outlined later.

Third, if you are a single person your income must be less than $422.00 a month or, if you are a couple, your monthly income must be less than $746.00.

Fourth, what you own is limited to items worth no more than $1,500 if you are an individual or $2,250 if you are a couple.

Income With regard to the maximum amount of monthly income that you may receive and still be entitled to SSI checks ($422.00 for an individual and $746.00 for a couple), if you are a couple who has been separated for more than six months, each of you will be treated separately.

Under the SSI program, "income" means more than just cash. It includes any checks you receive as well as items received in kind, such as food or housing from your family and relatives. If you are an eligible person or couple living in another person's household and receiving support and maintenance in kind from that person, your basic SSI monthly check is reduced by one-third.

The basic monthly SSI benefits are also reduced if the eligible person or couple is in a hospital or health facility for an entire month and Medi-Cal is paying over one-half the cost of the care. If only one person in a couple is in a hospital, each of their incomes is considered separately in determining the SSI payment.

Items Not Counted as Income None of the following are counted as "income" for the purposes of SSI eligibility:

- the first $20 a month received from any source, including part-time work, except aid to needy families or veterans disability pensions
- the first $65 a month from earnings; that is, from wages or net earnings from self-employment (Half of any additional earnings are deducted from the monthly check.)
- income above $20 a month other than earnings, including income from: Social Security checks; veterans compensation or pensions; pensions and annuities; gifts; worker's compensation; inheritances; support and alimony payments (These reduce SSI payments.)
- tax refunds
- assistance by a state agency that is based on need
- tuition and fees of grants, scholarships, and fellowships
- home-grown produce consumed by the individual and his or her family
- irregular or infrequent earned income if it totals no more than $30 in a calendar quarter
- irregular or infrequent unearned income if it totals no more than $60 a quarter

- foster care payments for a child who is not receiving SSI payments but who has been placed in the recipient's household by an approved agency
- one-third of child support payments received by an eligible child from an absent parent
- earnings (up to $1,200 a quarter but not more than $1,620 a year) of an unmarried student under 22
- income necessary for fulfillment of an approved plan to achieve self-support established for a blind or disabled person
- work expenses for an eligible person who is blind
- housing assistance from federal housing programs run by state and local subdivisions
- benefits, compensation, or items from ACTION programs run by state and local subdivisions
- relocation assistance provided because of property acquisition for federal or federally assisted projects
- incentive allowances and certain types of reimbursement for individuals in training under CETA programs administered by the state and local subdivisions
- grants or loans to undergraduate students from Department of Health, Education, and Welfare (HEW) education programs
- most federal judgment distribution payments to members of Indian tribes

What You May and May Not Own If you are single — or married but not living with your spouse — you can own savings accounts, stocks, bonds, jewelry, and other valuables worth up to $1,500 and still receive SSI payments. The amount for a couple is $2,250.

The following property is not counted in what you may own and still be eligible for SSI:

- personal effects or household goods worth less than $1,500 if you are single or $2,250 if you are a couple
- insurance policies with a face value of less than $1,500 if you are single or $2,250 if you are married — if the policies are worth more, then only the cash surrender value counts
- automobile, if used for transportation to a job or to a place for regular medical treatment — if not, then only that part of the retail value over $1,200 is counted

- your home — no matter what it is worth — and the land adjacent to it
- certain property essential to self-support and certain community stocks if you are a native of Alaska (inquire at your local Social Security office.)

Disability In most instances, "disability" under SSI rules and disability as defined by Social Security are the same. (What disability means under Social Security is outlined in Chapter Three.)

However, a few conditions that are considered to be disabilities should be mentioned here. For example, under SSI rules, drug addicts and alcoholics are considered to be disabled, but they must undergo treatment if the SSI program offers it to them. Note: All SSI payments for a disabled drug addict or alcoholic must be made to a representative payee on behalf of the disabled person. How this is done is explained in Chapter One.

Inmates or Residents of Public Institutions Inmates of public institutions are not eligible for SSI benefits, except in three cases:

- If a person is in a public or private health facility that receives substantial payments for the person from Medi-Cal, the person may be eligible although the amount is reduced. (For Medi-Cal payments to health facilities, see Chapter Nine.)
- If a person lives in a publicly operated community residency serving no more than 16 people, he or she may be eligible for SSI payments.
- If a person resides in a public institution primarily to attend approved educational or vocational training provided there, he or she may be eligible for SSI payments.

Amount of Benefits – Examples The federal and state agencies base the income limits on whether the money comes from earnings or other sources, and how much income you receive each calendar quarter — that is, each period beginning January 1, April 1, July 1, and October 1. For that reason, the following examples show monthly figures. SSI payment rates change frequently, and these examples should be used as illustrations rather than as a guide to what you will actually receive.

1

Sam Johnson is 66, lives alone in a small house he owns, and his only income is his Social Security benefit of $121.80 a month.

Income not from current earnings:		
Monthly Social Security benefit	$ 121.80	
Less $20	– 20.00	
Remainder: Countable income not from current earnings	$ 101.80	$ 101.80
Income from current earnings:	None	+ None
Total countable income for the month		$ 101.80
Basic SSI amount for the month ...	$ 402.00	
Less total countable income	– 101.80	
Monthly SSI payment	$ 300.20	$ 300.20
His Social Security benefit is		+ 121.80
So his total monthly income will be		$ 422.00

2

Now let's say Mr. Johnson is married and lives with his wife, who is 65. She gets $60.90 a month from Social Security. The couple's total Social Security is $182.70 a month.

Income not from current earnings:		
Couple's monthly Social Security benefits	$ 182.70	
Less $20	– 20.00	
Remainder: Countable income not from current earnings	$ 162.70	$ 162.70
Income from current earnings:	None	+ None
Total countable income for the month		$ 162.70
Basic SSI amount for the month ...	$ 746.00	
Less total countable income	– 162.70	
Monthly SSI payment	$ 583.30	$ 583.30
Their monthly Social Security benefits are		+ 182.70
Their total monthly income will be		$ 766.00

3

Mr. Johnson takes a weekend job that pays $100 a month gross wages. Here's how these earnings affect Mr. and Mrs. Johnson's total income.

Income not from current earnings:		
Monthly Social Security benefit	$ 182.70	
Less $20	– 20.00	
Remainder: Countable income not from current earnings	$ 162.70	$ 162.70
Income from current earnings:		
Wages for the month	$ 100.00	
Less $65	– 65.00	
Divide remainder by 2	2 / 35.00	
Countable income from current earnings	17.50	+ 17.50
Total countable income for the month		$ 180.20
Basic SSI amount for the month ...	$ 746.00	
Less total countable income	– 180.20	
Monthly SSI payment	$ 565.80	$ 565.80
Their Social Security benefit is		182.70
And Mr. Johnson's monthly earnings are		+ 100.00
So their total monthly income will be		$ 848.50

Living with Your Family You may find your SSI check reduced if you live with your family. In order to receive the full "in-your-own-home" SSI rate you must show that you are contributing your fair share. Social Security will want to know what you contribute toward food, rent or mortgage payments, utilities, and other household expenses.

As of January 1981, qualifying for the "own-home" rate puts $80 per month extra in your pocket. For this reason, you may want to arrange your family finances in order to reflect your contributions to the joint expenses.

If you can't provide your own physical care or if you require constant supervision, you may be able to receive the "board and care" rate even though you are living with your family. Currently this is about $60 per month more. But it is seldom to your advantage to take this additional money. If you do, you cannot receive the generally much richer level of homemaker services available through your county welfare department or Department of Social Services.

What If Your Assets Are Too High? Often seniors have an income that is low enough to qualify them for SSI but assets that disqualify them. For example, if you receive $232 in Social Security, own your own home, and have $7,500 in savings, you have several choices. One is simply to live off your savings until they have dipped below the $1,500 maximum. However, it often makes more sense to spend your savings right away on needed home repair and long-term purchases.

Mr. Colman would qualify for SSI (and Medi-Cal) if he didn't still own one, last, $10,000 Treasury Certificate. He sells the certificate and uses the money to fix his leaking roof, repair his furnace, and insulate his home. He has spent $8,500 of his savings. But his home is finally in good repair, and he qualifies for SSI and Medi-Cal.

You should remember that Social Security will want to know how you spent your savings. You can spend your money on legitimate expenses, repairs, and purchases. You cannot just put your money in someone else's name. This will be viewed simply as a paper transfer of assets, and your claim will be denied.

If your resources are only slightly above the allowed limits, you may still qualify for SSI checks if you agree to sell those assets that are above the allowed limits within a certain time. This rule is intended to help the person who owns property that provides little or no income but that cannot be sold quickly at a fair price.

The time limits within which such property must be sold are six months for land and three months for other property. If you receive SSI payments while the sale of your property is incomplete, you may have to pay back the amount of the payments when you complete the sale of your property. Also, if you receive payments but refuse to go ahead and complete the sale, you probably will be declared ineligible for SSI and have to refund the payments you have received.

Applying for SSI Benefits

Senior Applicants All persons 65 or older should apply at their local Social Security office for federal SSI payments. The state supplementary benefits will be included in the federal SSI monthly check, and there will be no need to apply at any state office for the state supplementary benefits. This procedure, however, may vary in some counties.

The procedure for making any claim at the Social Security office is outlined in Chapter One. In addition to the documents listed there, you will need any papers relating to income you may be receiving, such as bank statements, wage receipts, and the like.

If you are living with your relatives, you will need papers showing how much your living expenses are, such as rent receipts, utility bills, and food bills.

Disabled Seniors If you are a senior and disabled, the process differs somewhat. In such a case, the Social Security office can find out immediately whether you are receiving Social Security disability benefits. If so, and you qualify for SSI in addition, immediate payments may be authorized without the need for a medical review referral. But in the event that a determination does have to be made as to your disability, it is made by the state, as is the case with Social Security disability claims. (See Chapter Three.)

Eligibility for Other Benefits Since SSI payments are reduced by other income above the allowed limits, you must, if the Social Security employee so advises you, apply for any other money benefits due you. The employee should help you with this.

How Long Does It Take to Receive Checks? The time varies, depending on your application and circumstances as well as where you live in the state. For most seniors (65 or older), SSI benefits will generally be received within four to six weeks after they apply. However, many Social Security and SSI claims are delayed because of clerical errors and computer problems.

Disability and blindness claims may take longer because it may be necessary to obtain medical reports and evaluate them. (See Chapter Three.) These claims can take about three months or longer. However, the law permits the Social Security office to authorize payments in such cases immediately for up to three months where the claimant is obviously blind or disabled.

If you are in desperate financial straits and can convince the SSI worker that you are probably eligible for SSI payments, you can receive an interest free loan of $200. Most likely, though, you will be referred to the General Assistance program administered through your county's welfare department or Department of Social Services. This very minimal program may just barely keep you alive until your SSI check arrives.

Each county sets its own rules and rates for general assistance. However, all require that you be almost flat broke, and then they give very little. Furthermore, you must promise to pay the little they give you back when you receive retroactive SSI checks. If you own property, you will be required to sign a lien on this property, payable when the property is sold or upon your death.

New Changes in the Law Affecting Disabled Persons Disability payments under Social Security are outlined in Chapter Three. However, disabled seniors are frequently eligible for supplementary SSI payments, as noted above. A number of recent changes in the law affect these payments and are outlined here for your attention.

First, if you are a senior who has a blind or disabled child at home receiving SSI benefits, as of October 1980 your income and assets are no longer to be considered as part of the child's. This change should enlarge the payments to such beneficiaries.

Second, if you are a senior who is an alien and who has an immigration sponsor, as of October 1980 your sponsor's income and resources will be considered to be available to you for support. This, of course, reduces your prior benefits.

Third, as of October 1980 any income you receive for therapeutic workshop activities will be considered earned income. A greater part of this income can now be excluded in determining your SSI benefits, which, of course, will be to your advantage.

Appealing Claims The procedure for appealing claims is outlined in detail in Chapter One.

Yearly Review of Eligibility

The law requires that your SSI claim be reviewed once a year to determine whether you are still eligible. The Social Security office that processed your claim originally may review it by mailing you a questionnaire, telephoning you, or by a personal interview at your home.

In the yearly review, you are asked basically the same kinds of questions you answered when you applied for SSI, such as information about income, what you own, your living arrangements, etc. If your review is done by personal interview, be sure to ask the person appearing to identify himself or herself. If you have any doubts about the identity of the person calling, telephone the Social Security office and verify it.

Reporting Changed Circumstances You should report any changes in the information you gave the Social Security people when you applied. Such changes may affect your payments, but if you fail to send in this information you may have to pay back money that was not due you, you could receive less than you are entitled to, or under some circumstances you may be penalized.

If you make a false statement in the yearly review and receive money that is not due you, you will be penalized also. Note: You will not be penalized if you couldn't help reporting late or if you failed to report but it wasn't your fault.

You may make your report by mail, telephone, or in person — whichever is easiest. You can get the necessary reporting forms by calling or writing the Social Security office. If you don't use the form, be sure that you include the following information in your report:

- your name (or the name of the recipient)
- the claim number
- the change being reported
- the date the change occurred
- your signature and address

What to Report The following list of items to report to the Social Security office is not exhaustive but includes many of the more common things that should be reported.

- *Any change of address or residence*
  You should notify the office of any move you make or a change of mailing address — even if you have your checks deposited directly in a bank. You should also notify the office if you begin living in a different household. You should not delay reporting any change in residence or address.
- *If you enter or leave an institution*
  Notify the Social Security people promptly if you enter or are discharged from a public institution, hospital, skilled nursing facility, nursing home, intermediate care facility, or correctional institution. Your report should include the name of the institution and the date you entered or were discharged.
- *If you leave the United States*
  If you plan to leave the country for 30 consecutive days or more, notify your Social Security office, giving the dates you plan to leave and return. Note: You are not eligible for SSI for any month you are outside the country. You are not again eligible for checks until you have been back for 30 consecutive days.
- *Marital separation*
  You are to notify the office if you and your spouse start living apart or begin to live together again after a separation. The amount of your payments may depend on this information.
- *Change in marital status*
  You are required to notify the Social Security people promptly if you marry or your marriage is terminated. Again, the amount of your payments may depend on this information.
- *Income changes*
  You are required to notify the office promptly of any change in income you receive other than SSI. This requirement also applies to changes in the income of your spouse and child (under 18 or student under 21) who receives SSI checks.
  Note: You do not have to report the automatic general increases in Social Security checks (such as retirement or disability benefits). An adjustment in your SSI check will be made automatically. See above in this chapter for what counts as income.
- *Change in resources*
  Notify the Social Security office if there is any change in what you own, or your spouse owns, including: land, car, or other personal property. "Change" here means that you either bought

or sold such property not included in the list of exceptions. Reminder: On occasion, you will receive SSI checks provided you get rid of property and have made yourself eligible. If you have done that, notify the Social Security office promptly. And remember too that the property, cash, and savings of a parent of a child under 18 or student under 21 are considered those of the child or student and any changes must be reported.

- *If you are blind or disabled*
  Changes in the physical condition of a blind or disabled person should be reported. Also, if such a person takes a job, that fact should be reported.
- *If you are a student*
  A student under 22 should notify the Social Security office promptly if he or she starts or stops attending school regularly.
- *If you are a drug addict or alcoholic*
  You can get SSI checks as long as you continue with the required treatment. The payee of such checks should notify the office promptly if such person stops treatment.
- *Incompetency of recipient*
  If the person entitled to the SSI checks becomes unable to manage his or her affairs, the person caring for the recipient should report that fact to the Social Security office who will substitute that person as a representative payee.
- *Death of a person*
  The office should be notified of the death of the recipient of SSI checks, that of his or her spouse or other household member. Note: Any SSI check not signed and negotiated before the recipient's death must be returned. See above on how to return checks.
- *Any change as to whether you eat your meals at home or away from home.*

Legal Assistance

When and where to obtain legal assistance may be extremely important in SSI claims, since the federal and state programs involve complicated questions of eligibility, benefit levels, administrative procedure, and due process of law. Sources of legal help are outlined in Chapter Fourteen.

PART II
HEALTH, MEDICAL, AND SOCIAL SERVICES

6
Medicare and Private Health Insurance

Medicare

The federal Medicare program provides hospital and medical insurance for persons over 65 who receive or are entitled to Social Security benefits, SSI payments, or railroad retirement. Eligibility for Social Security benefits and SSI payments is outlined in Chapter One. Those interested in Medicare under railroad retirement should ask at their railroad retirement office for a free copy of *Your Medicare Handbook for Railroad Retirement Beneficiaries*.

Certain disabled persons under 65 are eligible for Medicare health care coverage. Persons over 65 who are not receiving or entitled to Social Security benefits can purchase Medicare coverage if they meet certain requirements. The requirements for Medicare coverage generally are outlined in this chapter.

The Medicare program is designed to pay for the treatment of acute medical problems. It very seldom pays for routine, preventative, or custodial care. In fact, you can expect Medicare to pay for less than half of your total health care costs.

The details of Medicare law and the covered benefits change frequently as a result of both new laws and new methods of implementation by the Social Security Administration. In this chapter and the next two on Medicare, we will be talking about benefits effective July 1, 1981. While these new benefits are law, they were not in effect at the time this book was written. And it is possible that the cost-cutting measures of the new administration may curtail or delay the implementation of some of them.

This chapter outlines Medicare law, rules, and policies, regardless of the type of coverage involved. Private insurance protection, particularly in relation to Medicare, is also discussed.

Medi-Cal, unlike Medicare, is intended to assist persons of all ages, including seniors, whose incomes are not sufficient to meet their basic health needs. Medi-Cal supplements the Medicare coverage by paying for most medical, hospital, and health supply expenses that are not covered by Medicare or are only partially covered. Medi-Cal is outlined in detail in Chapter Nine.

Parts A and B of Medicare There are two separate parts to Medicare health insurance. The *hospital insurance* part (sometimes called Part A) provides limited coverage for inpatient hospital care, post-hospital care, and home health care services. Hospital insurance is outlined in detail in Chapter Seven.

The *medical insurance* part (sometimes called Part B) provides for limited coverage of certain services of doctors, hospital outpatient services, and other forms of medical treatment, and the costs of medical equipment and supplies. Medical insurance is discussed in detail in Chapter Eight.

Services and Supplies Not Covered Regardless of the type of coverage, Medicare will never pay for medical expenses that are not reasonable or necessary or for custodial care.

The following list shows many of the important health services and supplies Medicare does not help pay for under either hospital or medical coverage. There are exceptions, however, to some of the items. The exceptions are discussed in the chapter indicated in parentheses.

Not Covered by Medicare

- acupuncture
- chiropractic services (see Chapter Eight)
- Christian Science practitioners' services
- cosmetic surgery
- custodial care
- dental care (see Chapter Eight)
- drugs and medicines you buy yourself with or without a doctor's prescription
- eyeglasses and eye examinations for prescribing, fitting, or

changing eyeglasses (allowed after cataract surgery)
- foot care that is routine (see Chapter Eight)
- foreign health care (see Chapter Seven)
- hearing aids and hearing examinations for prescribing, fitting, or changing hearing aids
- homemaker services
- immunizations unless required because of an injury or immediate risk of infection (anti-pneumonia vaccine allowed, July 1981)
- injections that can be self-administered, such as insulin
- meals delivered to your home
- naturopaths' services
- nursing care on a full-time basis in your home
- orthopedic shoes (unless part of a leg brace)
- personal convenience items that you request such as a phone, radio, or television in your room at a hospital or skilled nursing facility
- physical examinations that are routine and tests directly related to such examinations
- private duty nurses
- private room (see Chapter Seven)
- services performed by immediate relatives or members of your household
- services that are not reasonable and necessary
- services payable by workers' compensation or another government program
- services for which neither the patient nor another party on his or her behalf has a legal obligation to pay
- supportive devices for the feet
- services for which a third party insurer is liable (effective July 1981)

Applying for Medicare

Who Is Eligible? All persons 65 or older, including veterans, who are entitled to or receive Social Security benefits, SSI payments, or railroad retirement are eligible for Medicare hospital protection. On eligibility for Social Security benefits, see Chapter One.

Seniors who are 65 or older, U.S. residents or citizens, and ineligible for Social Security benefits or railroad retirement and who are "deemed insured" qualify for Medicare hospital benefits. "Deemed insured" refers to women born before 1909 and men born before 1910 who were covered by Social Security for at least 3 quarters during each year after 1966 before they reached age 65, *or* persons who became 65 before 1968. Inquire further about deemed coverage at your nearest Social Security office.

Disabled persons under 65 are eligible for Medicare coverage if they have been entitled to Social Security benefits for 24 or more consecutive months. This includes adults who have been receiving disability benefits since childhood.

Workers who are insured under Social Security and their dependents who need a kidney transplant and related medical services are eligible for Medicare coverage.

Persons over 65 who are not eligible for Medicare under any of the above provisions can buy Medicare coverage (discussed later in this chapter).

When to Apply If you are nearing 65, you should apply for Medicare coverage at your local Social Security office about three months before your 65th birthday. This should allow enough time to process your claim so that coverage will start the month you reach 65.

Note: When you apply for Medicare hospital insurance, you will be enrolled automatically for the medical insurance coverage of Medicare unless you tell the Social Security people you don't want it. The premium will be deducted from your Social Security check.

If you are under 65 but eligible under one of the above provisions, or over 65 and want to buy Medicare coverage, you should apply immediately — even if you are not ill or have no reason to think you will be in the near future. If you are hospitalized suddenly from an illness or accident, you may or may not be able to make your Medicare claim.

Where and How to Apply You apply for Medicare protection at your local Social Security office. If you are already receiving Social Security benefits and are over 65, you are automatically eligible for Medicare and your application can be processed fairly quickly. If you are eligible for Social Security benefits but not receiving them, as, for example, if you decide not to receive retirement benefits at 65, you will have to establish your Social Security eligibility first. That procedure is outlined in Chapter One.

If you are under 65 but eligible for Medicare as a disabled person or a kidney transplant patient, or are over 65 but not entitled to Social Security benefits, you will be required to give the Social Security people proof of your status. Proof of age is discussed in Chapter One and proof of disability is discussed in Chapter Three.

The Social Security office has the necessary Medicare forms and will help you fill them out when you apply. In most cases, it takes about six weeks for a Medicare application to be processed — depending, of course, on whether your eligibility for Social Security benefits has already been established.

You will be enrolled automatically when you become entitled to any Social Security benefit, and you will be sent a Medicare card about three months before you reach your 65th birthday or, if your Medicare eligibility is based on your disability, about three months before the completion of twenty-four months of entitlement. The Medicare cards indicate your eligibility for both hospital insurance and supplementary medical insurance. If you do not want Medicare medical coverage, you must decline it in writing a month or more before it becomes effective.

Cost Persons who are automatically eligible for Medicare because they are entitled to Social Security eligibility benefits pay nothing for hospital insurance under Medicare. Persons who are 65 or older but not eligible for Social Security benefits can buy hospital coverage by paying a monthly premium of $77 for the period ending June 30, 1981 and $89 a month for the following year. (This premium may go up as hospital costs rise.)

The basic monthly premium for medical insurance is $9.60 for the period ending June 30, 1981 and $11 a month for the following year. This premium may be raised only if there is a general increase in Social Security benefits during the previous year. Remember, if you want medical insurance, you must pay for it.

If you have one part of Medicare coverage but not the other (medical or hospital), you can sign up for the other part in the first three months of any year. For each year's delay in signing up, after you are eligible to enroll in Medicare, the monthly medical premiums go up 10%. Effective July 1981 you can enroll any time during the year. Furthermore, you can change your mind about the coverage an unlimited number of times and still buy back into the system.

All persons insured under Medicare must pay the premiums on their medical insurance. Certain health service prepayment plans have cost saving features, but these do not include Medicare insurance premiums, deductibles, or co-insurance payments. An exception to this rule is where your former employer continues to pay the plan premiums when you are retired.

Claims for Deceased Beneficiary

Mrs. Jones is critically ill and pays many of her medical expenses. After her death, her estate pays the remainder of the medical costs incurred before she died. Mrs. Jones was fully insured by Medicare.

Claims for payment of these bills under Mrs. Jones' Medicare policy should be made by her oldest family member or the legal representative of her estate. The family member will request from her Medicare office "Request for Medicare Payment" (HCFA-1490) and "Request for Information — Medicare Payment for Services to a Patient Now Deceased" (HCFA-1660). The legal representative, in making the claim, will request the first of the above forms and attach certain legal documents to it. Effective July 1981, either paid or unpaid medical bills may be submitted.

If you have any questions about the above procedure, contact Blue Shield and request their "Medicare Bulletin" (78-6), October 1978.

Your Medicare Card When you enroll in Medicare, you will be sent a Medicare health insurance card by the Social Security office where you applied. This card shows:

- what protection you have — hospital, medical, or both
- the date your protection started
- your health insurance claim number — usually nine numbers and a letter (sometimes another number follows the letter)
- your name, etc.

If both husband and wife are entitled to Medicare protection, they receive different cards with different claim numbers. Each person must use his or her own card. Note that your claim number may be very different from your Social Security number.

Carry your card with you at all times — an accident may happen when you least expect it. If you lose your card, call the Social Security office issuing you the card and give them your name, address, health claim number, and tell them where and when you lost the card. They will issue you a new one.

When you receive covered services, always show your card, unless the services are rendered before the effective date of your coverage, as shown on the card. Always write in your health insurance claim number, including the letter, on any medical bills you send in for payment and on any letters you write about such bills.

For covered services, present your card to any of the following:

- hospitals
- skilled nursing facilities
- home health agencies
- ambulance firms
- chiropractors
- doctors
- independent medical laboratories and X-ray labs
- physical therapy and speech pathology firms
- independent physical therapists who practice in your home
- kidney transplant facilities

If You Are Refused a Card If your local Social Security office has refused to enroll you in the Medicare program and you feel their decision is unjust, you should file a "Request for Reconsideration" as soon as possible. This and the other steps to appeal a Social Security decision are outlined in detail in Chapter One.

Sorting Out Claims, Forms, and Papers

If you use Medicare to any extent you will probably find yourself inundated with bills, processed claims, statements, and other forms. Private insurance protection will add to the volume of papers you collect. It may become quite bewildering if you are making several claims at the same time.

Sorting out this mass of papers and receiving correct payment on your claims will be much less complicated if you keep a record of each medical procedure (that is, each item on your bill). Include the following:

• date
• name of doctor, supplier, or hospital
• service or supply you received
• date you mailed claim
• amount you received from claim, if applicable
• date you mailed private insurance claim, is applicable
• amount you received from private insurance claim, if applicable

Part A claims — those for hospital benefits — generally cause fewer problems. This is because the hospital or home health agency processes the claims and then bills you for the part you must pay.

Part B claims — medical insurance — are more complicated. Generally you file the claim yourself, receive payment directly, and pay your doctor, laboratory, or supplier yourself.

You will be receiving statements from time to time indicating that you have met your deductible or that your claim has been paid. These look very much like medical bills. Don't panic! They are not. They should be labeled "This is not a bill." Simply keep these for your records.

Obtaining Help with the Paperwork Much of the billing in Medicare is done by health care providers. Nevertheless, it is very important for every senior receiving Medicare to be able to read and understand all the medical bills he or she receives. First, this helps prevent fraudulent billing practices. Second, even though Medicare covers many of the costs, there will usually be costs that you must pay. Third, if you wish to contest non-payment or partial payment you must have the facts readily available to you.

One thing you can do is inquire at your local senior legal assistance center and enroll in a Medicare forms class if one is offered. If not, perhaps a volunteer expert at the center will offer you help. Many of these centers have sample billings and will go through them with you.

Another method of handling the numerous forms involved, if your finances permit, is to hire a private company that specializes in handling Medicare claims for individuals. These companies (usually called Medi-Claim or something similar) will take all your forms, bills, papers, and the like, sort them out, make the proper claims, and generally handle all of your paperwork.

These companies usually charge a flat fee plus a percentage (from

10 – 35%) of the amount they collect on your Medicare claims. You will find them listed in the yellow pages of the telephone book under "Senior Assistance Organization Centers" or something similar, and also under a "Medicare Claim" listing. Be sure, before you pay an initial fee and hire a firm like this, that you thoroughly understand their terms of employment and fees.

How to Appeal Decisions on Claims

The procedures for submitting hospital and medical claims are outlined in Chapters Seven and Eight, respectively.

After your claim is submitted, by either you or the doctor or medical facility furnishing the services, you may be sent a notice by Medicare that (1) the claim is rejected because the services were not covered by Medicare or (2) only part of the claim is allowed. You always have the right to request a review of these decisions.

The notice you receive from Medicare, rejecting or partially disallowing your claim, will specify exactly what steps to take if you want to appeal the decision. The main thing to remember is that the Social Security administration reviews decisions on hospital insurance claims, whereas the insurance carrier reviews medical insurance claims.

Your first step, in any event, is to request a review. The proper forms may be obtained either from your Social Security office or the medical insurance carrier handling your claim. You must take this first step within six months after you receive the notice of the decision on your claim.

If you are still not satisfied after such a review, you are entitled to request a formal hearing if the amount Medicare would pay, were your claim fully allowed, is more than $100. The procedure to request a hearing is outlined in Chapter One.

If your Medicare claim involves $1,000 or more, you can appeal the decision to a Federal Court. To reach the $1,000 amount on a medical insurance claim, you may combine several claims, provided they are all within the time limit for appeal.

If you have any other specific questions on how to appeal a Medicare decision, contact your local Social Security office.

Your Liability for Medical Bills

Medicare generally does not limit the amount a doctor or hospital may charge a patient. It only limits the amount Medicare will pay. That does not necessarily mean, however, that you are legally liable for medical bills not paid by Medicare.

Under your medical insurance coverage, if a doctor or supplier accepts an assignment of the medical insurance payment, he or she agrees that the total charge to you for the covered services will be the reasonable charge approved by the carrier. ("Assignment" means that your claim against Medicare is transferred to the doctor or supplier and he or she collects from Medicare directly. This is discussed in more detail in Chapter Eight.) In other words, the doctor or supplier agrees with you in advance that you will be charged no more than what will be approved by Medicare.

You should find out in advance if the doctor or supplier will accept an assignment. If so, and you later receive a bill for an amount not paid by Medicare, don't call your lawyer right away. Even if the doctor accepts an assignment, Medicare pays only 80% of the charge, minus any part of the $60 deductible amount you have not met. The doctor or supplier can still legally bill you for the remaining 20% of the charge plus that part of the $60 deductible amount you may not have met.

Miss Dale's Medicard shows she is fully covered. In July she received a bill from her doctor for $75.00 for a routine physical exam. In September she underwent surgery. Her doctor accepted her assignment, and his bill for the surgery and medical tests came to $1,500 – a reasonable charge by the insurance carrier's standards. Before July Miss Dale had paid out $30.00 in medical costs. In October she receives a bill from her doctor for $405.00 for the physical exam and medical costs at the hospital. Should she pay it?

Yes. Miss Dale's physical exam was not covered by Medicare. Medicare paid $1,170.00 of her other medical costs (80% of the $1,500.00, minus $30.00 for the rest of the $60 deductible.) $1,170.00 from $1,575.00 (physical and surgery) leaves $405.00, for which she is liable. Of course, she should see if Medi-Cal might pay the balance.

Mr. Samuel has the same coverage as Miss Dale. His doctor accepts his assignment for a cataract operation and bills Medicare for $2,000.00 for the surgery. The carrier determines $1,500.00 is a reasonable amount and Mr. Samuel's doctor claims Mr. Samuel owes him $500.00 Should he pay?

No. The doctor, by accepting the assignment, agreed with Mr. Samuel that whatever he charged would be reasonable by the carrier's standards.

Although the bill is $500.00 over that amount, the doctor cannot hold Mr. Samuel liable for the difference.

Waiver of Beneficiary Liability Under federal law, Medicare cannot pay for medical services or supplies that are not reasonable and necessary or for custodial care. But you may not be liable for such costs if a law called waiver of beneficiary liability applies to you.

Under this law, if the doctor or supplier accepts an assignment of payment and you receive services or supplies not covered by Medicare for one of the above reasons, you are not liable for their cost — provided you could not reasonably be expected to know they were not covered.

In other words, if your doctor accepts an assignment of payment and then gives you services in excess of what is reasonable, you are not liable for payment if you had no good reason to know or believe they would not be covered by Medicare. This law helps protect patients and Medicare from being exploited by unscrupulous doctors and suppliers.

Mr. Brown is a retired agricultural worker (age 70) who hasn't been sick much and knows little about doctors or hospitals. He doesn't "feel right" and his doctor hospitalizes him for two weeks followed by a week in a care home – all with exotic medication. It turns out Mr. Brown had mild gastritis, and Medicare turns down most of the medical claim. Mr. Brown probably isn't liable to his doctor for the unpaid balance.

If You Can't Pay Your Medical Bills You may be liable for hospital and medical costs not covered or not fully covered by Medicare or Medi-Cal, but you may be unable to pay the whole bill or part of it.

Luckily most older people are in a good position to ask that their medical debts (and other debts) be settled at less than face value or be paid over a long period of time. This is because assets such as the home you live in and the car you drive and your pension and Social Security income generally are protected from court ordered attachments and garnishments. (Handling creditors and debts is discussed in Chapter Seventeen.)

Mr. Frederick lives in a modest home, drives a five year old car, has almost no savings, and survives on his Social Security income. He ordered medical equipment prescribed by his doctor. Even after Medicare's reimbursement Mr. Frederick still owed the medical equipment supplier $235. Mr. Frederick *contacts the supplier and offers to pay the bill at $25 a month. The supplier decides to accept the offer rather than take court action to collect the debt. This supplier knows that the court will not force Mr. Frederick to sell his home or car or to sacrifice his Social Security income in order to pay the debt.*

When Medicare Coverage Ends

If you are 65 or older and have Medicare hospital insurance arising from your Social Security benefits, you will have this protection until you die. Your medical insurance protection, however, depends on the payment of monthly premiums that are paid directly to Medicare or deducted from your Social Security checks.

You can stop the medical insurance if you wish, and beginning July 1981, you will be able to reenroll as often as you wish. But your premium will be higher the second time.

If you are buying hospital insurance, you cannot cancel your medical insurance without losing your hospital insurance too. You can, however, cancel your hospital insurance and still have medical insurance.

If you desire to cancel either or both parts of your Medicare protection, your local Social Security office will tell you how.

If You Are Disabled Before December 1980 disabled people under age 65 lost their Medicare coverage one month after they recovered from their disability. However, new Medicare law provides for a grace period of up to three years and other more liberalized provisions. This new law is described in greater detail in Chapter Three.

Payment

Medicare hospital payments are made directly to hospitals, skilled nursing facilities, and home health agencies by the insurance companies (generally Occidental Life in southern California, and Blue Shield in northern California). You need not submit a claim personally.

Whenever a health care facility sends Medicare a hospital insurance claim for payment, you will receive a notice that explains the decision made on the claim and how much Medicare has paid. Should you have any questions about the decision or the payment, contact the intermediary (insurance company) that sent you the notice. The name and address of the intermediary will be on the notice that is sent to you.

Insurance Carriers — Blue Shield and Occidental Life Medicare claims from the southern California counties (Los Angeles, Orange, San Diego, Ventura, San Bernardino, Imperial, San Luis Obispo, Riverside, and Santa Barbara) are processed by the Occidental Life Insurance Co. of California. Their address is:

P.O. Box 54905
Terminal Annex
Los Angeles, CA 90051.

You may telephone them at (213) 742-2111.

Medicare claims from northern California (those counties other than the ones above) are processed by the Blue Shield Co. They are located at:

MEDICARE
P.O. Box 7968
San Francisco, CA 94120.

Here are the telephone numbers at which you may call them toll free:

From Area Codes	**Call**
408, 415 (where message units are charged to San Francisco), 209, 707, 916	(800) 792-8040
415 (where no message units are charged)	(415) 445-9000
213, 805, 714	(800) 792-2982

Most of your questions concerning charges and billing should be referred to one of these two insurance companies.

Note: You must submit your claims to the insurance carrier for the area in which you receive treatment. For example, if a doctor treats you in Ohio, you must submit your claim to the insurance carrier in Ohio and not to Blue Shield or Occidental Life. Ask your doctor or supplier for the correct address at which to submit your out of state claims.

Those receiving Medicare under Railroad Retirement should submit their Part B claims to:

Medicare
c/o Traveller's Insurance
P.O. Box 30050
Salt Lake City, Utah 84125

You can call toll free to either (800) 453-5290 or (800) 453-9845.

If you receive Medicare benefits through United Mine Workers, your Part B claims should go to:

Medicare
United Mine Workers of America
Health and Retirement Funds
P.O. Box 9224
Van Nuys, California 91409

You can call (213) 506-5430.

Private Health Insurance

Medicare covers many but not all of your health care needs, as discussed in the following chapters. First, Medicare does not cover certain medical or health services at all: for example, long-term nursing home care. Second, Medicare pays only a portion of covered services, and you must pay the balance. Third, you must pay a deductible amount even if your coverage is complete.

A very common problem, then, for California seniors is deciding whether to buy additional health care coverage or whether to keep the coverage they already have. This decision is complicated by the fact that Medi-Cal supplements Medicare coverage and pays most of the costs not covered by Medicare. To make the decision more difficult, many private health care insurance policies contain very complicated, legalistic terms and conditions (often in small print) that affect the coverage of the policy if you have other similar insurance.

You should decide whether you need private health care insurance that will supplement Medicare *before* you become eligible for Social Security and Medicare benefits. If you are still working but planning retirement at age 65, you have an ideal opportunity to gather the facts you need to make this decision before spending unnecessary money. On the other hand, if you are already over 65 and receiving Medicare, you'll still need to make this important decision as soon as possible.

Do You Need More Health Care Coverage? Nobody these days — seniors least of all — can afford unnecessary insurance coverage. Premium costs are rising rapidly with no end in sight. Many seniors, frightened by the prospect of failing health, buy or retain policies that duplicate or overlap Medicare and Medi-Cal protection simply because they — understandably — want to make sure their medical costs are covered. However, the belief that "the more insurance policies I have, the more certain I am that I'm covered" is not always true.

If you have private health insurance at a low cost and with good coverage, don't hurry to replace it until you are sure it is unnecessary. For example, if you belong to a Health Maintenance Organization (discussed later) or have a similar type of group coverage, it may not be wise to replace it with a Medicare Supplement policy or a catastrophic illness policy.

New policies often require lengthy waiting periods before the coverage is effective, or they may exclude health conditions that your present coverage includes. But don't keep a policy that doesn't fit your needs or pocketbook just because you have had it for a long time.

Keep in mind that neither the federal nor the state government sponsors or sells health care insurance policies that supplement Medicare. Do not believe any advertisements or representations to the contrary.

You should definitely seek advice before deciding. Few seniors or persons of any other age group are experienced enough to make decisions on duplicate insurance coverage without help. If you are still working but planning retirement soon, seek the help of your personnel department if possible. Or, if you have coverage and trust your insurance carrier, ask their advice.

If possible, discuss your decision with a family member or friend who knows and understands insurance policies and is familiar with your financial situation and the Social Security benefits you will be receiving. And, where necessary, contact your local seniors' legal assistance center and obtain what relevant publications and advice they may have available.

Note: As a general rule, remember that if your income is sufficiently low to qualify you for Medi-Cal as well as Medicare, you will not need additional private health care insurance. Your medical needs will be well protected, unless you feel that in the near future your income might rise and disqualify you for further Medi-Cal assistance.

What to Look for in Private Coverage

Generally, you should be looking for private health care coverage that pays for the costs not covered by Medicare. Evaluate your current insurance policy or the one you may purchase in this light.

Some of the very expensive health care costs that Medicare does not cover are:

- the Medicare deductible costs
- some hospital costs
- the 20% that you must pay in Medicare medical coverage
- routine and preventive medical care
- custodial health care, such as nursing home care
- dental care
- extended psychiatric care

Remember that many private health care policies will simply buy you coverage where Medicare is most inclusive — hospital costs. Any additional coverage of these costs is expensive and usually unnecessary.

What Is Excluded under the Policy? Many health insurance policies exclude coverage for any preexisting health conditions you may have had before the policy became effective. Typical of these preexisting conditions are cancer, heart disease, strokes, and the like. In fact, some highly publicized policies designed especially to attract seniors exclude just about everything but the common cold — and a very mild one at that.

Do not be misled by the promise that no medical examination is required! Most policies issued with this claim are precisely the ones that exclude any prior health conditions that could possibly result in a claim.

Giving Your Medical History Most reputable insurance companies require a detailed medical history when issuing a health care policy. If your history is inaccurate or incomplete in any important details, the company can cancel the coverage. Beware of an insurance agent who, to obtain business, tells you that the required medical history is unimportant. This is not true.

What Are the Maximum Benefits? Every health care policy limits its coverage in terms of the maximum benefits payable. These limits may be stated in dollars or in the number of days covered. In any event, check this item carefully and compare the premium costs with the maximum coverage.

What Are the Renewal Rights? In California, health care and service insurance policies generally cannot be cancelled because you make a claim, unless *all* policies of that type in the state are cancelled.

Some of these policies may require action by you to renew the coverage within a stated period of time; others are renewed automatically unless you cancel them. The best health service policies are those that are guaranteed renewable for life. Be aware, though, that you get what you pay for, and these renewal terms may be more costly.

Coverage of Medicare Costs The ordinary private health insurance company that supplements Medicare coverage pays some or all of the deductible amount not covered by Medicare, as well as that part of the coverage services which Medicare has limited. Some policies also cover health services not covered by Medicare, and others do not. Note also that, as is true with Medicare coverage and payment, most private health insurance coverage is limited to reasonable charges — coverage will be excluded for any services the insurer finds unnecessary.

Specific Cost Coverage Some insurance companies offer specific coverage that is limited in scope, such as nursing home coverage, hospital confinement indemnity coverage (pays a fixed amount for each day you are hospitalized up to a designated number of days), and policies covering specified diseases, such as cancer. Most limited coverage policies specify payments only for a fixed amount for each type of treatment, and in most instances the benefits afforded by these policies are not designed specifically to fill any gaps in your Medicare coverage. Still, you may decide that one or more of these policies fits your particular needs.

Major Medical Major medical expense or catastrophic illness policies usually cover the extremely high cost of serious injury or illness, including some coverage excluded by Medicare. The problem with these policies for many seniors is that they generally have a large deductible and limited amounts not covered by Medicare. Often these policies will simply duplicate your Medicare coverage.

Items Not Covered by Most Policies In general, private health insurance policies (as well as Medicare) do not cover the following expenses:

- private nursing
- skilled nursing home care costs (above what is covered by Medicare)
- custodial nursing home care costs
- intermediate nursing home care costs
- home health care expenses (other than the number of visits covered by Medicare)
- physicians' charges (other than the reasonable charge paid by Medicare)
- drugs (except prescription drugs furnished during hospitalization or during a skilled nursing facility stay)
- care received outside the country
- dental care, immunizations, routine checkups, cosmetic surgery, general foot care, eyeglass and hearing aid expenses

Caution: Remember that many, if not all, of the above expenses may be covered by Medi-Cal.

Health Maintenance Organizations

Health Maintenance Organizations (HMOs), such as Kaiser, are one answer to purchasing medical care coverage on a piecemeal basis. HMOs also help solve such problems as the inadequate ratio of doctors to patients in some areas of the state, the maldistribution of health personnel, and the rising costs of medical care.

Basically, a Health Maintenance Organization insures health care and provides health services in return for a membership fee and premiums. People who join HMOs receive their health services directly from physicians and other health care providers who are affiliated with the organization. Generally, the health care is comprehensive and is provided 24 hours a day, seven days a week. This method of health care has become known occasionally as "prepaid group practice" and was established in this state as long ago as 1929 in Los Angeles.

Joining an HMO and paying the required premiums generally frees you from paying further medical costs and from the inconvenience of handling your own Medicare claims. However, you must use the HMO's doctors and services rather than ones of your own choosing.

Buying and Understanding Your Policy

Health insurance policies vary widely in coverage and cost, and, of course, the issuing companies vary widely in how they service their policies. Unless you have private, sound advice to assist you, you will probably need to contact at least four or five different insurance companies, ask that they send you sample policies, and compare them carefully. In making this comparison, you should list separately what your Medicare insurance will pay (or any other existing private insurance you have), and, on a separate piece of paper, list what the new policy you are considering will pay. If you need help in making such a list, ask the insurance agent to help you. If the agent refuses, go to another agent.

Most private health insurance issuers in California give consumers at least ten days or so to read the policy and decide whether or not they want to keep it. Look for such a clause and, should you decide you don't want the policy, go back to the agent or the company within the required time. They are obligated to refund all the premiums you have made within that time.

Don't be high-pressured into buying a private health insurance policy. If you do not understand the policy and its terms thoroughly, ask the agent to explain it to a third party who does understand it in your presence. In any event, take your time about making the decision.

You should receive your private health insurance policy within one month after you completed the application. If you do not receive it, contact the company or the agent in writing and ask them to notify you in writing why the policy has not been delivered. Should substantial further time go by without your receiving your policy, contact the State Insurance Department. Similarly, if you have returned your policy within the prescribed time limits but have not received any refunds that are due to you, contact the same department.

Checking on Insurance Companies

Insurance companies must meet the standards set down by the state Department of Insurance to do business in this state. These requirements and qualifications are basically for your protection. Insurance agents are also required to be licensed by the state, and you should ask any agents contacting you to offer you proof of their licensing as well as that of the companies they represent. If they cannot or will not do this, refuse to do any further business with them.

If you wish to obtain information on any insurance company or agent, call or write the

State Department of Insurance
700 "L" Street
Sacramento, CA 95814

The telephone number is (916) 322-3555.

7
Medicare — Hospital Coverage

In Chapter Six, Medicare and how it works generally were outlined. In this chapter, the hospital insurance part of the Medicare program will be explained. Be sure to read Chapter Eight after you finish this chapter. It deals with the other part of Medicare coverage — medical insurance — and the two parts work together in many instances. Remember throughout this chapter that Medi-Cal may pay for charges and services not covered by Medicare.

Again, many new Medicare benefits are effective July 1, 1981. These benefits may be subject to curtailment or delay in implementation due to proposed cut-back measures of the new administration.

What Is Hospital Insurance?

Medicare hospital insurance (Part A) helps pay for inpatient hospital care if:

- prescribed by a doctor
- the care you require can only be provided by a hospital
- the hospital participates in Medicare
- a hospital review board does not disapprove

Kinds of Hospitals Covered

Participating Hospitals Any recognized hospital that participates in the Medicare program can receive Medicare payments. If you are unsure whether or not the hospital participates, ask the hospital personnel or inquire at your Social Security office.

Non-Participating Hospitals — Emergency Treatment Generally, Medicare helps pay hospital bills only if the hospital participates in the Medicare program. There is an exception to this rule, however. If you are admitted to a non-participating hospital for emergency treatment and that hospital is the closest one equipped to handle your emergency, Medicare will pay about two-thirds of the cost.

The hospital should submit a claim for your emergency treatment. If it doesn't, and you get billed, contact your Social Security office and ask them to help you fill out a claim.

Psychiatric Hospitals Medicare will pay up to 190 days for care in a psychiatric hospital — in a lifetime. That is *all* they will pay. Period. Not only that, but if you were already in a psychiatric hospital at the time your Medicare coverage started, they will subtract from your covered days the number of days you had been an inpatient for the previous five months. In short, psychiatric hospital care is not one of Medicare's specialties!

However, the picture is not as grim as it might seem, since care in the psychiatric ward of a general hospital does not count as care in a psychiatric hospital and does not fall under the 190-day limit.

Mrs. Wright is a patient in the psychiatric ward of San Francisco General Hospital for 20 days. She is discharged and goes home for 30 days; then she is admitted to a psychiatric hospital for 40 days, goes home again for 4 days, and spends 10 more days in the psychiatric ward of San Francisco General.

Mrs. Wright has a benefit period of 90 days — as have all Medicare patients. Of these, she has used 30 (20 plus 10), and so she has 60 left. If she uses the remaining 40 days, she still has 20 days left in that benefit period (60 minus 40). But her lifetime psychiatric care insurance is now reduced to 150 days (190 minus 40).

If a patient enters a psychiatric hospital directly (without referral by a health care provider), the patient must pay a deductible of $204. The patient must also pay $51 per day until the 90th day if he or she remains in the hospital more than 60 days.

For psychiatric outpatient services, Medicare pays 80% of whichever of the following is less: $250 or 62.5% of the actual charges up to $500 maximum a year (or about $312.50).

Foreign Hospitals Medicare will not pay for hospital or medical services outside the United States except for three situations involving emergency care in Mexico or Canada. In the following three instances, Medicare will pay for necessary doctor's services and necessary ambulance transportation:

- You have a medical emergency while in the U.S. but a Mexican or Canadian hospital is closer than the nearest U.S. hospital that can provide the necessary services.
- You live in the U.S. but a Mexican or Canadian hospital is closer than the nearest U.S. hospital that can give you the required care — whether or not an emergency exists.
- When traveling in Canada (other than on vacation) to or from Alaska and an emergency occurs requiring you to be admitted to a Canadian hospital.

You can get help on claims for any of the above at your local Social Security office.

Christian Science Sanitoriums Medicare will help in paying for inpatient hospital care or skilled nursing facility care at Christian Science Sanitoriums, provided they are operated by, listed, or certified by the First Church of Christ, Scientist, in Boston, Massachusetts. Ask your local Social Security office for details. Caution: The services of a Christian Science practitioner, however, are not covered either by your hospital or medical insurance.

Skilled Nursing Facilities – Inpatient Care A skilled nursing facility is a specially qualified facility having the staff and equipment to provide skilled nursing care or rehabilitation services and other related health services. If you are in doubt, ask someone at the facility or at your local Social Security office.

Physician's Office Cost containment measures, effective July 1981, provide that certain surgical procedures can be performed in a doctor's office and be fully covered. These measures also provide for full coverage of lab tests and the like, performed in a doctor's office seven days before hospitalization.

Alcohol De-Tox Centers Beginning July 1981, treatment in a de-tox center will be covered under Medicare, Part A.

How Long Hospitalization Is Covered

Medicare hospitalization coverage is based on benefit periods. A benefit period starts the first day you are in a hospital and are covered by Medicare. Another benefit period will begin when you enter a hospital again after being out of the hospital or skilled nursing facility at least 60 days in a row.

Medicare limits the amount of coverage you can receive in one benefit period. However, there is no limit to the number of benefit periods you can receive in your lifetime.

Mrs. Garcia, covered by Medicare, enters Los Angeles General Hospital March 1. She remains there for 30 days, or until March 30. After recuperating until April 30, she is hospitalized again that day. Mrs. Garcia's re-hospitalization does not start a new benefit period – she was not out of the hospital the necessary 60 days. So the number of days that Medicare will cover her hospitalization remain the same (see below).

Mrs. Garcia enters and leaves Los Angeles General on the same dates initially, but she is not re-admitted until June 5. This time, she has been out more than 60 consecutive days, and the number of days covered by Medicare on her first stay doesn't count – a new benefit period starts for her.

Days Covered For each benefit period, Medicare will pay for all covered services as follows:

Days Hospitalized	Medicare Pays
1 – 60	All but $204.00 deductible
61 – 90	All but $51 a day
After 90 days	For 60 reserve days except for $102.00 a day (see below)

A new benefit period begins when you have been out of the hospital 60 days in a row.

Mr. Russel enters Los Angeles Memorial February 1 and leaves May 7. His covered services come to $10,000 for his 90-day stay. Medicare will pay for all services Mr. Russel received up to May 1, except for the $204 deductible and $1,530 ($51 a day for 30 days). Mr. Russel must pay the $1,734 plus whatever his services cost for May 1–7, if he doesn't use his reserve (below) or unless Medi-Cal picks up the difference.

The same facts as above, but Mr. Russel is not eligible for Medi-Cal, so he elects to use his reserve. Now, Medicare will also cover the 7 days in May, except for $102 a day, or $714. Now Mr. Russel only has 53 reserve days left and owes the hospital $1,797. He leaves quietly, remembering you can't win 'em all.

Mr. Russel is re-admitted September 15 (hoping nobody recognizes him). He has been out more than 60 days in a row and is entitled to the same benefits again, since a new period is started.

The reserve days referred to above can be used only once in your lifetime. Unlike the 90 hospital days in each benefit period, they do not start again. You can use your 60 reserve days all at once or some at one time and some at another.

Warning: Be careful with your reserve days. It may be to your benefit, in the long run, to try to make other arrangements for hospital payment if your stay runs over 90 days. If you choose not to use these reserve days, you must write down that choice and give it to the hospital ahead of time; otherwise your reserve days will be used automatically if they are needed. The statement might look something like this:

> To: ________________ [*name of hospital*] ________________
> You are hereby notified that I, the undersigned, elect not to use any of the reserve days, to which I may be entitled under Medicare, for my hospitalization commencing on________ , 19___.
> ________________ [*Signature*] ________________

Hospital Services Covered and Not Covered

Important Services Covered

- a semiprivate room (two to four beds in a room)
- regular nursing services
- your meals, including special diets
- rehabilitation therapy, such as physical, occupational, or speech therapy
- medical supplies (splints, casts, etc.)
- drugs furnished by the facility
- use of appliances (wheelchairs, walkers, canes, etc.)

Services Not Covered

- personal items such as television, radio, or phone
- private duty nurses
- extra cost of private room — other than as needed for medical reasons
- the first three pints of blood received in a benefit period (unless covered by a donor plan)

Permanent Kidney Failure The Medicare benefits for persons 65 or older include health insurance for permanent kidney failure, regular kidney dialysis treatment, or a kidney transplant. If you are under 65, you are eligible for such benefits if:

- You qualify for Social Security benefits or railroad retirement.

  or
- You are already receiving Social Security benefits or railroad retirement benefits.

  or
- You are the husband, wife, or dependent child of a worker who qualified for Social Security benefits or retirement benefits or who is receiving them.

In order to receive Medicare payments, the medical facility at which you receive medical services for permanent kidney failure must be approved by Medicare. The facility itself can tell you whether they are approved, or you can ask your doctor. The insurance carrier serving your area (to whom you submit your Medicare bills) will also know.

In addition to kidney transplant surgery and related hospital inpatient services, Medicare covers the following doctors' and medical services:

- outpatient maintenance dialysis
- doctors' services
- surgeons' fees for kidney transplant
- outpatient training in self-dialysis
- home dialysis equipment and supplies

If you are entering a hospital for a kidney transplant, Medicare coverage starts the month you are admitted to the hospital and receive the transplant or the month before, if necessary for preparation for such surgery.

If you are receiving maintenance dialysis treatments, Medicare protection begins on the first day of the third month after you start the treatments.

If you have permanent kidney failure, Medicare coverage ends twelve months after the month you no longer require dialysis treatments or have received a kidney transplant. Coverage continues, however, if maintenance dialysis must be re-started or another kidney transplant is required during the year after such surgery.

If you meet the eligibility requirements, you may receive kidney transplant help and related services from the Veterans Administration, the Indian Health Service, a federal employees' health plan, or Medi-Cal.

Skilled Nursing Facilities — Coverage

Skilled nursing care means care performed by (or under the supervision of) licensed nurses. Skilled rehabilitation services are those, such as physical therapy, performed by or under the supervision of a professional therapist. Both of the above services must be under the general direction of a doctor to qualify for Medicare payment.

It often happens that you are discharged from a hospital but need daily skilled nursing services or daily physical therapy that can be most conveniently provided by a skilled nursing facility.

Medicare will pay for this care if:

- You have been in a hospital 3 consecutive days, not counting the day you leave, before you enter the skilled nursing facility, *and*
- You are transferred to the skilled nursing facility for treatment of a condition for which you were hospitalized, *and*
- You enter the skilled nursing facility within 14 days (30 days as of July 1981) after you leave the hospital or skilled nursing facility, *and*
- Your doctor certifies you require the services of the skilled nursing facility, *and*
- The nursing facility's reviewing board does not disapprove of the transfer.

Medicare will not pay for custodial care in a skilled nursing facility. Nor will Medicare pay for your stay at such a facility if you need these services only occasionally, such as once or twice a week. However, again effective in July 1981, Medicare will not presume that certain medical conditions require only a set number of days of coverage. Each situation must be evaluated individually.

Below are the stories of two patients receiving care in skilled nursing facilities. They illustrate when Medicare will and will not pay:

Mr. Mead is 72 and covered by Medicare. He was hospitalized for two weeks after his third stroke, which left him unable to walk, talk, and take care of even his most basic personal needs. He is also incontinent, and very confused.

His doctor does not expect him ever to recover sufficiently to live independently. Mr. Mead was transferred to a skilled nursing facility, and Medicare did not pay.

Mrs. Krammer is 67 and covered by Medicare. She is a lively woman and generally in good health. However, she fell, broke her hip and her arm, and was hospitalized. During the week she was hospitalized, Mrs. Krammer underwent surgery and had a steel pin implanted in her hip. She no longer needs hospital care, but she does need nursing and rehabilitative services, such as physical therapy, which are available in a skilled nursing facility. Her doctors expect her to be home and walking within three months. Medicare covers Mrs. Krammer's stay in a skilled nursing facility.

Number of Days Covered Medicare will pay for skilled nursing care at such a facility for up to 100 days in each benefit period. To receive these benefits, however, you must need daily skilled nursing care or rehabilitation services.

Alternatively, your doctor may submit a special certification guaranteeing Medicare coverage for a prescribed number of days of such care, for certain medical conditions.

If you leave a skilled nursing facility and are re-admitted within 14 days (30 days beginning in July 1981), the 3-day prior stay in the hospital is no longer required. Furthermore, if you are still in the same benefit period, you can use the rest of your 100 days if you have some left.

Deductible Amount For the first 20 days in a skilled nursing facility, Medicare pays all costs that are covered. From the 21st day to the 100th day, Medicare pays all but $22.50 a day (the deductible amount). After 100 days, Medicare pays nothing.

Skilled Nursing Facility Services Covered and Not Covered Generally, the items and services covered by Medicare in a hospital will also be covered in a skilled nursing facility. However, your doctor's services in a skilled nursing facility will not be covered under Medicare hospital insurance (Part A). These may be covered by Medicare medical insurance (Part B). Medicare medical insurance is discussed in Chapter Eight.

Home Health Care

On occasion, you may need skilled health services in your home because of an injury or illness. For example, you may require these services following hospitalization. Also, some home health services may help you avoid further hospitalization or care in a skilled nursing facility.

This kind of care is covered by both parts of your Medicare policy — hospital and medical. The coverage is similar, but not identical. Medical coverage is explained below.

If your medical condition requires part-time skilled health care in your home, the hospital part of your Medicare coverage covers part of it. Usually these services are provided by home health agencies, which may be private or public agencies specializing in home care services such as skilled nursing services (For example the Visiting Nurses Association), physical therapy, and other therapeutic services.

Requirements for Coverage You must meet these six conditions before Medicare will pay for home health visits:

- You were hospitalized for at least three days in a row, not counting the day you were discharged, before your home health care was needed (no minimum hospital stay beginning July 1981).
- The care you seek is for further treatment of the condition treated at the hospital or skilled nursing facility.
- The care you need includes part-time nursing care, or physical or speech therapy (or occupational therapy in July 1981).
- You are confined to your home.
- Your doctor determines you need this kind of care and sets up a plan for you to receive it within 14 days of your discharge from the hospital or skilled nursing facility.
- The home health agency participates in the Medicare program.

What Is Covered in Home Health Care Medicare will help pay for the following services received from a home health agency:

- part-time skilled nursing
- physical therapy
- speech therapy
- occupational therapy (as of July 1, 1981)

If you require one of the above services, Medicare will also help pay for:

- part-time services of home health aides
- medical social services
- medical equipment and supplies furnished by the home health agency

Medicare will not help pay for:

- full-time nursing care
- drugs and medicines
- home-delivered meals
- homemaker services (meal preparation, shopping, bathing assistance, dressing, etc.)

Number of Visits Covered Under new Medicare law, effective July 1, 1981 you will be eligible for unlimited home health visits provided your doctor prescribes them and the home health evaluator finds them reasonable. In reality, you can expect your visits to be limited. But they will no longer be limited by an arbitrary maximum number of visits.

So remember that the following applies only to home health services received before July 1, 1981:

The home health services you receive under your medical insurance are counted in visits. Each time you receive a home health service this is counted as a visit, whether the visit is for the same service twice in one day (or more) or different services twice in one day (or more).

If the coverage requirements are met, Medicare will pay up to 100 home health visits after the start of one benefit period and before the start of another. Benefit periods are explained earlier in this chapter. This coverage is good for as long as twelve months after you leave a hospital or skilled nursing facility.

For certain medical conditions that require longer home health care, your doctor may submit a special certification guaranteeing coverage for a prescribed number of home health visits after you were hospitalized.

Payment of Home Health Care Claims The payment of Medicare claims generally is outlined below. Note, however, that Medicare pays the full cost of covered home health services for each benefit period — you may be charged only for any services Medicare does not cover.

Payment

Medicare hospital payments are made directly to hospitals, skilled nursing facilities, and home health agencies by private insurance companies called intermediaries. You need not submit a claim personally.

Whenever a health care facility sends Medicare a hospital insurance claim for payment, you will receive a notice that explains the decision made on the claim and how much Medicare has paid. Should you have any questions about the decision or the payment, contact the intermediary (insurance company) that sent you the notice, or call your Social Security office. The name and address of the intermediary will be on the notice that is sent to you. (For a discussion of your personal liability for hospital bills, see Chapter Six.)

8
Medicare — Medical Coverage

The Medicare medical insurance program helps pay for a wide variety of health care services and health supplies prescribed by a doctor. The different kinds of care and services covered and what part of your medical expenses is covered are explained in this chapter. Again, we will be talking about Medicare law that is effective July 1, 1981. Remember that these benefits may possibly be curtailed or delayed because of the new administration.

Also remember while reading this chapter that Medi-Cal may pay the costs and services that Part B of Medicare does not cover. (See Chapter Nine.)

Doctors' Services

Your Medicare Part B coverage — medical insurance — helps pay for any covered services you receive from a medical doctor. This coverage is provided whether the services are in the doctor's office, your home, or any other location in the U.S. Your medical insurance can also pay for some doctors' services you may receive as an inpatient in Mexican or Canadian hospitals, in certain situations. See Chapter Seven under "Hospital Insurance — Foreign Hospitals."

Medicare payments are made through private insurance companies who contract with the government. The companies handling claims from hospitals, skilled nursing facilities, and home health agencies are called intermediaries. Those companies handling Medicare claims from doctors and suppliers are called carriers. The way you submit Medicare medical claims and how they are paid is outlined in this chapter.

Other Practitioners

Chiropractic Services These generally are not covered by Medicare, with one major exception. That exception is manual manipulation of the spine to correct a partial dislocation (subluxation) that can be shown by X-ray. Other services rendered by a chiropractor are not covered by Medicare.

Podiatrist's Services These generally are covered, except for routine foot care. "Routine foot care," as used by the Medicare people, includes treatment for flat feet, hygienic care, removal of corns and warts, etc. However, Medicare will cover part of routine foot care if you have a medical condition affecting your lower limbs, such as diabetes, which makes routine foot care necessary. In July 1981, the removal of planter's warts will also be covered.

Dental Care This is generally not covered by Medicare, except if you suffered an injury requiring surgery of the jaw or other bone structures or a setting of the jaw or facial bone fractures. The following common types of dental care are not covered:

- filling, removal, or replacement of teeth
- surgery for an impacted tooth
- root canal therapy
- other surgical procedures involving the teeth or gums

Psychiatric Services The services of a psychiatrist for outpatient treatment of a mental illness are covered only up to $250 a year. See Chapter Seven.

What Services Are Covered?

The following are some of the major doctors' services that are covered by Medicare medical insurance:

- medical and surgical services, including outpatient services and home care
- diagnostic tests related to your medical treatment, including those made by a certified, independent laboratory
- office services, such as X-rays, services of office nurse, medical supplies, drugs administered by the doctor or nurse, and physical and speech pathology services

- medical supplies, such as casts, splints, etc.
- emergency room services
- ambulance transportation
- services of comprehensive rehabilitation centers

Outpatient Physical Therapy and Speech Pathology Physical therapy or speech pathology services are covered by Medicare if either is reasonably necessary for your medical condition. Coverage differs, however, depending on where and from whom you receive these services.

If you receive either physical therapy or speech pathology services in your doctor's office, Medicare will cover the usual 80% of the bill after the $60 yearly deductible is met.

If you receive these services directly (but prescribed by your doctor) from a licensed independent therapist in his or her office or in your home, Medicare will pay only $100 a year. Beginning July 1981, the maximum payment to a physical therapist is $500 a year.

If you receive these services in a medical facility, such as a hospital, skilled nursing facility, clinic, home health agency, rehabilitation agency, or public health agency, that is approved by Medicare, the organization may charge you only for the deductible or any part of it ($60), 20% of the remaining reasonable charges, and for any services not covered by Medicare. The organization will bill Medicare directly for its services. These services must be approved by your doctor in order to be covered.

Ambulance Services Medicare coverage includes ambulance service, provided the service meets Medicare requirements and your health would be endangered by other transportation. Covered ambulance service includes that from your home to a hospital or skilled nursing facility or between these facilities and services to your home. Ambulance service from the scene of an accident to a hospital is also included. Generally, however, the service must be in your area unless there is no medical facility nearby.

If you choose to go in an ambulance to a medical facility outside your local area, Medicare will pay — but only the amount reasonably necessary to transport you to the nearest medical facility.

Medical Equipment and Supplies Various necessary medical equipment and supplies are included within Medicare coverage if they are prescribed or ordered by your doctor. These include:

- prosthetic devices, such as artificial limbs, heart pacemakers, colostomy supplies, corrective lenses following cataract surgery, and orthopedic shoes when they are part of leg braces
- portable diagnostic X-ray services
- medical supplies, such as dressings, splints, casts, and similar supplies ordered by your doctor

Durable Medical Equipment Medicare coverage includes some of the cost of medical equipment such as wheelchairs, oxygen equipment, home dialysis equipment, and other medical equipment for use in your home. Assistive devices such as raised toilet seats are generally not covered.

You may buy or rent the equipment, but Medicare will only make monthly payments on its cost. These payments may help pay part of a monthly rental charge or go toward the purchase price. Medicare will stop payment if the equipment is no longer medically necessary.

Home Health Care Hospital insurance for home health services is outlined in the preceding chapter, and the use of home health services is discussed in Chapter Ten. Medical coverage for this care is very similar, but there are some important differences.

Before July 1, 1981, you were allowed a maximum of only 100 visits per calendar year, and you had to meet the standard $60 deductible before Medicare would pay. Then you could expect Medicare to cover the entire cost of your approved home health care.

However, as of July 1, 1981, Medicare home health benefits will be expanded. First, you will not be required to meet a $60 deductible. Second, Medicare will pay all authorized home health costs. Third, there will be no arbitrary maximum number of visits in a calendar year.

Medicare coverage is available for these services if:

- you need nursing, physical therapy, or speech therapy (or occupational therapy as of July 1981)

- a doctor determines your need and sets up a plan for the services
- you are confined to your home
- the home health agency participates in the Medicare program

Comprehensive Rehabilitation Centers Another new addition to the Medicare benefits beginning July 1981 is the inclusion of comprehensive rehabilitation centers as recognized providers under Part B. For details regarding possible Medicare coverage of services provided by the centers, contact the centers themselves or your Medicare insurance carrier.

Blood Costs Either hospital or medical insurance can help pay for blood except for the first three pints. If you are an inpatient in a hospital or skilled nursing facility, your hospital insurance helps pay for any blood cost for the fourth pint of blood in each benefit period.

If you are an outpatient at a medical facility, or are receiving other Medicare-covered services, your medical insurance helps pay for all blood after the third pint — provided you have met your $60 deductible amount.

If possible, arrange to have your blood costs covered by donors if you are not already part of such a plan.

How Much Medicare Pays

When you receive bills or pay for any of the above medical services or supplies that are covered by Medicare, here is the general rule as to what they will pay: after you have incurred $60 in reasonable charges for such services (the deductible amount), Medicare will pay 80% of the reasonable charges for the covered services during the rest of that year. Some exceptions to this general rule are explained below.

What Are "Reasonable Charges"? What you must pay for medical supplies differs, of course, depending on the doctor and supply manufacturer, where you live, etc. The Medicare law, recognizing this, requires the insurance carrier to base its payments on what charges are reasonable, rather than trying to fix certain charges for medical services and supplies that apply anywhere to any doctor.

The way it works is that the Medicare insurance carrier determines, on July 1 of every year, what the reasonable charges are for covered services in the insurance company's particular area. The insurance company arrives at these figures as follows:

- The so-called customary charge for such services is determined for the prior year. Customary means the charge most frequently made.
- The prevailing charge is then determined. This is an amount that is high enough to pay for three out of four customary charges. But even this amount is limited further by an "economic index" formula — a way the government figures out how much it costs the doctor or supplier to do business.
- The charge submitted by the doctor or supplier for covered services is compared to the customary and prevailing charges for that item. The insurance carrier pays the lowest of the three amounts.

Beginning July 1981, your coverage will be based on the customary and prevailing charges at the time you receive treatment — not those in effect when you submit your claim.

The above rules do not, of themselves, limit what a doctor can charge you — only what Medicare will pay. However, under the "waiver of beneficiary" rule outlined in Chapter Six you may not be liable to the doctor or supplier for any charge that exceeds the reasonable amount. And, if you feel that you are being charged an unfair amount for medical services, you should refuse to pay — depending on the circumstances. For help on this, see Chapter Thirteen.

Exceptions The rule outlined above is subject to two major exceptions — those in which Medicare pays 100% of the covered services and those in which Medicare coverage is limited even as to what amount is reasonable.

The first group of exceptions is as follows:

- If you are an outpatient at a qualified hospital, Medicare will pay 100% of the reasonable charges for the services of pathologists and radiologists, even if you have not met the $60 deductible amount. However, you cannot use these charges to meet your deductible.

- Medicare will pay 100% of the reasonable charges for home health care that is covered.
- Certain surgical procedures performed in the doctor's office in lieu of hospitalization, beginning July 1981, are 100% covered under Medicare.
- Laboratory and blood tests done in a doctor's office seven days or less before hospitalization are 100% covered effective July 1981.

The second group of exceptions is as follows:

- The most Medicare will pay for outpatient doctors' treatment for mental illness is $250 a year.
- The most Medicare will pay for home and office services from a licensed, certified, independent physical therapist is $100 a year ($500, effective July 1981).

Medicare — How to Claim Benefits

When to Submit a Claim There is no point in submitting a claim for Medicare payments until you have already incurred at least $60 in medical expenses that year (the deductible amount). Exception: The first exception in group one above requires no deductible amount, so if you have been an inpatient in a qualified hospital and have bills from pathologists or radiologists, you need not wait.

When you look at your medical expenses for the year to see if they total $60 yet, remember to count any bills that your doctor or supplier has sent directly to Medicare. This procedure is called "assignment" and is discussed below. Be sure also to count any bills you received during the last three months of the prior year. This is called the carry-over rule and allows you credit for that amount on the next year's deductible.

When you have met the yearly deductible amount, or qualify for the exceptions discussed above, you should send a Medicare claim in to Blue Shield or Occidental Life (see Chapter Six for addresses) each time you receive covered services during the rest of that year. Don't let the bills collect — it's more difficult to keep them straight and you won't get paid as quickly.

Time Limits You have slightly over a year to submit your claim. For example, claims for services rendered from October 1, 1980 through December 30, 1980 must be submitted by December 31, 1981. Claims submitted after the time limit will not be paid.

Don't send in bills you incurred before the date you were covered (the date on your Medicard). It will just delay the paperwork and they won't be paid anyway.

How to Submit a Claim First, you need a form called "Request for Medicare Payment." Your Medicare insurance carrier should send you a blank form every time a Medicare payment is sent to you. Or you can get this form at your nearest Social Security office, doctor's office, or supplier's office. The form is often referred to as Form SSA-1490. It consists of Part I and Part II.

Generally you will fill out Part I of the form yourself. Make sure your name and health insurance claim number are written exactly as they appear on your Medicare card. The address you give will be the address your check is sent to, whether or not this is your permanent address.

Ask your doctor or supplier to agree to be paid directly by Medicare. This is called an "assignment" and will limit the amount you must pay on your medical bill.

If you are fortunate enough to get your doctor to agree to an assignment, claiming your benefits should be easy. Simply fill out Part I of the form yourself, and the doctor will do the rest. He or she will then send the completed form to the Medicare insurance carrier and bill you for your portion of the charges.

Most likely, however, your doctor or supplier will not accept assignments, and the Medicare payments will be sent directly to you. First complete Part I, paying careful attention to Item 4, in which you have to describe the illness or injury and the treatment you received. In order for Medicare to pay, you must show that you had an illness, injury, or condition that required the treatment you received. If you do not, Medicare will assume that the treatment you received was preventative or routine and will not pay.

Your doctor can fill out Part II, or you can simply staple your doctor's itemized bill to the form. If you attach the bill, be sure to write your name and claim number on it. You can submit either a paid or an unpaid bill.

A bill must include:

- the date, place, and description of service

- the charge for each service
- your name and Medicare number (including the letter at the end of your number)

You then send in the form and, if you have received them, the itemized bills, to the Medicare insurance carrier named on your card (usually, Occidental Life or Blue Shield). If your card doesn't name the company, ask at your Social Security office, and, while you are at it, request a copy of "Your Medicare Handbook" free of charge — it lists all the Medicare insurance carriers, their addresses, and the areas they serve in the various states. You can send in several bills from one doctor or supplier — or from different doctors or suppliers — with the same form. Remember, if you receive treatment out of state, you must submit your claim to the insurance carrier who processes claims for that area.

Some doctors who do not accept assignments will complete their patients' forms and send the forms to the insurer. This is done only as a courtesy. It does not mean that the doctor has accepted an assignment. Your Medicare reimbursement will still come directly to you.

Your Medicare payment will come attached to an "Explanation of Medicare Benefits." Read this explanation carefully, paying special attention to what is not covered. Often a benefit will be denied because a doctor has not provided sufficient justification for the treatment. When this happens, ask your doctor to provide the insurance carrier with more specific information.

Private insurance claims are submitted after you have received your Medicare reimbursement. You can usually send a copy of your "Explanation of Medicare Benefits" computer printout to your private insurer.

Claim for Person Who Died When someone covered by Medicare hospital insurance dies, payment will be made directly by Medicare to the hospital, skilled nursing facility, or home health agency where the person died.

Doctors' bills or medical supply bills are paid directly if the doctor or supplier accepts an assignment. If not, payment is made to the person paying and submitting the bills with proof of such payment. This person will need these forms:

- Request for Medicare Payment (Form 1490)

- Statement Regarding Medicare Payment
- Medical Services to Deceased Patient

Copies of these forms are available at your local Social Security office.

Notice from Insurance Carrier Each time you submit a claim, the insurance carrier will send you a notice that states whether the claim has been accepted under Medicare law, and the amount paid or to be paid for each service or supply you received. Generally, along with this notice, you will receive another Form SSA-1490 (Request for Medicare Payment) for your use next time.

You Are Refused Reimbursement You may receive a notice from the insurance carrier that your Medicare claim was refused — usually on the ground that the medical services were unnecessary or that the charge was not reasonable.

If you feel the decision was unfair, you can ask the Social Security office to review your claim — submitting any additional medical evidence you may wish. If you are still not satisfied after the review, and your claim is for more than $100, you can request a formal hearing from the Social Security people. This procedure is discussed in Chapter One. For legal help in preparing for a review or a formal hearing, also see Chapters One and Fourteen.

9
Medi-Cal

Medi-Cal is a state and federal program that pays for the health care of low-income and needy Californians of any age. This assistance does not need to be repaid by either the person receiving the help or his or her heirs.

The Medi-Cal program is extremely important to many senior Californians who rely on it for help with their medical care costs. Twenty-four percent of Californians receiving Medicare also participate in the Medi-Cal program.

Medi-Cal is a more comprehensive and inclusive benefit than Medicare. For example, Medicare pays only a portion of the cost of treatment for acute care, diagnosed medical problems, and illnesses. Medi-Cal pays for these types of health care and also for routine, preventive, and custodial care in many cases.

Medi-Cal helps eligible seniors in the following specific ways:

- It fills in the gaps in Medicare coverage, such as the deductible amounts and the period of treatment limitations.
- It pays the Medicare medical insurance premium (Part B).
- It pays for the health care of needy and low-income seniors who do not qualify for Medicare.
- Under some circumtances, it pays unusual medical costs for persons who are normally not needy.

Even Californians who have sufficient income and property to be very comfortable should be aware of their potential Medi-Cal benefits. When private medical insurance, Medicare, monthly income, investments, and savings are exhausted by exceptional medical costs, Medi-Cal is every Californian's last protection.

Medi-Cal receives partial funding from the federal Medicaid program. Medicaid has been targeted for massive funding cuts by the new administration. While this chapter describes current Medi-Cal coverage, federal funding cuts are likely to affect the benefits received by California seniors.

Eligibility

Medi-Cal is administered by the state through the local county welfare departments (also called, in some counties, departments of social services, public assistance, or social welfare). Most questions regarding your eligibility, lost cards, and changes in circumstances should be directed here.

There are four ways to qualify for Medi-Cal:

- All persons who receive an SSI or AFDC payment each month are automatically eligible.
- Persons 65 or older or disabled not receiving SSI payments or other public assistance, but who have insufficient income to sustain their medical needs, are eligible.
- Persons not receiving SSI payments because their income is too large, but who do not have enough to pay for all necessary medical care may be eligible.
- Those persons up to 64 years of age who receive no public assistance and are medically indigent are eligible.

The state also sets specific requirements that determine your eligibility in addition to the above qualifications. These requirements deal with property, income, and residency. (The first two change from time to time to reflect the current cost of living and changes in administration.) When these requirements are met, your Medi-Cal card is mailed to you monthly, and you need not contribute to the payment of your medical bills. Note: Even if you fail to meet the property or income requirements, you may still be eligible for Medi-Cal, provided you meet the residency requirement. How this can happen is discussed later.

When you apply for Medi-Cal for yourself, the application also includes your family. As of February 1981, "family" means you, your spouse, and your minor children. Your total family property and income are combined and then compared to the property and income limitations for the number of people in your family. If your property and income are within the limits set by the state, you and your family are eligible for Medi-Cal and all will receive coverage.

The exceptions to this rule are situations in which you can apply for coverage only as an individual: if you live out of the family home, such as in a nursing home; or if you live with your adult children. In this latter situation, however, if your adult family contributes to your support by providing room and board, an amount reflecting this support will be considered as income for the purpose of determining your eligibility.

Residency Requirement To qualify for Medi-Cal, you must live in California and intend to remain here. There is no longer any minimum period of time that you must have resided here.

Non-U.S. citizens can receive Medi-Cal if they have a "green card." If you do not have a "green card," you will be required to sign a statement to that effect, which will be forwarded to the U.S. Immigration and Naturalization Service.

Property Limits "Property," for the purposes of Medi-Cal eligibility, includes:

- land
- houses
- cash and savings
- insurance policies with a cash value
- investments
- other belongings that have a cash value

When determining your eligibility for Medi-Cal, in respect to the property limitations, the following items are exempt (not included):

- necessary household goods and furnishings
- one automobile or other motor vehicle needed for transportation
- land (other than your home in which you live), provided it has a net market value of less than $25,000 and is producing a net income of at least 6% of its value per year
- wedding rings
- the home you live in

The property limits for Medi-Cal eligibility, not counting the above exempt property, are as follows:

- single person — $1,500
- couple — $2,250

- each additional minor child — $50

As long as your property is within these limits at any time during the month, you meet the property requirement for the entire month.

Income Limits Your family's monthly gross income — minus mandatory payroll deductions, union dues, work expenses, and necessary mileage expenses — is compared with a state table of "maintenance need." Assuming you are under the property limits, you will qualify outright for Medi-Cal if your income is less than this maintenance need. As of January 1981 the maintenance need standards were:

- one person, $328 a month
- two people, $500 a month
- three people, $625 a month
- four people, $733 a month

Excess Property You may still qualify for Medi-Cal even though you own property that is in excess of the limitation discussed above. This exception applies if the property you own is not "readily accessible," which means, in effect, that you cannot readily convert the property to cash. Examples of this kind of property might include undeveloped land, a business interest that is not readily reducible to cash, or perhaps even a house for which there is no current market at a fair price.

If you own this kind of property, you can still be certified for Medi-Cal eligibility provided you develop a plan that can utilize or sell the property within six months from the time you apply for Medi-Cal and provided you follow through with the plan. Your eligibility within this six-month period will depend to a great extent on whether or not your efforts to realize income from the property are good faith efforts. Remember that during this six-month period you are subject to a periodic and continuing review of your eligibility.

Mr. Wright is sick and becoming sicker as he sees the mounting pile of unpaid doctors' bills. He owns his own home, which is exempt from Medi-Cal property limits. His income is $300 a month — below the Medi-Cal income limits. However, he owns a one-fourth interest in the family ranch, which is now valued at $20,000. The ranch produces no income, and Mr. Wright is too ill to develop it. His interest in it puts him $3,500 over the property limit for Medi-Cal eligibility.

He is certified for Medi-Cal, provided he either sells his interest in the ranch or has his interest in it producing income within six months. When this happens, Mr. Wright's income limits may be affected.

Mrs. Rogers has $1,450 in cash assets but owns a small rental property. She applies for Medi-Cal and is told she is over the income limit and must contribute. She is also told to dispose of the rental property within six months. At the end of that time, she has received two bona fide offers for the market value of the property but refused both because she didn't like the potential buyers. Her Medi-Cal eligibility is terminated, the welfare department stating that she did not act in good faith.

Again, this exception depends on your making a good faith effort to convert the excess property to cash. If, for example, you put up your excess property for sale at a reasonable price and it simply fails to sell, your Medi-Cal eligibility will not be terminated. You must, however, make a further effort.

If your cash, savings, etc. exceed the maximum limitation, you may bring yourself within the limit by paying necessary expenses until you are within the limit. (This is often called "spending down.")

Mrs. Fisher, a widow, is ill, lives in her own home, and is within the income limit, but has $2,000 in her savings account—$500 over the maximum allowed. She pays her doctor $300 of what she owes and spends $250 on automobile repairs that were necessary. She now qualifies for Medi-Cal, and they pick up the rest of her medical expenses.

Caution: Do not interpret this to mean that before you apply for Medi-Cal you can transfer assets simply in order to meet the eligibility standards. If you have made a transfer of property (including cash) within the two years before your application, it is presumed that the transfer was not bona fide. The burden of proving otherwise is on you. Thus, in the above example, Mrs. Fisher will have to submit to her eligibility worker documented proof (bills) that the excess money was spent on necessaries rather than to avoid eligibility requirements.

Excess Income You may still qualify for Medi-Cal even if your income is above the limit, provided you are within the property limit. You must, however, contribute a "share of the cost" in such a case.

Your share of cost is determined as follows: the maintenance need for a family your size is subtracted from your family's gross income (minus the Medi-Cal allowed deductions). You must pay or obligate yourself to pay the difference. This means that you can qualify for Medi-Cal benefits no matter what your income, if your medical expenses are high enough.

Mr. and Mrs. Roberts' monthly income, minus deductions, is $841. They meet Medi-Cal's property requirements. On January 2 Mr. Roberts becomes quite ill and within a week runs up $460 in medical bills. He applies for Medi-Cal. The maintenance need standard for two people, $500, is subtracted from the Roberts' income. Their share of the cost is $341, and both Mr. and Mrs. Roberts have Medi-Cal coverage for the month of January. And while Mr. Roberts is recuperating, his wife is a busy woman. She has scheduled her routine physical, her dental care, and her appointment with an optometrist for this month in order to take advantage of her Medi-Cal coverage.

Like Mrs. Roberts, many seniors not normally eligible for Medi-Cal can try to schedule their routine and preventive medical care during a month or a period when they have other medical expenses. Their share of the cost is the same no matter what their actual medical costs are. Some moderate-income seniors find that by scheduling their non-Medicare covered care in one month, applying for Medi-Cal, and paying their share of the cost, they are able to save a substantial amount on their yearly medical bills.

Applying for Medi-Cal

Your Social Security office will process your Medi-Cal application at the same time you apply for SSI. When you are certified as eligible for SSI, you automatically become eligible for Medi-Cal. A separate application is not needed.

Seniors not currently eligible for SSI must make their Medi-Cal application through their county welfare department. Call first to ask about their application procedure. Whatever their method of handling applications, you may apply in person, by telephone, or through a representative.

Retroactive Coverage Medi-Cal coverage begins with the month of application, not the month you are certified as eligible. You may also have the right to three months retroactive coverage. For these reasons it may be important that you apply before the end of the month.

Pete Folger enters San Diego Memorial hospital in early January and incurs large medical expenses that continue through March. On March 30 he discovers Medi-Cal and immediately makes a telephone application. He is certified as eligible for continuing treatment, as well as for his expenses and coverage during January, February, and March.

The Interview Your county welfare department will interview you in order to determine your eligibility. An eligibility worker will ask that you fill out a large number of forms and that you provide documentation of your income, property, assets, residence, living expenses, work expenses, vehicle registrations, medical expenses, and any other items considered relevant to your financial condition. You must provide the same information for any persons the welfare department determines to be part of your household.

The welfare department will assist you in filling out the forms, if needed. (Most people, regardless of age, need assistance, so don't hesitate to ask.) If you don't speak English, a worker who speaks your language generally will be available. You may also bring a friend or relative to help you. When medical problems make it impossible for you to visit the welfare office, a worker will come to your home.

Throughout the interview, the worker must treat you courteously. He or she must explain the rules for determining eligibility and should refer you to any other benefits for which you might be eligible.

At the end of the interview your eligibility worker may inform you there and then that you are eligible, tell you that you will receive written notice on the status of your application, request that you provide further documentation, or deny your application outright. Whatever the result, you will receive written notice later of the action on your claim.

Notices of Action The welfare department is required to inform you of anything that will affect your Medi-Cal benefits. You can expect to receive a volume of these "Notices of Actions." Read each one carefully. They will concern everything from eligibility matters — application, ongoing eligibility, and discontinuance —

to changes in what Medi-Cal covers. Each notice will inform you of your right to appeal the change.

Your Continuing Responsibilities

In order to receive Medi-Cal, you must promise to furnish updated information regarding your situation. This means that you must inform the welfare department promptly of any changes in your circumstances. (Report changes to your Social Security office if you receive SSI.) You must also cooperate with the welfare department in a periodic redetermination of your eligibility. This redetermination, usually an interview, can occur monthly or less often. Persons under 65 and not disabled or blind are required to complete a written form each month indicating their current income and assets and mail this to the welfare department.

Regardless of how often your case is reviewed, you must report within ten days any of the following:

- change in income
- change in assets
- transfer of property or assets
- change in insurance coverage
- change in family composition
- change of address

Note: The Medi-Cal people are chiefly concerned that the benefits of the program go to those for whom they are intended. Generally, their investigative processes are not overly harassing or burdensome. However, you should be aware that in the case of fraud the system can be very punitive. It is not unusual for Medi-Cal to prosecute to the full extent of the law to collect money paid out through fraud. They will even go after the person's estate to collect, when possible.

Right to Appeal Decisions

You have the right to a fair hearing whenever you disagree with a decision regarding your Medi-Cal benefits. As stated earlier, each time something happens to affect your benefits you will receive a "Notice of Action" in the mail. This notice indicates your right to a fair hearing and tells you how to request one. You can request a fair hearing at the following addresses:

Office of the Chief Referee
State Department of Benefit Payments
744 P Street
Sacramento, CA 95814

For Los Angeles County residents only:

Fair Hearing Section
P.O. Box 10280
Glendale, CA 91209

Obviously you should try to resolve the differences with your county worker first. However, if they are not resolved to your satisfaction, do proceed with your appeal. Your county worker is required to assist you in preparing and submitting a request for a fair hearing. Often a senior legal assistance center can be a great help in the appeal process.

Your Medi-Cal Card

You will receive a computer-printed blue and white Medi-Cal card at the beginning of each month you are eligible for the program, and you may receive cards for past months if you applied retroactively. This card verifies that you are eligible for Medi-Cal and is used by the doctor, hospital, or supplier to bill Medi-Cal for your treatment. Keep this card with you at all times.

The left portion of the card shows your name and address, and whether you participate in Medicare, have private insurance, or are a member of a health plan. This portion also indicates the month the card is valid. A card dated August 1981 will only pay for medical services rendered in that month.

The right side of the card contains eight stickers, all with your name and Medi-Cal number. On two of the stickers is written "MEDI." The remaining six stickers have "POE" (Proof of Eligibility) written on them. For the differences between the two types of stickers, see the next section, "Services and Items Covered."

Normally, the Medi-Cal computer sends out cards on the first of each month. If you do not receive your card or if you lose your card, a new one can be issued by your local welfare department. County-issued cards look different from the computer printed cards but they can be used in the same manner.

Services and Items Covered

Your card comes with only two "MEDI" stickers each month. You will receive no more. Certain services can be obtained only by using these stickers. They are:

- eye care (optometric services)
- chiropractic services
- audiology services
- psychology services
- occupational, speech, or physical therapy
- foot care (podiatry services)

If you need more than two visits for these services, you will just have to wait until the next month.

Most medical services will be obtained by using a "POE" sticker. You are entitled to an unlimited number of these. Often a doctor will make a photocopy of your Medi-Cal card rather than take a sticker. For "POE" services this is just as effective.

For some services your doctor must first consult with the state's Medi-Cal evaluators before payment can be authorized. This is called prior authorization and, for you, usually means a delay in receiving treatment. Prior authorization is required for the following:

- hemodialysis services (kidney treatment)
- nursing home care
- dental services
- hearing aids
- non-emergency medical transportation
- artificial limbs and braces
- non-emergency inpatient hospital care
- crutches, wheelchairs, and other durable medical equipment

Prior authorization is not needed, except as noted, on the following "POE" services:

- doctor's services (visits to a doctor's office, with few exceptions, do not require prior authorization)
- laboratory, X-ray, and radiation treatment
- blood and blood derivatives
- home health agency services (one every six months without prior authorization)

- eyeglasses, artificial eyes, and eye appliances (one pair of eyeglasses every two years)
- medical screening for persons under 21
- family planning services
- psychiatric and allergy services in a doctor's office or outpatient clinic (eight in a 120 day period without prior authorization)
- drugs (many drugs, however, do require prior authorization)

Keep in mind that many services not routinely covered will be paid for if your doctor provides sufficient justification to the state's Medi-Cal evaluators. Doing this, however, requires an extra effort on the part of your doctor. And often you must ask or remind your doctor to make this effort.

Coverage Outside of California

Medi-Cal is valid outside of California under certain circumstances. When, as a result of an injury or illness, your health would be endangered by postponing treatment until you return to California, Medi-Cal will pay for your treatment. In non-emergency situations, medical services must be approved by Medi-Cal consultants before the service is given. Contact your welfare department for information on how to take care of out-of-state expenses.

These restrictions do not apply if you live near the state line and routinely use the services of doctors and suppliers in another state. However, services in Mexico or Canada cannot be used unless a medical emergency exists.

Your coverage ends when you permanently move out of the state.

Other Insurance Coverage

Medi-Cal will bill your other insurers if you have outside health care coverage. Generally, you need not worry about this. You simply present your Medi-Cal card for services, and whatever complications the other coverage presents are handled by your doctor, Medi-Cal administrators, and the other insurers. In this situation you would be well advised to reconsider the advisability of continuing your additional health care coverage. Some of the considerations on this question are outlined in Chapter Six.

If you have other applicable coverage — Medicare, Blue Cross, etc. — you will have stated so on your initial application. If you acquire such coverage later, you must notify your welfare department. And if you are injured in an accident in which another individual or insurer may be liable, you must notify your county eligibility worker of the facts of the accident. It may be that Medi-Cal will be reimbursed for your medical expenses.

Some seniors participate in private "prepaid" medical insurance plans such as Kaiser Health Plan, CHAMPUS, and the Ross Loos Health Plan. These plans require members to use the Plan's facilities exclusively if they want coverage. If you are a member of such a plan, you must use it rather than Medi-Cal. But you may use your Medi-Cal card for services not covered by the plan.

Seniors who receive SSI or AFDC (Aid to Families with Dependent Children) can elect to participate in another type of prepaid health plan if one is located in their area. These prepaid health plans contract with the state to provide all the necessary medical care for those who enroll in the program. You do not have to find your own doctor. For information about these you can call, toll free, (800) 952-5528.

Examine these plans carefully before you enroll. You will be required to get all your medical services from this plan. If you are dissatisfied with the plan or with your doctor, you will not be able to change immediately. For help on how and when a change can be made, call the above number and ask them to send you the necessary information and forms.

Securing Medical Services

No doctor or supplier is required to accept your Medi-Cal coverage as payment for his or her services. Often health care providers are reluctant to take Medi-Cal patients because Medi-Cal requires additional paperwork and frequently reimburses providers for less than their usual fee.

When a doctor or supplier does take your Medi-Cal card, he or she agrees to accept as full payment whatever Medi-Cal pays. You cannot be asked to make up the difference between the doctor's usual charge and any lower rate that Medi-Cal pays.

Even though some physicians will not take new Medi-Cal patients, most will continue to treat their regular patients who become eligible for Medi-Cal. For this reason, think twice before you change physicians.

If you are unable to find a doctor who will treat you and accept your Medi-Cal coverage, call your county medical society. You will be referred to local health care providers who participate in the Medi-Cal program. Remember also that all county hospitals and clinics will accept Medi-Cal.

10
Supportive Health Services in the Home

The desire to remain as independent as possible, to live at home with one's friends, family, and possessions, and to avoid the regimentation and restriction of a nursing or convalescent home is paramount to many seniors. This is not always easy, however. Health problems and reduced physical abilities, the death of family and friends, isolation, and the pinch of inflation all work against seniors who want to remain in their homes. For most seniors, staying at home means adjusting to the changes in their lives and being able to accept the help of others.

Fortunately, this desire on the part of seniors coincides with stated public policy and the thinking of current movers and shakers in senior programs. As a result, many private and public programs and resources exist specifically to help older people live as independently as possible.

This chapter describes health-related supportive services designed to keep seniors healthy, at home, and out of institutions.

What Are Supportive Health Services?

Home supportive services are those services, programs, and people which make living at home possible or easier for seniors. These services can help you survive another day. Or, for some, they can assist in recovering lost abilities and enjoying life again.

They include nutrition programs, adult daycare, social activities, counseling, homemakers, home nursing, physical, occupational, and speech therapy, health screenings, and social work. Many of these services cost little or nothing.

When Are Supportive Services Needed?

Mrs. Goldberg, 67, just lost her husband. She sits alone in her home watching TV and waiting for a long distance call from her children. She is not eating properly, and as a result, her diabetes is worsening. Her once tidy home is a mess, and the dining room table is littered with piles of unpaid bills.

Mrs. Robinson is an alert 87. She lives alone in her own home. Although healthy, she is unable to do heavy housework or yardwork. And cooking a balanced, hot meal for one person hardly seems worth the effort.

Mr. Michaelsen, 78, now lives with his son and daughter-in-law. Basically, he takes care of himself, but he must be nagged to go to the doctor, eat properly, and do much else other than watch TV. His daughter-in-law feels that she never has a moment's freedom. And Mr. Michaelsen feels that he is never free from her constant nagging.

Mrs. Albert, 65, has just returned home from the hospital after having a massive stroke. She may recover many of her former abilities. But now she is totally dependent on her very tired husband for all of her daily care.

Each of these seniors can and should receive outside help. They need not rely solely on their own and their family's resources. This kind of help is available and should be used when there is:

- a major illness
- a loss of physical or mental abilities
- a major loss of income or savings
- a death in the family
- acute loneliness
- a chronic medical or emotional problem
- an increase in home accidents

How to Find Supportive Services

Home-supportive programs are generally located in and administered by local communities. As a result, they vary widely throughout the state. Some areas provide a rich level of services; others simply do not. Furthermore, the same service may have a different name and be managed by different agencies throughout the state.

This means that you will have to rely on local sources in order to obtain accurate information about the home-support services you will use. Remember even the experts are often unaware of all the services that exist. If you have a problem requiring supportive services, ask several professionals for their recommendations. And keep on asking, since programs change frequently.

Generally, your best sources of information are your local Information and Referral Service, the social service section of the local welfare department, and your physician.

Information and Referral Service This local service should have up-to-date information on programs in your community. It is most helpful when you are able to identify what you need. Look in the yellow pages of your telephone directory under "Senior Citizens' Service Organizations" for the phone number.

Welfare Department A social worker within the social service section of your welfare department is a good resource, both to discuss what services you might need and to provide you with information on how to find and secure the services. In fact, many needed support services are administered by the welfare department. The phone number of the welfare department is in the telephone directory under the name of your county.

Personal Physician For medical conditions requiring home care, change in lifestyle or health habits, or mobility problems, your physician can be a source of information regarding community services. However, this is often not a doctor's area of expertise. For example, your doctor knows that your medical condition demands that you stay off your feet, but he or she probably won't know how you can get your housecleaning done with outside help.

Discharge Planner If you have been hospitalized, a discharge planner working at your hospital may be able to assist you in planning for your home care. This person, usually a nurse, will have access to your medical charts, and consult with you, your family, and your doctor. He or she will be familiar with the local health resources and can both advise you and make the practical arrangements for your care.

The remainder of the chapter describes many of the home support services that may be available to you in your community.

Home Health Agencies — Can They Help You?

Mr. Perry is a 73-year-old bedridden gentleman who is now incontinent. His family provides for his care, but a home health agency nurse changes his catheter weekly.

Mr. Yee is home now with his family after being hospitalized for a severe stroke. A home health agency nurse monitors his health on a weekly basis. A physical therapist helps him restore use of his muscles and instructs him on the use of mobility aids such as walkers. An agency home health aide assists him in bathing, personal grooming, and personal care. The medical social worker meets with him and his family to help them sort through the financial and emotional problems related to his illness and to plan for his future needs. Since Mr. Yee's speech was affected by his stroke, a speech therapist assists him in regaining his ability to communicate. And an occupational therapist instructs Mr. Yee and his family on the safest and easiest ways to adapt to his new physical limitations.

Mrs. Randolph is recovering from knee surgery at home. Initially, an agency nurse attends to the healing of her surgical incision. For two months a physical therapist helps her regain knee strength and adjust to crutches. Finally, an occupational therapist instructs her on how to live with her permanently impaired ability to walk safely and comfortably.

Home health agencies are generally private agencies. Some are non-profit and others are profit-making ventures. A few are funded by government grant monies. These agencies provide all or some of the following services:

- professional nursing
- practical nursing
- physical therapy
- speech therapy
- occupational therapy
- medical social services
- home health aide service

The focus of home health agencies is to provide their patients with the medical and practical support they need to remain at home during periods of illness and recuperation, to assist patients in regaining their former level of functioning, and to give patients the practical means to adapt to their physical limitations.

Perhaps the most important attribute of home health agencies is the very practical, individual level of care they provide. They help you stay at home during an illness, and then they try to give you and your family the skills to live with your new limitations. Simple things, like how to arrange your furniture for safety and how to transfer from your wheelchair to a toilet seat, are explained and practiced.

Referrals Referrals to home health agencies are generally made by the patient's doctor. If you think you need the help of a home health agency because of a new health problem, ask your doctor to make a referral. Most doctors customarily refer to one or two local agencies. If you think another agency might give you better service, ask that your physician refer you to the one of your choice.

Medicare Payment Payment for home health services under Medicare is discussed generally in Chapters Seven and Eight. However, you should remind your physician to refer you to home health services at the time you are ill. Medicare will not pay for services related to an old or chronic complaint.

Medicare pays 100% of the cost of approved home health service. You can receive these services in your own home, the home of a relative, a retirement residence or community, or in a residential care home. Medicare will not pay for home health services while you are hospitalized or in a nursing home.

Medi-Cal Payment Seniors receiving both Medi-Cal and Medicare need not worry about the limitations of Medi-Cal coverage. However, those who receive only Medi-Cal may find their home health benefits very limited.

Private Payment Most home health agencies will accept an individual's own direct payment and/or the payments of private insurers. But bear in mind that home health services are quite expensive when paid for on a private basis.

Publicly Supported Home Health Agencies In some communities, these programs are available free or at a reduced rate on a very limited basis.

Home Refitting for Physical Limitations

A well-placed handrail, a transfer seat for the bath tub, or a ramp for a wheelchair can make the activities of daily life simpler and safer for many seniors. And, for some seniors, home refitting and convenience and safety aids are essential if they are to remain in their homes.

The problems are knowing what is needed, securing the items and the installation, and then learning how to use the new refittings or devices correctly. This is a question of both logistics and finances.

The professional in the best position to advise you here is an occupational therapist. He or she can evaluate your home and your physical limitations, recommend what is needed both for safety and ease, and teach you the proper use of the items. An occupational therapist may be available to you free of charge through Medicare payments to a home health agency. In a few areas, occupational therapists will help you for a reduced rate. In any event, the services of an occupational therapist are usually well worth the cost, even if you must pay for them out of your own pocket.

Some devices to assist you in safely taking care of your personal needs are available through Medicare and Medi-Cal. Home refittings and the cost of their installation are not; these you must pay for yourself. However, some community programs will assist disabled seniors in refitting their homes at a nominal or reduced cost.

County-Funded In-Home Support Services

Mrs. Tyler lives alone and barely survives on the SSI income she receives. She walks only with the aid of a walker and as a result finds shopping, housecleaning, and normal household tasks extremely difficult. Her county welfare department has determined that she needs ten hours of household help each week. Mrs. Tyler hires her nephew to provide this help. The nephew is paid $4.69 for each hour he works.

In-Home Support Services is a county-administered program designed to give needy persons who have impaired physical or emotional functioning assistance with housekeeping, shopping, meal preparation, personal care, and, in some cases, supervision. To qualify for this program you must be both financially needy and, to some extent, disabled. Help comes in the form of either a person sent by the county to your home for a given number of hours or money paid directly to the person that you hire.

Application should be made through your local welfare department.

Financial Eligibility If you receive either SSI or Medi-Cal, you meet the financial requirements for In-Home Support Services.

If you do not, you may still qualify. Basically, this is handled in a manner similar to Medi-Cal. (See Chapter Nine, under "Excess Income.") First you must meet the Medi-Cal property requirements. Any monthly income you receive over the monthly maximum SSI amount you must use to pay for support services.

Mrs. Wright has a monthly income of $500. The current maximum allowed income is $402. Mrs. Wright must contribute $98 toward her support services at the county set hourly rate of $4.69 an hour. The welfare department authorizes Mrs. Wright 38 hours of services a month. She pays for the first 21 hours ($98 divided by $4.69), and the county pays for the balance.

Amount of Services If you meet the eligibility requirements, a social worker will be sent to your home to evaluate your needs. This worker looks at the tasks involved in daily living (cooking, bathing, shopping, etc.) and determines which ones you cannot manage yourself. For each task in which assistance is required, a certain amount of time is allotted. The county then takes the allotted time, multiplies it by a set hourly rate ($4.69 for example), and that becomes the total maximum amount the county will pay. No matter what your actual needs, this program will pay no more than slightly over $700 monthly for your home care.

Furthermore, 24-hour supervision will generally not be paid for. You may need someone with you all the time to see to your safety and to attend to your medical and personal needs, but there is no payment available for this. The only exception is in the case of persons whose primary disabilities are mental or emotional.

Mrs. Sanchez is bedridden and totally dependent on others for all her personal needs. No payment is authorized for her supervision.

Mr. Jones is confused and if not watched will wander out onto a busy street. Payment for supervision is authorized.

Who Can Provide Support Services? You can hire almost anyone — your son, your daughter, your granddaughter who lives with you, or even your best friend. Unfortunately, you cannot hire your spouse. The government will hold you to your marriage vows! You must care for each other "in sickness and health" — and for free.

Homemaker and Choreworker Services at a Reduced Cost

Each locality receives federal Older Americans Act monies to provide persons over age 60 with homemaker and choreworker services. But different areas use these available funds in very different ways. However, most try to provide low-income seniors who do not qualify for county administered In-Home Support Service (mentioned in the previous section) with affordable household help. Generally, funds for these programs are severely limited. Contact your local Information and Referral or your Agency on Aging for further information.

Private Homemaker and Companion Services

Many seniors who do not need extensive nursing care may need help with personal care, household tasks, shopping, meal preparation, and escorting. Some may also need assistance with heavy cleaning, yard care, and household repair. (The latter are sometimes referred to as chore services.) Still other seniors may need someone to be with them when their family is not at home.

Most communities have several private agencies providing these services. Agency employees can include registered nurses, vocational nurses, and nurse's aides. As these agencies often have trained employees and can be profit-making ventures, they are generally more expensive than standard household help. But their added reliability and their skilled workers can be worth the additional cost. Minimum hour requirements and fees vary, so be sure to contact several agencies for specific information.

Your best source for these services is your local senior center and your Area Agency on Aging Information and Referral Service.

Twenty-Four-Hour In-Home Care

The housekeeper, that reliable woman, who would live with and care for an older person for a modest salary, is unfortunately a creature of the past. And the cost of full-time nursing is beyond the means of all but the wealthiest of seniors. As a result, the family is the primary resource for seniors who require 24-hour-a-day care and wish to remain in their homes.

Home Visitors

In many communities seniors who are confined to their homes can request that a volunteer visit them regularly. These volunteers, often called Friendly Visitors, provide homebound seniors with outside contact, companionship, and the security of knowing that someone will check in on them at expected times. Call your Information and Referral service or your local Volunteer Bureau if you are interested in such a service.

Check-In Services

Telephone reassurance programs (such as "Lifeline") are available in most communities and provide regular contact for persons who live alone and have chronic health problems or are anxious about their safety. Usually the person receives a call at an agreed-upon time. A family member, neighbor, or the police are alerted to check on the person if there is no answer. This service is available at little or no cost.

Some communities are experimenting with a new program similar to telephone reassurance that uses a radio. The senior carries this device and can alert others that he or she needs assistance simply by pressing a button. The device is equipped with a timer, which if not reset will summon help. A moderate fee is charged for this service.

To obtain further information, try your local senior center, a large hospital near you (these systems are also used to summon medical help), or the telephone company in your area.

Santa Cruz County has begun a program called Postal Alert, in which a red dot is placed inside a participant's mailbox. If the mail is not picked up from these mailboxes, the postal carrier will notify a local hospital.

Low-Cost Health Care and Health Screenings

Medicare does not pay for routine or preventive health care. As a result, financial pressures force many seniors to neglect their non-emergency health needs. While the message "that an ounce of prevention is worth a pound of cure" has not yet reached Washington, some efforts to provide seniors with low-cost health care are being made at the local level.

Most senior centers provide regular blood pressure checks to seniors. In some centers and senior complexes, the health screenings are more extensive and include the following:

- vision testing
- test for early signs of glaucoma
- hearing test
- foot inspection
- blood pressure test
- urine test to screen for possible diabetes and kidney disease
- medical history
- medication evaluation
- nutrition assessment
- inspection of teeth, gums, tongue, palate, and cheeks

Your county health department will be able to tell you where and when such screenings occur.

Municipal Health Services Programs The federal government has granted funds for five municipal health services programs, one of which is located in San Jose. The programs are designed to provide quality primary health care, health education, and preventive services to senior residents in the area, and to create and operate four community health clinics.

These clinics accept Medicare and Medi-Cal payments as well as private insurance. Special benefits are available to county residents, including discounts on health care costs. Hopefully, other such clinics will be established for California seniors in the near future. Check with your local Information and Referral or your county health department to see if such clinics are located in your area.

Dental Care at Reduced Cost The California Dental Association sponsors Senior-Dent, a program to provide moderate- and low-income seniors with dental care at reduced prices. Participating dentists give seniors a 10% or greater reduction on their usual fees.

To be eligible, seniors must be 65 or older, have no Medi-Cal or other dental insurance, and have a household income of less than $12,000 a year. Generally no financial statements are required, although an individual dentist may request one.

Interested seniors can find out more about the program and receive the names of participating dentists by calling, toll-free, (800) 262-1213.

Senior Nutrition Programs

Two types of meal programs are found in most communities — home delivered meals and congregate meals. Generally, the meals are served to persons 60 or older or disabled persons.

Remember, if you receive SSI and have disabilities that prevent you from cooking your own meals, you are entitled to a small restaurant allowance. Contact your nearest Social Security office if you believe that you might qualify.

Home-Delivered Meals Programs such as Meals-on-Wheels usually provide their participants with a midday, home-delivered meal five days a week. Some areas also offer weekend service. Specialized diets such as diabetic and low-salt are available in some programs. In order to receive home-delivered meals, you must be unable to cook for yourself — not just find home-delivered meals more convenient. These meals come at moderate cost, and often reduced prices are available to low-income seniors. Be advised that the waiting lists can be very long.

Congregate Meals Many senior centers offer midday meals which are low-cost, hot, and nutritious, as well as offering the bonus of sociable, shared dining. Generally donations are required.

Food Stamps

The Food Stamps Program is sponsored by the U.S. Department of Agriculture and administered by your local welfare department. Application should be made through your welfare department. This program can help low-income seniors buy more food than their income alone would allow.

Participants in the program receive monthly food coupons or stamps. These stamps can then be taken to participating stores and used as money. Most food items can be purchased with food stamps.

Like most government benefit programs, the Food Stamps Program gives you the right to appeal any eligibility decision. At the time of your application, your welfare department will advise you of your appeal rights and procedures.

Currently, persons receiving SSI are ineligible for food stamps. However, if your spouse receives SSI and you do not, you are still eligible.

Generally a family or household applies for food stamps together, and all their income and assets are pooled in order to determine their eligibility. However, if you can show that you and your household usually don't cook or buy food together, you may be able to apply separately.

The property limit is $1,500 for most households. However, when at least two people live in a household and one of them is 60 or older, the maximum is $3,000. The house you live in is exempt from the property limit.

Your income determines the amount of food stamps you will receive. A number of deductions are made from your gross income. After a series of calculations, a figure called "food stamp program income" is determined. You are eligible for food stamps if the income is below the maximum — currently $316 for one person and $418 for a couple. The lower your income, the more food stamps you will receive. In January 1981, the maximum given single persons was $70 a month.

Even if you do not have cooking facilities, you can be eligible for food stamps. Be sure to check with your welfare department.

Senior Centers

For seniors who are mobile, a senior center is the best source of support and assistance in the community. Although the traditional social and recreational activities remain important, most centers now provide many more services. A new concept in delivery of senior benefits called Focal Points is bringing more senior services to local senior centers.

Senior centers and the services they provide are discussed in detail in Chapter Nineteen.

Adult Day Care

Mrs. Arthur is a 76-year-old woman who has some minor health problems and now walks with the use of a cane. Several years ago she began to have difficulty living alone and moved in with her daughter. The daughter works full-time and cannot be with Mrs. Arthur during the day. Some months ago, Mrs. Arthur began to forget to eat lunch and take her daytime medications. When neighbors found her wandering in the street on several rainy days, it became apparent that Mrs. Arthur could not be left alone during the day. Mrs. Arthur now goes to an adult day care center while her daughter is at work.

Adult day care is an organized day program for seniors and other adults. The programs generally have either a medical and health orientation or a social orientation. However, in addition to supervision, social activities, and recreational activities, these centers often provide seniors with health services, nutritional programs, occupational, physical, and speech therapy, and counseling services. For a senior's relatives or caretaker, adult day care can provide a period of respite and some freedom from worry, and at least postpone the appointment of a legal guardian or conservator.

The focus of these programs is to keep seniors who require some form of supervision in their communities, with their friends and families and out of institutions for as long as possible.

Adult day care programs are administered by community agencies or the state Department of Health. Most centers will accept seniors in walkers or wheelchairs, those who need supervision, and those who need help with their medications. Persons who are confused or have emotional problems, if manageable, are generally accepted. Bedridden people are not accepted.

Adult day care is not available in all areas. Some of the counties that do have these services are Contra Costa, Orange, Sacramento, San Bernardino, San Diego, San Francisco, San Mateo, Santa Clara, and Mendocino.

The costs vary. Some centers will accept Medi-Cal payment. For more information on local resources contact the Information and Referral Service in your area or:

Department of Health Services
Adult Day Care Section
714 P Street
Sacramento, CA 95814

Temporary Nursing Home or Residential Care

Mrs. Lopez lives with her son, daughter-in-law, and four teenage grandchildren. She is confined to a wheelchair and requires her family's help with most of her personal care. Her son, his wife, and their children are taking a much needed skiing vacation in Idaho. While they are on vacation, Mrs. Lopez will be staying in a carefully selected nursing home.

Mr. Ronald is discharged from the hospital after having a stroke. The prognosis for his recovery is excellent, but for the time being he will need nursing care and extensive physical therapy. Mr. Ronald receives these services for a month in a nursing home. And then he goes home.

Nursing homes and residential care homes are described in detail in the following chapters. But remember that short-term care is available at these homes. Going to one does not mean a life sentence. Some will take patients on a short-term basis, as short as a weekend, in order to give their families a period of respite. Most also provide a genuine rehabilitative program designed to return patients to their homes. In fact, some patients can recover more quickly and comfortably in these facilities.

These homes will be listed in the yellow pages of your directory under "Convalescent Homes."

Psychiatric and Counseling Services

Unfortunately, a senior's personal or emotional problems may be dismissed by family or professionals as senility or "just part of being old." Certainly, a portion of the senior population does become more confused, irritable, inflexible, forgetful, irrational, and mentally less quick as they become older. These people often legitimately need the support and guidance of their families or a governmental agency. (See Chapter Thirteen.)

Many seniors, though, have personal difficulties whose primary cause is not the organic deterioration of their brain cells. A person who required psychiatric assistance throughout his or her younger years is likely to need continued help when older.

The circumstances of many seniors' lives bring additional personal problems. Financial worries, discrimination, adjustment to leisure time, new physical limitations, medical problems, change of living arrangements, increased dependency, and the deaths of loved ones are all difficulties that strain a person of any age. For every age, depression, confusion, and inability to cope with daily life are typical short-term responses to these problems. However, for seniors, the inability to recover from major setbacks can bring disastrous consequences, permanently impairing a senior's ability to be independent and live at home.

The law gives seniors the same rights to counseling and psychiatric services as other citizens. But, equal rights do not always translate into equal services. Often communities simply lack counseling services that are usable by seniors or facilities that provide emotionally upset seniors with adequate protection.

New state legislation, effective in 1981, requires that some mental health funds be earmarked for the specific benefit of seniors. Hopefully this will make needed counseling services more available to seniors throughout the state.

Generally counseling services are available at a reduced cost to a low-income senior. Often Medi-Cal, Medicare, or private insurance will pay all or a portion of the cost of psychiatric care.

Mental Health Services All counties provide community mental health services to their residents. A senior or his or her family need not have a severe emotional problem to use these services. Outpatient counseling will also be provided for such common problems as grief, unhappiness, isolation, and not getting along with the people you live with. This counseling can be individual, family, or within a group. All community mental health programs have inpatient facilities for emergency and crisis situations. Mental health agencies also operate 24-hour crisis telephone lines for people of all ages.

Some communities have fairly extensive mental health services for seniors. These include outreach programs that provide counseling and evaluation services in your home, senior support groups, and education programs. Seniors with impaired mental functioning may have a worker come to their home. Inpatient facilities for seniors in crisis or emergency situations have been developed in some areas.

Private Counseling Agencies Local agencies such as Family Service, Catholic Social Service, and the like provide counseling services to people of all ages. Some have services specifically tailored to seniors. These agencies usually charge a fee that is based on your ability to pay.

Grief Counseling The death of a loved one often affects the physical health and functioning of the survivors. Grief is a natural reaction to loss but, when prolonged, can inhibit a senior's ability to be independent. Many communities have both volunteer and professional programs to assist people in recovering from losses such as this.

The Welfare Department

The social service bureau of your local welfare department is an excellent starting point in your search for local support services. The welfare department is also your last resort.

When you, your family, or your friends cannot find the resources that you need or a solution to your problem, the welfare department can be called. A social worker can do the following:

- assess your situation and recommend potential community resources
- help you work out an emergency problem
- make an emergency home visit
- investigate possible abuse or neglect
- help you make other arrangements for your care, if living at home is no longer possible
- assist you with long-term planning
- assess the situation of a person believed to be incapable of caring for himself or herself

11
Residential Care Homes

Mrs. Eddy is 86 years old and for the past seven years has been living in a retirement residence. She is basically healthy and active but has become more frail, accident prone, and forgetful in the past year. She now needs daily reminders to take her medication and to eat properly. When she injured herself for the third time in a month, it became apparent that she needed more supervision. She, her family, and her doctor decided that residential care would be appropriate. Mrs. Eddy now lives in a suburban residential care home near her family. She has her own room, filled with her things, but she shares the home with two other older residents and the residential care home's owner and family. The owner provides Mrs. Eddy with her food, does her laundry and housecleaning, and gives her company, and sometimes a little needed nagging.

Differences Between Residential Care Homes and Nursing Homes

Older people and their families should not confuse residential care homes with nursing homes. Nor should they view residential care homes from the perspective of "to be avoided at any cost." Residential care homes are not nursing homes — most are not even institutional in character.

First, residential care homes generally provide no nursing care, and people who live in them are called "residents" rather than "patients." Although residents may have some minor medical problems, they are for the most part healthy people.

Second, residential care homes are individualistic operations and vary greatly. You may be able to choose the type of home that suits your taste and convenience. You may find you can choose from the following examples: a family home that cares for one older person, who is treated somewhat like an extra family member; a remodelled home that accommodates six older people and a resident caretaker; and a large, dormitory-like facility with central dining, social activities, and full staff supervision.

Third, in a residential care home you need not be cut off from your community, from participating in your usual social activities, and from living a reasonably normal, non-institutionalized, daily life.

This type of living situation is ideal for a senior who wishes or needs to be relieved of most of the daily burdens of cooking, cleaning, and shopping, and also to have fairly constant companionship or supervision. In a good residential care home, an older person is likely to find the same security, assistance, respect, and caring attention he or she would find in the home of a relative or friend.

The term "residential care home," often abbreviated to RCH, is a licensing term for what can also be called a "board and care home," a "family care home," or a "rest home."

General Requirements for Residential Care Homes

Residential care homes are housing facilities for persons who do not require nursing care but do require some help with their daily living. They offer room, board, and minimal personal care. This includes, in most instances, meals (including special diets), necessary transportation, minimal personal care (hygiene, clothing, etc.), day and night staff availability, and medication when prescribed by a physician.

Residents generally must be ambulatory and, where necessary, able to use wheelchairs, canes, crutches, and so on. A few residential care homes are licensed to care for persons in wheelchairs. Almost all require that seniors can feed themselves and attend to their toilet needs without help. Usually a physician must certify that the applicant is able to do these things before the senior will be accepted.

Finding the Right Home

As previously mentioned, residential care homes vary tremendously. Some are awful places, run-down, located in high crime areas, serving barely adequate food, and providing questionable supervision. Others are ideal facilities, such as the one described in the example earlier. Some are small family operations that care for two or three persons. Others are large-scale businesses caring for hundreds of patients.

Generally either a family member or a professional social or health care worker will assist an older person in finding a residential care home. This family member or professional person can be of tremendous help in weeding out obviously inappropriate facilities, in seeing to the logistics of the move, and in attending to the financial arrangements.

However, the prospective resident must be included in the selection process and must have a major say in the decision. The senior will be making the facility his or her home. The success of this living situation is likely to depend on such factors as whether the company is congenial, what type of food is served, and whether the senior can continue to garden and keep his or her own furniture. A senior should make several lengthy visits to a residential care home before making a final decision.

Prospective residents and their families should consider the following when making a decision:

- location — close to friends, family, and activities
- cost
- physical surroundings and environment
- cleanliness and maintenance
- quality and type of food served
- congeniality of staff and other residents
- regulations regarding resident behavior and rights
- medical back-up and assistance provided during short-term illness
- transportation provided
- quality of supervision
- general atmosphere
- possibility of resident pursuing hobbies or interests

If you are interested in finding this type of accommodation, contact your county welfare department and ask for a referral worker, or contact the State Department of Health, Facilities Licensing Section. The addresses and phone numbers of the district offices can be found in Chapter Twelve.

If you have no luck here, ask the Area Agency on Aging or your local senior citizens' center. If you are an SSI beneficiary and have a case worker, direct your inquiries to him or her. Finally, try your church. Many religious organizations are very active in this field and can be of great assistance.

Costs

Depending on where the facility is located in the state, what services and amenities are provided, and what profit the owner decides to make, you can expect that the fees will be $375 – $1,000 a month. If you have special needs, you can expect to pay an additional amount. Although the best homes are not always the most expensive, the better homes do cost more. Expect to spend at least several hundred dollars a month over the minimum amount if you want privacy, good supervision, activities and stimulation, and a relatively comfortable environment.

If you enter a residence, you will be required to sign an admission or rental agreement that states the monthly and special charges, provides for notice to move and/or for the owner to change the stated rates, and a medical release authorizing the owner to give you medical assistance in an emergency. Extra medical care may be provided only for brief illnesses, such as colds. Remember, however, that you can still receive Medicare-paid home health benefits while living in a residential care home. (See Chapter Ten.)

SSI benefits can be raised slightly when you enter a residential care home. This raise is paid to cover your increased costs while living out-of-home. Actually your personal income will decrease to a very modest amount (about $50 a month), and the home operator will be paid directly by Social Security for your care. In order to receive this higher "board and care," you or your representative must apply at the Social Security office.

Many residential care home operators are reluctant to accept SSI recipients because SSI pays them so little. Before entering the facility, be sure to ask about their policy on SSI admissions, even if you are not receiving SSI at the time. You may exhaust your funds and be forced to apply for SSI benefits later.

SSI beneficiaries who have been living in their own homes may lose both their SSI and Medi-Cal benefits when they move to a residential care home. This is because their homes are no longer exempt from the property limits of both programs. If this is your situation, be sure to consult with your local senior legal assistance center or other experts before deciding to move to a residential care home.

Licensing

Residential care homes must be licensed. Although a few small homes are still licensed by local welfare departments, most residential care homes are licensed by the State Department of Health. All facilities are visited at least yearly. When licensing violations occur, follow-up visits are made to ensure that violations are corrected.

Resident's Rights

Seniors living in residential care homes have their full rights as citizens and adults, unless a court has ordered conservatorship or guardianship on their behalf. This means that you can visit and communicate with whom you wish, authorize your own medical care, leave the board and care home, spend your own money, voice your political, moral and religious beliefs, and complain to officials if necessary. A residential care home operator, however, can require that you exercise these rights in a manner that is safe, considerate to others, and reasonably convenient to all involved.

You, as a resident, also have the right to adequate food, housing, respectful treatment, supervision, and other services that may have been spelled out in a written agreement with the residential care home operator. In most situations, you cannot be moved or ejected from the facility without adequate notice. Again, these provisions should be detailed in your agreement with the operator.

Most facilities forbid intoxication or the consumption of alcohol on the premises. Furthermore, all medications are generally taken under the supervision of the staff.

Note: Many persons who move to residential care homes are physically healthy but confused and need supervision. If this is the situation in your family, it may be appropriate for someone else to handle the resident's financial affairs. How to do this is discussed in Chapter Thirteen.

When You Have a Complaint

It is impossible to live in a residential care home and not have an occasional grievance or complaint. This is simply part of living in another person's home or in a more organized facility. Sometimes the operator will be curt, sometimes the food will taste appalling, and sometimes things will be unfair.

However, if you have a recurring complaint or frequent complaints, you, and perhaps your family or your social worker, if you have one, should discuss the areas of concern with the operator. If these problems cannot be worked out to your satisfaction, it is probably best that you consider moving. You may get what you want by resorting to the formal complaint procedure described below, but you are likely to destroy whatever friendship and rapport you have with the operator in the process.

Ombudsman Residents, their families, and operators have access to the local Ombudsman. (Ombudsman is a Swedish word meaning a neutral person who can arbitrate disputes.) While an Ombudsman has no power to impose a solution, he or she can help all parties work out their problems regarding care, finances, and behavior without resorting to formal complaint procedures. Your local Ombudsman can be located by calling Information and Referral or the district office of the State Department of Health.

Formal Complaint Procedures You should report any major violation of your personal rights, violations of your written agreement with the operator, and any deterioration in care, food, housing, or supervision. Do this even if you have decided to leave the residential care home. You will be protecting other residents.

Formal complaints should be directed to the agency that licenses the residential care center. In most cases, this will be the district office of the Facilities Licensing Section, State Department of Health. These complaints are made in a manner very similar to nursing home complaints. See Chapter Twelve for a detailed description of complaint procedures and an example of a sample complaint.

Complaints regarding homes licensed by local welfare departments should be made to the residential care licensing section of the welfare department. If the resident has a welfare social worker, the complaint should also be directed to him or her. The complaint should be made over the telephone and, if it is quite serious, also in writing. Formal complaints should be made in writing and should indicate the times, dates, and persons involved in the problem. Include as much detail as possible. And try to be as organized as possible in your description.

The welfare department must act on your complaint, if, on the surface, it is found not to be simple harassment. You are entitled to receive written notification of the results of the licensing worker's investigation, upon your request.

12
Nursing Homes

Everything you've ever heard about nursing homes is probably true for some nursing homes at some time — but doesn't have to be true. Nursing homes are a large national industry, as well as being places where infirm seniors receive care.

There are many good nursing homes in California, despite the drawbacks that do exist. Many nursing homes obey the law, provide excellent care, and do their best to take a personal interest in the lives of their patients.

On the other hand, many nursing homes are nightmares. The patients in these facilities are, for the most part, isolated, frail, and dependent, and so they are easily exploited by unscrupulous proprietors who provide inadequate food, unsafe conditions, filthy facilities, and lack of even the most minimal care.

Of course, none of this should happen. Families should take care of their elder members; nursing homes should be well and humanely run; licensing agencies should be ever vigilant; and taxpayers should provide the funds to see that every sick older person receives adequate care.

But pointing fingers and listing the "shoulds" does not change the present reality. Nursing homes are not going to disappear. For many reasons, many families are simply unable to care for a sick older person. And, given the present state of the health care industry and the cost and level of financial support provided for health care, exploitation and poor care are bound to happen.

Some seniors go into nursing homes planning to return to their own homes after a short convalescence. Others plan to stay indefinitely. Both groups are equally concerned about the quality and appropriateness of the care. But for the long-term residents, the nursing facility must be a place that can be called home. For this reason, the rest of this chapter focuses on long-term residents and their families and the problems that arise for each.

What Is a Nursing Home?

The term "nursing home" is broad and confusing and is often used to describe such facilities as convalescent hospitals, rest homes, board and care homes, and residential care homes. However, as used in this chapter, "nursing home" describes a state licensed facility that provides 24-hour care and medically supervised professional nursing care. The State of California licenses two types of nursing homes:

- intermediate care facilities (ICF)
- skilled nursing facilities (SNF)

Unlike residential care homes described in the previous chapter, both intermediate care facilities and skilled nursing facilities provide care related to the physical conditions or problems of their patients. The people who live in these institutions are generally called patients rather than residents. In order to be admitted to either type of facility, a physician's order is required. The physician must also monitor the patient's medical condition.

Intermediate care and skilled nursing facilities are very similar. However, patients in intermediate care facilities are likely to have stabilized, chronic health problems requiring long-term custodial nursing care. Patients in skilled nursing facilities generally require even more nursing care and more involved treatment, and they are often short-term residents admitted for a rehabilitation or convalescent program. Because of the added services required by these patients, skilled nursing facilities are usually the most expensive type of care.

State law defines a skilled nursing facility as any institution or unit of another institution that operates 24-hour skilled nursing service for the care and treatment of chronically ill or convalescing patients. Included are facilities that treat persons with mental retardation, and emotional, behavioral, and alcohol-related problems. In these facilities, either a registered nurse or a licensed vocational nurse must always be on duty. Patients in skilled nursing facilities may be either ambulatory or bedridden.

Similarly, an intermediate care facility is any institution or part of an institution that provides supportive, restorative, and preventive health services to its patients in conjunction with a socially oriented activities program. The facility must also maintain 24-hour services and supervision, including board, room, personal care, and intermittent nursing care. Licensing requirements provide that either a registered nurse or a licensed vocational nurse must be on duty eight hours a day, seven days a week. Patients must be ambulatory but may use assistive devices such as walkers.

Now 87, Mr. Gilden has become rather frail. He is also nearly blind and almost deaf. The gentleman is still alert and ambulatory, but in recent years he has acquired both a heart condition and diabetes. When his daughter became ill, she could no longer care for him. Mr. Gilden now resides in an intermediate care facility.

Mrs. Middleton lived alone until she fell victim of a stroke, which left her with very slurred speech, unable to walk, and, for the most part, incontinent. She is now cared for in a skilled nursing facility.

When Mrs. Gonzales broke her hip, she was hospitalized, surgery was performed, and she was discharged for several weeks to her son's home. She received the Medicare-paid help of a home health agency while her surgical incision was healing. Once healed, Mrs. Gonzales went to a skilled nursing facility to undergo an intensive rehabilitation program. In several months Mrs. Gonzales was home.

Is Nursing Home Care Necessary?

It has been estimated that 40% of the patients in nursing homes are placed there unnecessarily. This wastes money and means that the patients lead less full and pleasant lives.

The problem is: when *is* it necessary to place a senior in a nursing home? This question probably causes more anguish, frustration, guilt, and confusion than any other when dealing with the problems of seniors. And why not? What harder decision is there than that to take a family member from the home and entrust his or her care and life to an impersonal institution — perhaps to die there? For many families, however, the decision must be made, and the mixed feelings must be resolved.

To a great degree, the decision depends on the seniors themselves. Some older persons are capable of sustaining themselves at home with medical help and supportive services, and even of contributing to the household despite severe and crippling illnesses. Others are less determined and simply cannot remain at home without being a danger to themselves and others.

Then there are the family and friends. People are often placed in nursing homes simply because their family and friends do not have the emotional strength, time, energy, facilities, or stamina to care for them. Most families are unable to drop their jobs and other commitments in order to attend to an infirm elderly person in the family home.

The result, then, is that the decision becomes largely a matter of practicalities. Given the people involved, their personalities and means, their strengths and weaknesses, what do love, fairness, and common sense dictate? Obviously, what might be necessary for one family, at one time, might not be necessary for another at another time. If you or a member of your family are involved in making this decision, you must — as best you can — leave your guilt and sadness aside and try to weigh the alternatives that may work for the senior and for you.

And there are alternatives. Even very ill and confused older people can receive good care outside of nursing homes. For that matter, the care in a nursing home, almost without exception, can be duplicated in the home with supportive health care services. (See Chapter Ten for some suggestions.)

Families and friends can be trained in simple practical nursing techniques; medical and nursing services can be brought into the home; medical equipment and assistive devices can be used at home; and some daily patient care can be provided by support agencies.

Consider whether the senior is in fact well enough to seek placement in a senior residence or a shared housing program, where another senior can provide the needed care. Or perhaps the senior — with some encouragement and help — might qualify for a residential care home.

With all of these alternatives comes some degree of risk. Help may not be immediately available in an emergency, and 24-hour-a-day supervision may not be provided. No senior wants to experience a medical emergency alone, and few families relish the possibility of receiving a call to say that Grandma has fallen again. But this may be the price of a senior's independence. Nursing home care will diminish these risks, but it is also likely to diminish the quality of a senior's life.

Ask Your Doctor Consult your physician about the appropriate level of care, since all facilities require a physician's clearance or recommendation. Discuss the alternatives and options that are available. Your doctor is also in a position to know many of your medical and psychological needs and should be able to suggest an appropriate level of care. He or she may be able to recommend a good facility. However, use the physician's recommendation as a suggestion only. Doctors customarily refer to a limited number of facilities, and you may be more comfortable in a facility that is not among your doctor's choices.

Talk to a Discharge Planner Discharge planners are fairly new to the health care field. They are usually nurses who work in hospitals and assist patients and their families in planning for post-hospital care. They have access to the patient's medical records, they consult with the patient's doctor, and they are familiar with local health care facilities and programs. Discharge planners can help you decide what type of care is needed, and they will help with the practical arrangements for both home care and out-of-home care. Some welfare departments will also provide this assistance to persons who are not hospitalized.

Selecting a Nursing Home

Most people who enter nursing homes are helped to make a selection by their family, friends, or a professional person. However, the person who will be living in the nursing home should be included as much as possible in the decision. This person should be informed of the process even if he or she seems unable to understand or is opposed to nursing home placement. Furthermore, the future resident should visit the selected facility before entering, unless there are strong medical reasons that make this impractical.

The patient's physician will indicate whether intermediate care or skilled nursing care is appropriate. Then you can begin to decide which facility will be suited to the future resident's needs. The district office of the State Department of Health's Facilities Licensing Section can furnish the names of local, licensed intermediate care facilities and skilled nursing facilities. Many communities publish a handbook with the names and descriptions of local residential care homes and nursing facilities. Contact your Information and Referral Service to see if such a handbook exists for your area.

Then try to define what your limitations will be. This will eliminate any number of facilities. Some possible considerations that may limit your choices are:

- location — does the prospective patient need to be near family, friends, or community activities?
- benefits — are you looking for a facility that accepts Medicare, Medi-Cal, or SSI?
- cost — what is the maximum that the patient or his or her family is able to pay?
- physician — which facilities does your doctor recommend?

After you have narrowed down your choices, call each facility and ask if there are vacancies, and if not, ask whether a vacancy is expected soon. You may wish to postpone the time of placement temporarily if an excellent facility has only a short waiting list.

Visit the Facility First Check the facility's record with the licensing agency. Then make an appointment with the administrator — never select a facility before you visit it. When you talk with the administrator, ask to see the admission agreement, or contract, licenses, and licensing citations, if any. Have the administrator go over the agreement with you and keep a copy. Check the agreement for the following:

- how long the contract runs (the term)
- specifically, the services and accommodations to be provided by the facility and the rates or charges for these services and accommodations
- specification of the rights, duties, and obligations of each party who signs the contract, in addition to the rights and duties required by state law
- extra charges
- policy when private funds are exhausted (this should be in writing)
- reasons for discharge
- policy on transfers

Spend a considerable amount of time looking over the facility. Talk to other staff besides the administrator, if available, and to other residents. Do you hear laughter or conversation? Have the staff worked in the facility for more than several months? Observe, and for purposes of comparison, note in writing:

- convenience of location — to the doctor, to the patient, to shopping, etc.
- environment and general atmosphere of the neighborhood
- appearance and demeanor of the home's residents
- staff appearance and attitude
- quality and quantity of food and food service (be around at meal time)
- medical staff and facilities (where medical services are included)
- posted and current state and local licenses to operate
- posted list of patients' rights
- cleanliness of the facility — public access areas, bedrooms, kitchen, and grounds
- visiting privileges — hours, children permitted
- a schedule of financial charges and payment requirements
- recreational activities and facilities
- availability of social services
- safety practices and safeguards against fire and injury
- arrangements for religious services, if desired
- availability of rehabilitative services such as occupational and physical therapy, if it is a skilled nursing facility
- special characteristics or services

Generally, it is advisable to make a second, unannounced visit before making a final selection. Try to visit during a meal or during a shift change. Evenings or late afternoon visits will often show you how the facility is run when staffing is low and the administrator is not around.

The final test should be these simple questions: Is this a place I or my friend or relative can call home? Does it provide a moderate degree of comfort, decent food, and the possibility of good relationships, self-respect, dignity, and something to live for?

The Role of Family and Friends

Families who care about their relatives usually feel a certain amount of guilt when a relative is placed in a nursing home. This is simply part of the package. However, don't let your guilt prevent you from doing what you can to help your relative in the new situation. Often feeling guilty prevents relatives from visiting or causes them not to recognize obvious problems. Some things you can do to help your relative are:

- Visit regularly.
- Continue to include the relative in your family life.
- Listen to your relative's complaints. These are likely to be valid.
- Observe the programs, condition, staff, and quality of care in the facility.
- Make complaints, when indicated, for your relative.
- Contribute financially to your relative's care, if appropriate.
- Be aware of what medications your relative is receiving and why these medications, particularly tranquilizers and sedatives, are being given.

Payment for Nursing Home Care

The basic cost of care in either a skilled nursing facility or an intermediate care facility ranges from about $25 a day to $80 a day. Generally the cost of intermediate care is somewhat less than skilled nursing care. What a facility charges depends on their staffing levels, the skill and training of and the salaries paid to employees, the physical plant, the quality of the food, the richness of the activity program, the locality, the quality of care provided, and the profit made by the facility. Furthermore, the patient's individual needs and preferences (private room, for example) may add to the cost. Generally, the cost of doctor's visits, medications, personal laundry services, and rehabilitative services are not included in the basic costs.

Medicare Payment Your Medicare coverage is likely to be of little use in paying for long-term nursing home care. Medicare Part A will not pay for any nursing home care that is even remotely custodial in nature. You must be in a nursing home for a genuine short-term rehabilitative program, and, even then, Medicare is likely to reject your claim. Furthermore, the facility must be certified as Medicare-eligible and willing to accept your Medicare coverage.

Even if you manage to persuade Medicare to accept your claim, the cost of nursing facilities is generally much higher than what Medicare will pay you. Both your eligibility for Medicare coverage and the reimbursement rates for nursing home care are discussed in Chapter Seven.

Medicare Part B, however, will cover many of your other medical costs while you are receiving treatment or care in any nursing facility. See Chapter Eight for information on your Part B Medicare Benefits.

Private Insurance Some private medical insurance policies pay the cost of limited skilled nursing care. However, most of these policies either provide similar coverage to Medicare or only supplement Medicare. These policies are unlikely to be of much assistance if you require custodial or long-term care.

Life Care Contracts Life care contracts are discussed generally in Chapter Fourteen. They frequently are offered by nursing facilities and must be scrutinized carefully, since they usually involve the transfer of the patient's home or savings to the nursing facility, and the home is frequently the elderly person's only financial asset.

These contracts generally provide that older people transfer title to their homes to the nursing care institution and are thereby assured of care from the institution for the rest of their lives.

Medi-Cal Depending on your medical needs, Medi-Cal can cover the cost of nursing home care. Medi-Cal coverage is much more liberal than Medicare coverage and often pays for needed custodial and rehabilitation-oriented care. A physician's order and the prior authorization of Medi-Cal's evaluators are needed. Additionally, the facility must be certified Medi-Cal eligible and be willing to accept Medi-Cal payment.

Private Payment The majority of patients enter nursing homes under private pay arrangements. Either they or their families pay the nursing home directly the $800 – $2,500 a month required for their care. Obviously, at this rate, a person's income and savings are quickly depleted. When this occurs, most nursing home patients become eligible for Medi-Cal. However, many nursing homes take private payment but do not accept Medi-Cal. As a result, patients are often forced to move when their resources are depleted. Our advice: choose a nursing home that accepts Medi-Cal, unless you are quite wealthy or expect to be in a nursing home only a short time.

Mr. Myers has a Social Security income of $382 a month and $5,000 in a savings account. He entered a skilled nursing facility that cost approximately $1,100 a month. Medicare would not pay for his nursing care, and because of his $5,000 in savings he was ineligible for both SSI and Medi-Cal. For three-and-a-half months Mr. Myers paid the nursing facility $1,100 a month from his income and savings. Then his savings dropped below the $1,500 property limit for Medi-Cal and SSI. He applied for and received both Medi-Cal and SSI. Since his nursing home accepts Medi-Cal, Mr. Myers was able to transfer over to Medi-Cal coverage. Both his Social Security and new SSI income help defray the nursing home costs. Mr. Myers is allowed to keep a very small sum for his personal needs.

Loss of Medi-Cal and SSI Benefits Both of these programs exempt your home from their property limitations as long as you live in it. If you are a long-term nursing home resident, you may find that your former home is no longer exempt from both programs' property limitations. This may cause you to lose your Medi-Cal and SSI eligibility and use the value of your home to pay for your care. If you are in such a situation, contact your county welfare department eligibility worker or your senior legal assistance center for help. (Your representative can also do this for you.)

Licensing Requirements

Both intermediate care facilities and skilled nursing facilities are licensed by the Facilities Licensing Section, State Department of Health. Local facilities are licensed and investigated by one of the nine statewide district offices.

All nursing facilities must renew their licenses each year and are inspected two to three times during the course of the year by the Department of Health. Licensing regulations cover a variety of items, including patient care, staffing, physical environment, services, and legal duties to the patients. When violations are noted, follow-up visits are made to ensure correction. When facilities do not have a license for the current year or have a provisional license for only six months, they may be experiencing licensing difficulties. With such facilities, it is wise to exercise caution.

The Department of Health also has the major responsibility for investigating any complaint made against such a facility. The process for making a complaint is discussed at the end of this chapter.

The following is a list of the current district offices of the Facilities Licensing Section, Department of Health:

District Office	Counties Served
Berkeley 2151 Berkeley Way Berkeley, CA 94704 (415) 843-7900	Alameda, San Francisco
Fresno 3374 E. Shields Avenue Room D-32 Fresno, CA 93726 (209) 488-5691	Fresno, Kern, Kings, Madera, Mariposa, Tulare
Los Angeles 241 N. Figueroa Street Room 346 Los Angeles, CA 90012	Los Angeles (Note: in Los Angeles County, nursing home inspections are conducted by the county rather than the state. This is the office to contact first with respect to making an inspection.)
Sacramento 2422 Arden Way Bldg. "B", Suite 35 Sacramento, CA 95825 (916) 322-6110	Alpine, Amador, Butte, Calaveras, Colusa, El Dorado, Glenn, Lassen, Merced, Modoc, Nevada, Placer, Plumas, Sacramento, San Joaquin, Shasta, Sierra, Siskiyou, Stanislaus, Sutter, Tehama, Trinity, Tuolumne, Yolo, Yuba

San Diego 1350 Front Street Room 2062 San Diego, CA 92101 (714) 236-7381	Imperial, San Diego
San Jose 888 North First Street San Jose, CA 95112 (408) 277-1784	San Mateo, Santa Clara, Santa Cruz, San Benito, Monterey
Santa Ana 28 Civic Center Plaza Room 850 Santa Ana, CA 92701 (714) 558-4001	Inyo, Mono, Orange, Riverside, San Bernardino
Santa Barbara 3704 State Street Suite 309 Santa Barbara, CA 93105 (805) 682-2541	San Luis Obispo, Santa Barbara, Ventura
Santa Rosa 2800 Cleveland Ave. Suite 9 Santa Rosa, CA 95401 (707) 542-6813	Contra Costa, Del Norte, Humboldt, Lake, Marin, Mendocino, Napa, Solano, Sonoma

Legal Duties State law imposes on nursing homes certain legal duties. Among these are the following:

- Maintain the premises and equipment and conduct its operations in a safe and sanitary manner.
- Provide a wholesome and nourishing diet that is sufficient to meet generally accepted standards of proper nutrition for its patients.
- Provide any therapeutic diet prescribed for any individual patients.

- Keep full and complete records of patient, discharges, medical and general health status, including medical records, personal and social history, and cards showing the identity and address of the next of kin or other persons who are responsible for the affairs of each patient.
- Keep financial records.
- Keep drugs and medicines in a safe, locked place that is set aside for this purpose. No patient or unauthorized person may be permitted access to the place where drugs and medications are kept.

Referral Fees An administrator, an employee, or representative of a nursing facility is forbidden to pay, directly or indirectly, any sum of money to any medical person or organization for the referral of patients. Likewise, all administrators and employees of nursing facilities are forbidden to solicit or accept payment of any money from a funeral home, physician, pharmacist, hospital, etc., for the referral of a patient to the nursing home.

Safety of Patient No nursing facility may employ or otherwise permit any person to serve in the home if the person has a communicable contagious disease or other condition that would be dangerous to the health or welfare of other patients. And, no person may be admitted or permitted to remain a patient if:

- They are dangerous to themselves or other patients.
- Their condition or conduct is such that they would be unduly disturbing to other patients.
- They are in need of medical procedures that cannot be given in the nursing home.

Transfer of Patient Other than in cases of emergency, patients may ordinarily not be transferred from a facility or discharged for any reason unless they have personally received notification of the discharge or transfer or it has been given to their next of kin or legal representative.

When a nursing facility stops operating or is about to stop operating, it must inform the State Department of Health that it intends to discontinue its operations. This facility must also inform the patients, their next of kin, or legal representatives, of its intention to close to give the patients sufficient time for a transfer. Where patients have no next of kin or legal representative, the nursing facility is ordinarily responsible for obtaining a suitable transfer of the patient before it discontinues its operations.

Patient's Property A nursing facility is required to provide for the safekeeping of patients' personal effects, funds, and other property in the nursing home. However, these facilities may, in order to avoid responsibility, require that patients' money and property be excluded or removed from the facility and kept in a separate place.

Nursing facilities must keep complete and accurate records of all money and other personal effects and property of the patients received by the facility for safekeeping.

Any other money or other property belonging or due to patients in a nursing facility, or available for their accounts, which are received by the facility, must be designated as "trust" funds. These funds must be kept separate from the funds and property of the facility and other patients, or specifically credited to the patients and may be used or spent only for their accounts.

Upon the request of the patient (except when ordered otherwise by a court), but not more often than once every three months, nursing facilities must furnish patients or their legal representatives, if any, a complete and verified statement of all money and other property that belongs to them, specifying the amounts of items received, together with where they came from and how they were spent. But in any event, both skilled nursing facilities and intermediate care facilities generally must furnish a statement once a year as well as when the patient is discharged or transferred.

Note: If any governmental agency or any private charitable agency contributes money or other property to a patient, the latter is entitled to receive a yearly statement as well as upon his or her discharge or transfer.

The admission of a patient to a nursing facility does not permit the nursing facility or any of its employees to manage, use, or dispose of any property of any patient admitted. Neither does the admission of the patient alone give any such person any authority or responsibility for the personal affairs of the patient, other than what is necessary for the safety and orderly management of the facility.

Nursing facilities must furnish bonds in order to ensure their faithful and honest performance in respect to the funds and property of the patient.

The law forbids a facility or its employees to act as a guardian, trustee, or conservator for any patient of the facility or for any of that patient's property. The legal protection that a patient may need in his or her personal and financial affairs is discussed generally in Chapter Thirteen.

Patient's Rights All facilities participating in Medicare or Medi-Cal are required to have available a written statement of the patient's rights and obligations. These must be prominently displayed. When patients are admitted, their rights must be explained, and they must sign a statement that they have been informed of these rights.

All patients in these facilities, unless under care of a guardian or conservator, have the following rights:

- to be fully informed of their rights and of all rules and regulations of the nursing home governing patient conduct
- to be fully informed of the services available in the facility and of the charges for services
- to be fully informed by a physician of their medical condition (except where limited by a physician and where medically inadvisable); to have the opportunity to participate in the planning of their medical treatment and to refuse to participate in experimental research
- to refuse treatment to the extent permitted by law and to be informed of the medical consequences of refusal
- to be transferred or discharged only for medical reasons, or for their welfare or that of other patients or for nonpayment for their stay and to be given reasonable advance notice
- to be encouraged and assisted throughout their period of stay to exercise their rights as patients and as citizens, free from restraint, interference, coercion, discrimination, or reprisal
- to manage their personal financial affairs, or to be given at least quarterly an accounting of financial transactions made on their behalf if the facility accepts this responsibility for them
- to be free from mental and physical abuse and from chemical and (except in emergencies) physical restraints except as autho-

rized in writing by a physician for a specified and limited period of time, or when necessary to protect the patients from injury to themselves or to others

- to be assured confidential treatment of their personal and medical records
- to be treated with consideration, respect and full recognition of their dignity and individuality, including privacy in treatment and in care for their personal needs
- not to be required to perform services for the facility that are not included in their plans of care for therapeutic purposes
- to associate and communicate privately with persons of their choice, and to send and receive their personal mail unopened, except where this right may be limited by a physician and is not medically advisable
- to meet with and participate in activities of social, religious, and community groups at their discretion, except where limited by the physician as a medical necessity
- to retain and use their personal clothing and possessions as space permits, unless to do so would infringe upon the rights of other patients
- if married, to be assured privacy for visits by their spouse and and if both are patients in the facility, to be permitted to share a room (unless medically inadvisable)
- to have daily visiting hours established
- to have members of the clergy admitted at the request of the patient or person responsible at any time
- to allow relatives or persons responsible to visit critically ill patients at any time (unless limited by the patient's physician for medical reasons)
- to be allowed privacy for visits with family, friends, clergy, social workers or for professional or business purposes
- to have reasonable access to telephones both to make and receive confidential calls

Making a Complaint About a Nursing Home

Any nursing home will occasionally violate some of its licensing requirements in minor ways. These petty violations are seldom cause for worry, and, when a facility is basically good, are probably not worth the trouble of making a complaint.

However, any major abridgement of your rights as a patient, such as deterioration in food or facility maintenance and cleanliness, lapse in care, theft of property, cruelty to patients, or unlawful behavior, should be reported.

The usual mechanism for making formal complaints is to bring the matter up first with the facility administrator, then the local Ombudsman, and finally the Facilities Licensing Section, State Department of Health. If you wish, you can bring the matter directly to the attention of the licensing agency rather than going through the usual channels.

When you have a major complaint, try to gather specific data and make a written record of your observations, noting date, times, personnel involved, and a description of the problem. For example: "On June 3rd from 7 – 11 P.M. patient Mary Smith's bedpan remained unemptied in spite of her frequent calls. Nurse Susan Jones was on duty." Try to establish a pattern or a frequency of the problem. One incident will probably be treated as a mistake, and you will have to be satisfied with only an apology.

The law requires that no patient may receive a lesser quality of care, or punishment, because he or she has made a complaint. However, the quality of life in a nursing home is often measured in little things such as warm words or a gentle turning in bed. At best, patients who make complaints are likely to receive somewhat less tender care. For this reason it is often preferable for a relative or friend to make the complaint rather than the patient or resident.

When you make a formal licensing complaint, it is often advisable to have the assistance of a local senior legal center's representative. This is particularly true if you are a patient at the facility.

Facility Administrator Most grievances and problems can be resolved simply by talking the situation over with the administrator in a nursing home.

For example, a patient is unhappy because she must sit in her wheelchair for several hours rather than being allowed to return to bed. After discussion, she finds that sitting is a prescribed part of her treatment program. Or, perhaps the administrator discovers that an employee has been disrespectful and reprimands the employee.

The Ombudsman Beginning in 1980, the long-term care Ombudsman program became a vehicle to resolve problems in California nursing homes. "Ombudsman" is a Swedish word describing a neutral, independent person who is used to help solve problems. Each area in the state has an Ombudsman program. This person (or persons) is by law given access to all long-term care facilities in his or her area. The Ombudsman is not only the patient's advocate but is also available to families, nursing home administrators, and concerned members of the community. Having no power to impose solutions or fines, the Ombudsman generally works to mediate disputes. The Ombudsman can assist in arbitrating problems involving:

- physical care
- medical care
- pharmaceutical services
- personal dignity
- food
- meaningful activities
- rehabilitation
- legal or financial problems
- regulatory red tape
- appropriate placements

When disputes cannot be worked out with the assistance of the Ombudsman, complaints can still be made to the licensing agency.

The Ombudsman is a required witness when nursing home residents wish to make a directive to physicians, under the California Natural Death Act. This act is discussed in Chapter Thirteen.

Contact your local Information and Referral Service for the phone number and location of your local Ombudsman.

Department of Health Nursing home licensing complaints should be directed to the Department of Health. (Los Angeles residents should contact the county department of health.) Addresses and phone numbers of local offices are found earlier in the chapter.

Your complaint should be as specific as possible and in writing. Keep a copy for your records. A suggested form for the complaint follows at the end of the chapter.

Once the Facilities Licensing Section of the Department of Health receives your complaint, it must assign the matter to an evaluator for a preliminary review. The Department of Health must make an on-site inspection within ten days, unless your complaint is found to be without reasonable basis in fact and intended solely to harass the nursing home. If your complaint is dismissed for this reason, the name of the evaluator must be given to you, and you can appeal his or her decision to the supervisor.

Generally, the person making the complaint may accompany the investigator on an inspection of the facility. The inspection must be unannounced. Any employee who gives advance notice to a facility is required by law to be suspended without pay for a period of time.

A citation will be issued when the investigator decides that the facility is in violation of the state licensing regulations. Three types of citations can be issued:

- Class A — violations that present imminent danger or substantial probability of death or serious physical harm to patients ($1,000 – $5,000 fine for each violation)
- Class B — violations that have a direct or immediate relationship to the health, safety, and security of the patients but are not Class A violations ($50 – $250 fine for each violation)
- Class C — violations that have only a minimal relationship to the health and safety of the patients and relate mostly to operation and maintenance (no fine)

The investigator must issue a written citation within three days. Facilities not wishing to contest the citation must pay their fines within four working days. Facilities wishing to contest the citation must indicate this within four days also. All uncorrected Class A citations must be publicly posted.

Anonymous complaints will be accepted. However, the Department of Health is under no obligation to investigate these. If you feel a patient is in imminent danger and believe an immediate investigation is necessary, call the Department of Health and let them know the emergency nature of your complaint. Then follow up with a written complaint indicating the date and time of your call.

Sample Complaint

Date:

State Department of Health[1]
Facilities Licensing Section
(address of office in county where nursing home is located)

Dear Sir/Madam:

I have good cause to believe there is a violation of California Administrative Code, Division 5, Title 22, by a nursing home and request an inspection of it.

The name of the nursing home is ________________ ________________________________, and it is located at ____. The name of the facility's administrator is __________.

The circumstances giving rise to this complaint are as follows: *(be as specific as possible)* ____________ ____.

I request an inspection due to a condition that poses an immediate danger to the health, safety, and security of the patients in the nursing home described above. I am (or am not) interested in accompanying the inspector on his/her inspection of the facility as provided for by state law.

I request that the name of any patient involved be left off any copies that are made of this complaint. If there is not an immediate inspection made by you in response to this request, I expect a written letter from you explaining why this request was denied.

Sincerely,

____
(your name)

____
(your address)

____
(your telephone number)

[1]Complaints in Los Angeles County are made to the County Board of Health, initially.

Other Agencies That Can Receive Complaints Most professionals working in nursing homes or providing medical services to nursing home patients are licensed by a board or agency within the State Department of Consumer Affairs. If your complaint concerns one of these professionals, you can complain directly to their licensing board at the following addresses:

Board of Examiners of Nursing Home Administrators
1020 N Street
Sacramento, CA 95814
(916) 445-8435

State Board of Registered Nurses
1020 N Street
Sacramento, CA 95814
(916) 322-3350

State Board of Vocational Nurses and Psychiatric Examiners
1020 N Street
Sacramento, CA 95814
(916) 445-1793

State Board of Pharmacy
1021 N Street
Sacramento, CA 95814
(916) 445-5014

State Board of Medical Quality Assurance
1430 Howe Ave.
Sacramento, CA 95825
(916) 920-6352

(This list applies to all doctors, psychologists, hearing aid dispensers, physical therapists, and medical and professional corporations.)

13
Protective Services

This is an unpleasant subject. It is unpleasant for seniors; it is unpleasant for families; and it is unpleasant for the professionals who must intervene on behalf of seniors.

But the reality is that some seniors are simply unable to manage their own affairs. Many only require assistance with financial matters. But a few must have the most basic decisions — where to live, what to eat, and what medical treatment to use — made for them.

Perhaps the most unpleasant reality is the physical abuse and neglect sometimes inflicted on older persons by their families, the public, and public policy. We hear of frail elderly persons assaulted by their own children. Daily news stories casually report robberies, physical assaults, and worse to seniors — on the streets, on public transit, and even in their homes. And most of us have seen an elderly person wandering aimlessly, unkempt, searching in garbage cans for something to wear or eat. Others confine themselves to cheap rooms, mental hospitals, or nursing homes under abysmal conditions.

A number of studies have shown the pressing need for reform of the procedures designed to protect mentally and physically infirm persons. More than three million persons 65 or over require protective support. This number would double if the help of friends, relatives, or social agencies were taken away.

The assistance given to such persons is usually called "protective services." This chapter will be of more help, however, if the reader thinks of protective services as those services which are appropriate where older persons are unable or unwilling to care for themselves. These services are outlined in detail later in this chapter. The services, or assistance, that may be given to an older person who needs help in maintaining himself or herself are called supportive services or supportive care. Some of these services are discussed later but many are outlined in Chapter Ten.

The Need for Supportive or Protective Care

The typical recipient of supportive and protective services is an aging widow, widower, or couple experiencing difficulty with changes in living arrangements, payment of bills, transportation, medical treatment and insurance, credit, ability to deal with salesmen, contractors, and governmental organizations. In some instances the difficulties may have arisen from physical disability or weakness, mental deterioration, low income and inflation, and in other instances from psychological depression resulting from these and other problems.

Mrs. Lewis, a widow (age 76), had to give up her home and take an apartment because of heart trouble. Her eyesight is dim and her hearing is blocked. She no longer reads or listens to music, which she formerly enjoyed. To the few friends who visit her, she seems apathetic and depressed. She eats very little and hardly ever leaves her apartment any more. Her friends wonder if they should do something.

Mr. Morrison, a former engineer (age 81), is pleasant to others but can't find his way around the house or follow a conversation. Several times when he left the house he became lost. His wife is in poor health but prepares his meals and looks after him. She worries about what will happen to him if he survives her.

Mr. Perry (age 85) lives alone in a filthy room in the city's slums. He wanders the streets and alleys, talking to himself and collecting junk and garbage. On several occasions he has been robbed of his Social Security and SSI checks. He appears ill and emaciated. Twice his landlord called the fire department to put out fires he started in his room. The neighbors who care wonder if they should call the police or something.

Obviously, all these people could use help — but not necessarily the same kind of help. Mrs. Lewis' situation, for example, may call for limited, supportive assistance to forestall her worsening condition. Mr. Morrison, on the other hand, may be helped the most by a guardianship or conservatorship to which he might agree. For Mr. Perry, perhaps intervention by a public or private agency to protect him despite his own wishes is warranted. A lot depends, of course, on who gives the assistance and when.

Incompetent or infirm elderly persons are frequently preyed upon through fraudulent schemes offered as investments, false promises of inexpensive services, oral agreements, and written agreements that contain nothing but legal jargon or fine print. (See Chapter Seventeen, Consumer Protection.) In many instances, homes have been lost, estates depleted, valuable personal property given away for a fraction of its value, and cheap or worthless goods or services bought at many times the real value. Furthermore, people have been locked in hospitals and residential care facilities of different types — sometimes without need.

Supportive Services or Care

Supportive services or care are designed chiefly to provide some kind of continuous assistance to an older person who can and should remain in his or her own home and does not require daily, 24-hour supervision. Numerous studies have shown conclusively that older people do better and live more useful, productive lives when they remain in their own surroundings than when they move to some kind of institution.

These services are useful both to the senior who is independently managing his or her own affairs and to the senior whose affairs are managed by others. By appropriately using these resources, many seniors and their families are able avoid the restrictions of guardianship and conservatorship.

Ideally, of course, the immediate family of an older infirm or incompetent person is best qualified to give the person supportive care. Such a family, however, frequently has its own pressing needs that make care difficult if not impossible.

Another problem, frequently encountered, is where relatives become a part of the problem by their inability to deal effectively with the elderly relative or their distance from him or her. And relatives, of course, have been known to seize the assets of an older person and place them in custodial care as one means of avoiding probate.

In the absence of care by the family, the core of supportive services consists of visits by social workers, various community services such as visiting nurses, homemakers, medical clinical services, special transportation, hot prepared meals delivered to the older person's residence, and periodic visitors or telephone checks. These services are discussed in Chapters Ten and Nineteen.

Intervention Protective Services

The rest of this chapter outlines the various legal alternatives available when older people are incompetent or mentally ill and, in the opinion of those closest to them, are unable to care for themselves adequately. When an older person recognizes this need and can participate in planning to meet it, the nature of the service is supportive. In a protective plan, guardianship or conservatorship, for example, is ordered by the court.

Admittedly, these categories are not mutually exclusive. The point is to grasp what services are available to an older person who needs them in his or her own situation.

Legal Incompetency — What Is It? Legal incompetency cannot be defined with any precision — even by judges and lawyers. For the purposes of this chapter, we will use the definition used by California courts when appointing a guardian.

A person is legally incompetent when, because of advanced age or some physical or mental disability, the person is unable to care for his or her person or property properly. Because of the age or disability, such a person is likely to be cheated or defrauded by others.

Of course, whether a person is ever found to be legally incompetent by a judge depends on the circumstances.

Mr. Sutter, age 76, lives with his family, who cares for him. He "talks" often with his former wife, who has been dead for ten years. Much of the time he is incoherent, and he is unable to care for his physical needs very well.

The chances are that Mr. Sutter's family can adjust to his behavior and make allowances for it. If, on the other hand, Mr. Sutter was alone in a city, he might well be found legally incompetent by the authorities.

Mrs. Jenner, age 83, has recently been approached by members of a religious group that has been indicted for fraud. Mrs. Jenner, despite advice to the contrary, sends the group substantial amounts of money and intends to leave her property to them.

Is Mrs. Jenner legally incompetent? It is difficult to say — drawing the line between foolishness or eccentricity and legal incompetency is difficult. Each case must be decided on its own facts. Remember always, however, that your right to manage your own affairs and person cannot easily be taken away from you. Furthermore, this right cannot be taken away without some sort of legal proceeding.

Commitment to an Institution When older persons are unable or unwilling to consent to planning for care outside their homes, they have been committed traditionally to mental hospitals by a procedure called civil commitment. Even now, nationally, about 30% of persons in mental hospitals are over 60. State hospital care is generally custodial rather than therapeutic. The psychological impact is frequently severe, and mortality rates are high. Furthermore, the care is extremely expensive.

Fortunately, in California, older persons are no longer committed en masse to state hospitals for custodial care. Generally, only a violent or dangerous older person will be committed on a long-term basis to a psychiatric institution. Physically healthy, mentally ill, or senile persons are more often placed under guardianship, sent to residential care homes, and medicated.

If you are faced with the responsibility of planning for someone in need of protective support and care, discuss this problem with professionals in the mental health field as well as with your lawyer. Occasionally, it makes sense to commit an older person to a psychiatric hospital for emergency treatment and evaluation. Involuntary commitment involves complex legal as well as ethical considerations and few persons — especially relatives of the older person — are qualified to make such decisions on their own. Note: Keep in mind the fact that Medicare coverage for mental health institutions is very limited and does not apply at all to custodial care. (See Chapter Six.)

Other Possible Solutions Besides commitment, legal intervention for incompetent older persons may take any of the following, usually preferable, forms:

- guardianship
- conservatorship
- power of attorney

- creation of joint tenancy
- substitution of relative as payee

Most of these options may be chosen freely by an elderly person. Others may be imposed voluntarily by state government action or the decision of private parties, such as family members. Therefore, all of these options must be evaluated for their usefulness to the older person and for the degree of protection they provide.

Warning: Be sure to seek legal help for any of the above procedures. Do not attempt to draw up papers yourself — they probably will not be correct and will endanger both the elderly person you are trying to protect as well as yourself.

Guardianship Guardianship is a legal proceeding in which some person or agency is appointed to manage the personal and/or business affairs of an incompetent person, who is called the ward.

Although legal guardianship may be appropriate in some cases, there are usually problems involved. For example, guardianship involves a finding (by a court) of incompetency. The result is that the infirm or confused older person has an almost total lack of control about his or her living arrangements, investments, and other such decisions. Needless to say, this total isolation from control of one's affairs brings on feelings of uselessness low self-esteem, and further mental and physical deterioration.

Furthermore, even well-meaning relatives who are appointed guardians for the older person may make wrong decisions, resulting in great financial loss to the ward.

Certain social agencies or the county public guardian may serve as guardian, provided they are willing to do so and are appointed by a judge. In addition, corporations, such as the trust department of a bank, may serve as property guardians (but not as personal guardians).

California has adopted the Uniform Veterans Guardianship Act. Generally the state laws provide for two systems of protection of property of minors and mental incompetents, one of which applies if the property came, in whole or in part, from benefits paid by the Veterans Administration and its minor or incompetent owner is or has been a beneficiary of the Veterans Administration; and the other of which applies to all property.

Mrs. Bouroughs (age 83) has been diagnosed as senile by her physician. Although in fairly good health for her age, she is unable to maintain herself or her property — consisting of several homes and income from other investments. On several occasions, she has tried to give her property to friends who are deceased and has attempted suicide when her family intervened. Her family, however, wants to care for her at home with skilled nursing and medical assistance. An adult member of her family should consider guardianshp of Mrs. Bouroughs' person and estate, since she would never agree to any form of voluntary assistance.

Found wandering in the streets confused and hungry, 74-year-old Mr. Rogers needed assistance. When no relative could be found, the court ordered Mr. Rogers placed under the care of the county public guardian. The guardian's office placed this gentleman in a residential care home, looks in on him occasionally, and manages his finances.

Conservatorship Legal conservatorship of seniors or their estates provides for court-supervised financial and/or personal management involving the same legal safeguards as guardianship, but without the stigma of incompetency. The conservatees (the older persons) have a legal right to consult with the conservators (the persons appointed) about their affairs. They also retain a right to make certain contracts of their own. Generally, the conservator must take adequate consideration of the wishes of the senior as part of the decision making process.

In conservatorship of an estate, disposition of the assets of the senior is allowed only where need and justification can be shown to the court, either before or after the assets have been disposed of.

In cases where conservators cannot obtain the approval of the court in regard to the disposition of the senior's property, they may be penalized personally or have to forfeit their bonds.

In some probate courts (for example, in Los Angeles County), judges require that conservators promise under penalty of perjury that the senior will not be placed in any health care facility against his or her will. Many such seniors live in their own homes or apartments and often retain their own furniture. And in some instances, the senior may be permitted to drive an automobile or travel at will on public transportation.

Conservatorship can be terminated when a person has recovered and no longer needs the protection.

Power of Attorney The purpose of a simple power of attorney is to provide the legal means for another person to handle your business and financial affairs. Legally competent seniors who are ill, who do not wish to manage their routine financial affairs, or who are confused and bored by paperwork may wish to give someone else their power of attorney. This procedure can be useful if your financial affairs are relatively uncomplicated and if your income and assets are not large.

In California, a general power of attorney that gives the attorney in fact (the person to whom the power is given) power to generally manage the affairs of the senior must be what is called a "durable" power. "Durable" means that the power expires automatically one year after it is signed and must be renewed to be valid. This protects people from fraud and forgetfulness.

You can obtain the forms for a power of attorney from your bank. Power of attorney will enable another person to act in regard to the senior's interests in the bank — for example, his or her checking or savings account, safe-deposit box, credit cards, etc. For a more general power of attorney form, ask at your local Senior Legal Assistance Center if you don't have an attorney.

When the power of attorney is restricted in its use, in most cases the attorney in fact is a relative or close friend who should be willing to serve without compensation. Furthermore, this person must be trustworthy enough to take care of the older person's interests without the necessity of giving bond. Also, the person or organization may be a social service or welfare agency, such as the American National Red Cross.

Mr. Peters (age 85) is physically and mentally alert but has been advised by his doctor that his poor eyesight will deteriorate into blindness in the near future. Mr. Peters contributes to his grandson's education from monthly benefits he receives but does not need. He should consider asking his son to act as his attorney in fact, through a power of attorney, to make sure the trust payments to his grandson continue as he wishes, should he become incapacitated.

Miss Williams is in a nursing home recovering from a recent hip injury. She owns her own home, several apartments, and other business interests. While she is undergoing her current treatment, she doesn't want to be inconvenienced by managing her routine financial affairs. Miss Williams has her attorney draw up a very specific document giving her niece a limited power of attorney. The niece sees to the daily running of Miss Williams' business affairs.

Caution: A senior must be legally competent in order to make a valid power of attorney. If his or her competency is questionable, the power of attorney can be challenged. Furthermore, a power of attorney will end automatically one year after signing. Consequently, if an older person becomes disabled, the power of attorney may terminate at the very time he or she needs it most. Also, be very careful to whom you give a power of attorney. That person has legal control of your financial affairs.

Joint Tenancies Joint tenancy is a way of expressing the share that two or more people own in a property or fund. Joint holdings are often used within families to serve convenience, provide mutual assistance, or safeguard ownership. If man and wife or parent and child hold funds jointly, one of the two may act if the other cannot. Joint tenancy usually applies only to assets or income under mutual control.

Jim and Mary Reynolds own their own home in joint tenancy, some stocks and bonds, and have a small income from Social Security benefits. Jim owns in his own name a parcel of valuable property which he recently inherited. Both are 80 and Jim's doctor advised him that his chronic heart condition could worsen in the near future. Jim worries about Mary's ability to survive, financially, should he die and his property go into probate. Jim should consider putting his property into joint tenancy with Mary, enabling her to sell it reasonably quickly should the necessity arise suddenly. But remember that transferring holdings to joint tenancy may affect the parties' eligibility for SSI, Medi-Cal, and other benefits.

Substitution as Payee of Benefits The job of managing money received by an incompetent senior is authorized by federal law, which authorizes certain agencies to appoint a substitute for the person entitled to receive federal funds. The need for this action may come to an agency's attention in various ways, such as notice that the beneficiary is in a hospital, a call or letter from a friend, or a claim for disability benefits. Once word is received of the beneficiary's alleged incompetence, all federal agencies except the Social Security Administration stop making payments until it is determined whether or not the older person is in fact incompetent.

Usually, the agency's procedure is to inquire whether the senior can manage money. When the senior is found incompetent, the agency tries to select a substitute who is generally concerned for the senior's well-being and is willing to serve, account for expenses, and inform the agency of other major events in the senior's life. The substitute need not be a relative.

If this procedure is suitable for your problem, contact the federal agency sending the senior's benefit payments. How to do this when the benefits come from Social Security or SSI is explained in Chapter One.

Miss Patrick (age 80) has been suddenly hospitalized for a severe illness that incapacitates her. Her nephew John, who looks after her, should notify the Social Security Administration in his area of his aunt's incapacity and request that he be named substitute payee of her monthly Social Security payments.

Private Care Companies

In the recent past, a private approach to organized protective services has been developed and serves this state. It is called Planned Protective Services, Inc., a non-profit charitable, federal and state tax exempt, nonsectarian California corporation. This organization was incorporated to provide court-supervised, bonded, expert, professional personal and financial management, through conservatorship, to the elderly infirm. It is planned that this corporation will expand, and you might check in the white and yellow pages of your telephone book to see if they have a branch near you.

One of the more interesting aspects of the protective services offered by these corporations is the lack of red tape involved. In cases of immediate crisis, because of the professional experience of the corporations in their field, and due to their excellent reputation with the courts, the judges, hospitals, and the medical profession, an agency such as Planned Protective Services, Inc. is often appointed as temporary conservator within as little as 48 hours after the first crisis call.

Compared with the average attorney cost of from $50 to $75 per hour and the bank or trust company charges of from $30 to $50 per hour, organizations such as Planned Protective Services, Inc., charge about $20 per hour. In the case of the Los Angeles organization, due to its efficiency, it has been able to guarantee that it will care for the older person for life, even though medical care and hospitalization costs eventually deplete all of his or her assets. They never receive payments in advance, and only if the court determines that the services provided were necessary and reasonable is payment endorsed by the supervising judge.

Services Provided by Banks

In most areas of the state, banks and trust companies regularly serve as legal representatives for the estates of incompetents. Their fees for this service are minimal, and by and large they do an excellent job, including the regular accounting that must be done by law. However, they are not allowed to handle the senior's personal protection (called conservatorship of the person). A friend or relative is usually most suitable for this task.

Mrs. Paul (age 80) is in good physical health and lives with her daughter and son-in-law. She receives rentals from various properties and owns certain stocks that are blue chip investments. Mrs. Paul cannot sign a check in the proper place or understand her monthly bank and stock statements. Recently, her daughter learned that Mrs. Paul's stock broker urged her to speculate in "growth" stocks and options, which she does not understand, but she agrees with her broker in order to be pleasant. The daughter should consider petitioning the court where she lives for a conservatorship of her mother's estate, naming a bank as conservator.

Protection from Abuse and Neglect

Since her husband died, Mrs. Redmond has lived with her daughter and son-in-law. She hands her monthly Social Security check over to her son-in-law and dips into her savings in order to help her family out. Recently her son-in-law demanded that she turn all her savings over to him so that he could pay his pressing bills. When she refused, he shouted at her and finally hit her several times. Rather than apologize, the son-in-law told her that she was lucky they gave her a home and didn't send her to a nursing home. She wrote out a check.

The national Administration on Aging has found that abuse of seniors by their families is a national concern. This may consist of physical abuse through violence, verbal abuse, theft, or the withholding of food, medical care, or personal care.

Seniors are frequently treated like children or in a manner that lowers their self-esteem or self-worth. Although this treatment may not constitute abuse, when it becomes aggravated it may well threaten the psychological or physical health of the senior.

The majority of the abused seniors are female, physically or mentally impaired or both, and live with an adult child or some other family member. And most abused seniors either deny that maltreatment exists or passively accept it.

What Can You Do? It would be a big step forward for seniors to lobby for mandatory reporting laws, such as those employed in child abuse cases. This way concerned agencies would be able to assist abused seniors with or without their consent. If you are concerned, write your legislator about the desirability of such laws.

Adult Protective Services State law requires the state Department of Social Services to establish and supervise the Adult Protective Services program authorized by Title XX of the Social Security Act.

The purpose of this program is to prevent or remedy danger to individuals who are unable to protect their own interests, who are neglected or maltreated by others because of their inability to protect themselves, or who are deprived of their benefits or exploited generally.

If you are a California senior, you are eligible for this protection no matter what your income is. Your county welfare department, upon receiving a report or referral alleging abuse, neglect, or mistreatment of a senior, must investigate the matter promptly.

The social worker from the department who investigates the situation may refer the matter to the police or to a local mental health agency. He or she may also arrange, where appropriate, for a conservatorship, out-of-home care, or for better in-home care.

In making these recommendations, the social worker must respect the senior's right to make an independent decision — where that is appropriate. In some situations, however, mandatory intervention may be necessary.

For further information on Adult Protective Services, including the telephone number to call, ask at your local county welfare department in the white pages of the telephone directory. Or, if you already have a case worker who is assigned to your SSI claim, contact that person.

Protection from Crime

Most seniors will be aware, before they read this text, of the basic lessons on how to protect themselves in their homes or on the streets. Nevertheless, here are some suggestions on how best to protect yourself and your property when needed without police protection.

In the home, you should, if possible, install some kind of peephole and never open your door until you know who is outside. Never leave a note on your door stating you're not at home; use only your last name and initial on your door, on the mail box, and in the phone book. Replace locks when you move to a new residence.

When a person calling on you claims to be a salesman, repairman, etc., ask to see adequate identification before letting him or her in.

If you return home and suspect someone is inside your residence, don't go in — call the police immediately!

When driving, keep your windows rolled up and your doors locked. Keep your purse (or valuables) out of sight. Do not, of course, pick up hitchhikers — even a woman alone. If you have car trouble, raise the hood and stay inside until help arrives.

When walking, avoid dark, deserted streets or alleys; walk with someone else if possible, stay near the curb and away from entryways and bushes, and, if possible, walk near other pedestrians.

Above all, don't be afraid or embarrassed to call the police if you suspect trouble.

Senior Escort Service Many cities and counties, in cooperation with their law enforcement agencies, maintain a senior escort service designed to better safeguard seniors out of their home. More information on this service, which is discussed in Chapter Nineteen, can usually be obtained from your local police or sheriff's department.

Police Classes on Tear Gas In both southern and northern California, the law-enforcement authorities are offering classes in the use of defensive tear gas techniques. The classes cost about $35.00 per person, with discounts for groups and disabled persons.

This promises to be a very effective method for seniors to better protect themselves while in public. If you are interested, contact your local police or sheriff's department and request further information.

Aid to Victims of Crime If you are a person who is a victim of a crime that has caused you financial loss, you may file a claim for reimbursement. This reimbursement may consist of a cash payment for medical expenses up to $10,000, a cash payment for lost wages or support up to $10,000, and up to $3,000 for job-training or rehabilitative services.

If you receive such reimbursement, it does not affect any benefits you get from public assistance, such as SSI payments.

A victim of crime should file a claim for reimbursement with the California State Board of Control (look in the white pages under "California, State of"). The application must be filed within one year after the date of the crime. For further information and help in filing such a claim, contact your local legal assistance center or your Ombudsman. The necessary form will be available at the Board of Control, and they will be glad to mail you one.

Lifeline Program

Lifeline is basically a remote control device from which a call for assistance can be made simply by pushing a button. Although the device is connected electronically with your telephone, the Lifeline works even though your phone is off the hook or if there is a power interruption. In the event that you are unable to push the button, a timer on the unit which you pre-set automatically activates a signal for help.

Lifeline has been used successfully in cases of medical emergency and personal assaults. Agencies and hospitals in the state are just beginning to offer this device to their neighboring communities.

Generally, there is a small installation charge and a monthly rental fee of about $10.00. In most instances, the Lifeline device is hooked up to a hospital that, upon being signaled, will send persons to investigate. These persons are usually neighbors or friends you have pre-designated to be called.

This device is recommended highly for seniors who live alone and want protection. If you want further information on Lifeline and have none in your community, contact (415) 579-2360 (Auxiliary of Mills Memorial Hospital, 100 So. San Mateo Drive, San Mateo, CA 94401).

Note: Do not confuse this device with that program offered by the telephone company called "Lifeline" which offers low-cost telephone service under specified conditions.

PART III
OTHER BENEFITS, RIGHTS, & SERVICES

14
Legal Problems and Solutions

Obtaining adequate legal advice and assistance, at an affordable price, is becoming an increasingly serious problem for California seniors. Ninety percent of seniors depend to some extent on benefits administered by the maze of federal, state, and local bureaucracies. The rules and regulations governing these benefits are complex and in many instances contradictory. Few seniors can afford to hire legal help at the going rate to ensure that they receive the benefits due to them.

As a result, many seniors remain unaware that they are entitled to certain benefits, many lose their rights to receive benefits for reasons they fail to understand, and many suffer from lack of knowledge about their general remedies under the law. For seniors with special needs who are economically dependent or have marginal incomes, this can be devastating.

This chapter discusses many of the situations in which a senior may need legal assistance, as well as where help may be found, and the cost of obtaining it.

Some Common Legal Problems

Mrs. Fong, age 86, is in poor health, almost blind, and dependent on her wheelchair. Her son feels she is unable to care for herself and petitions the court to be appointed her conservator. He also requests that she be placed in a nursing home. Mrs. Fong is mentally alert and wants to stay in her home, but she doesn't know what to do.

Mr. Kohlenberg, age 90, has complained to his county's housing authority about his landlord's refusal to install lighting in the apartment hallway. Now Mr. Kohlenberg is served with an eviction notice by his landlord.

Mr. Spencer, age 80, is bedridden with a heart problem. He receives Social Security retirement benefits, SSI, and Medi-Cal. Recently his senior service center sent a volunteer as a temporary live-in to assist him with his personal care and maintain his house. The county welfare department has now notified Mr. Spencer that his SSI payments will be reduced because of the extra help.

The above examples illustrate only a few of the common legal problems that California seniors are likely to encounter and that ordinarily require legal assistance. Others involve:

- Social Security and/or SSI benefits
- Medicare and/or Medi-Cal benefits
- patients' rights in nursing homes
- fraudulent consumer transactions
- protective services, including guardianship and conservatorship
- employment problems, including mandatory retirement and age discrimination
- landlord-tenant problems, including the enforcement of housing codes
- private insurance disputes
- veterans' benefits
- wills, property transfers, and other individual legal transactions
- marriage and divorce
- tax problems

Private Lawyers

Seniors who have legal problems involving a large amount of money, divorce, or criminal matters should engage the services of an attorney. Usually, doing otherwise is simply a case of being pennywise and pound foolish.

However, if you have a legal problem involving government benefits, simple consumer complaints, or government regulations, you are likely to find the services of a senior legal center cheaper and more effective than a private attorney. Lawyers are expensive, and most will charge you a consultation or "screening" fee that may be beyond what you can comfortably afford.

Furthermore, most private attorneys do not handle many administrative law cases. These cases — involving Social Security, Medicare, Medi-Cal, and other benefits — constitute a large part of the work handled by legal service programs for the elderly.

Additionally, when a private attorney does agree to accept an administrative law case, he or she will usually deduct from any settlement a substantial percentage. This deduction is not made by private, nonprofit legal services.

Nevertheless, you may want to retain private legal counsel for a variety of reasons. If you do, you'll find that lawyers in this state are expensive; their fees range from about $40 – $100 an hour; most demand an immediate retainer before they will work on the case; in addition, the fee range mentioned above does not include court costs and the other costs that are a part of every lawsuit.

Group Legal Services; Prepaid Plans In many counties there are group legal services available, which you will generally find advertised in the yellow pages under "Attorneys." Some of these offer substantial discounts on professional services.

If you are a member of a prepaid legal services plan, you should, of course, use those services. Similarly, if you have already used an attorney for other legal services such as making a will, you'll probably want to continue with the same person. If you are unfamiliar with the resources in your community, ask other seniors for recommendations.

Don't be afraid to shop around a little with regard to finding a lawyer. For example, there is nothing wrong with calling various attorneys from the phone directory, freely stating the nature of your problem, and inquiring as to whether they will take the case and, if so, how much their fees will be.

Lawyers' Referral Services These are available in many counties. This type of service offers a low-cost screening (about $15), in which your case is reviewed by an attorney and two or three referrals are made to other private attorneys. This kind of service may be useful to you, but remember that the fee covers *only* the initial interview — usually limited to 30 minutes — and your case is not processed. You will find these services also listed under "Attorneys" in the yellow pages. If you have trouble locating them, contact your Information and Referral service.

Reduced Fee Programs The Bar Association in some counties sponsors a reduced fee program that provides private legal services for low- and moderate-income seniors. The income limits average from $400 – $700 per month for a single senior and about $500 – $900 for a couple with dependents. The fees are reduced to about $20 – $32 per hour, depending on your situation. Check with your local Bar Association for further information about these programs where you live.

Volunteer Private Lawyers There is a relatively small but increasing number of law firms that devote part of their time, on a volunteer basis, to assisting minorities and seniors. You can find out who these attorneys are by contacting the Bar Association where you live or by asking at your local paralegal office.

Retired or semi-retired attorneys are another source of legal assistance. These professionals may have special empathy with their clients. They may do this work individually, or as part of the local Bar Association's sponsorship, or in teams. For example, one group has about 60 retired attorneys who accept elderly clients on what is called a *pro bono* basis — that is, they charge what the client can afford to pay. Check with your local Bar Association.

Senior Legal Assistance Centers

Community senior legal assistance centers offer by far the best and most affordable source of legal help for seniors. Even the counties that offer little other help to seniors maintain a senior legal assistance center. You will always be able to find this center by checking with your Information and Referral worker (listed in the yellow pages under "Senior Citizens' Organizations").

You have a right to expect the following from your local senior assistance legal center:

- available, competent legal assistance concerning threats to your income, health, or independence
- education about your legal rights and the legal resources available to you
- an outreach program that helps you if you need legal assistance but are unaware that it is available or have no access to it

Most senior legal assistance centers are staffed by one or two attorneys who are available if needed, after paralegal or volunteer personnel determine whether professional help is called for. Many of these volunteers have become experts in the legal problems encountered by seniors and are more effective than some private lawyers in helping solve their problems. In fact, it is not unusual for these volunteers to have backgrounds in law or other professional fields closely allied to law.

At most legal assistance centers, you will be given easy-to-read pamphlets and brochures that deal specifically with your problem. If you need further information and want to find it on your own, you will be given access in most instances to the center's law library. In addition, most senior legal assistance centers post on their bulletin board any recent changes in the laws that affect you and your benefits. Many centers publish newsletters containing the same type of updated information, free of charge. Put your name on the mailing list for any of these publications.

Statewide Organizations The state and federal governments subsidize a number of organizations that work with seniors and maintain or sponsor legal assistance centers. Of these, perhaps the best known and most accessible is a Federal program called ACTION.

ACTION also maintains and trains paralegal help for seniors. In Southern California, the ACTION office maintains the

National Senior Citizens Law Center
1709 West 8th Street
Los Angeles, CA 90017
(call (213) 483-3990)

In Northern California their main office is at

211 Main Street
San Francisco, CA 94107
(call (415) 556-1736)

For the ACTION office nearest you, look in the white pages under "United States Government."

The Gray Panthers is another group that, although it tends to specialize somewhat, does offer excellent legal advice to seniors. (Look in your telephone book under "Senior Citizens' Organizations" or under the name.) Similarly, the state and federal offices on aging sponsor a number of centers throughout the state that are easily found by contacting the State Department on Aging or your local Information and Referral number.

Privately Sponsored Legal Centers In addition to the funded legal assistance centers for seniors, a number of private organizations — business, religious, philanthropic — maintain similar facilities for seniors. Examples include the Catholic Social Service, the Jewish Community Centers, the Unitarian and Lutheran programs, the American Association for Retired People, and National Teachers' Association.

Generally legal assistance centers are not part of the general senior centers. They tend to be independently operated. In multi-purpose centers, however, they are often combined. By and large, these privately sponsored legal assistance centers are excellent sources of help for seniors with legal problems. And few of them require that the senior seeking help be affiliated with the sponsoring organization.

Legal Workshops Various organizations and Area Agencies on Aging conduct occasional workshops on the legal problems of seniors. These are usually announced in newsletters or posted on senior center bulletin boards. For example, one such agency in San Diego County conducts periodic classes for seniors on Medicare and Medi-Cal billing. In Northern California, the SALA group (Senior Adult Legal Assistance) in Palo Alto conducts similar classes from time to time.

Enrollment in Legal Services Courses

Whether or not you have a specific problem, many schools and universities offer part-time or night courses in senior citizens' rights. In some cases, your tuition may be deferred. These courses are interesting in themselves, are usually taught on an informal, non-legalese manner, and may qualify you to assist other seniors in a paralegal position. One of the most prominent of these courses is offered by the University of California at Berkeley.

Paralegal Assistance

"Paralegal," as used here, refers to persons who perform a variety of different functions relating to legal rights but who are not licensed attorneys. Paralegal teams or individuals are extremely important to the adequate enforcement of the rights of senior. In fact, it is doubtful whether many of them would receive any legal assistance at all without the help of paralegal persons and organizations.

Paralegal personnel can be of great assistance to you in very practical, day-to-day problems, such as interviewing you and gathering the facts necessary to an understanding of your problem, preparing drafts of legal documents, doing legal research, and taking steps to solve law-related problems.

Perhaps one of the most important ways that paralegals can be of assistance to you is by providing full representation through the hearing stage in administrative cases. Administrative cases are those in which the contentions of the parties are not heard in court, at least initially, but are decided by some board or hearing officer. Social Security cases are among the most common cases of this type. (For appeals in Social Security cases, see Chapter One.) For many seniors, appeals in such cases would be impossible without paralegal assistance.

Who Are Paralegal Workers? People working in paralegal offices come from all walks of life. Often they are seniors themselves. Paralegal work offers them good employment opportunities, and they are in a better position to understand the problems of other seniors. Almost all paralegal people work under the supervision of an attorney, and, as a rule, they are knowledgeable and competent.

Generally paralegal people receive some formal training along with practical experience. Some of the legal areas in which paralegal people receive particularly good training are real estate, taxation, trusts, and wills and estates. In addition, many of them are highly skilled in writing contracts. Law students, who often serve as paralegals, generally do an excellent job in these legal areas.

Finding Paralegal Help Fortunately, there are many sources of paralegal help for senior Californians. Both the federal and state governments have several public funding programs that include the funding of paralegal assistance for the elderly. In addition, many national and state organizations offer similar assistance. Among the most prominent is the National Paralegal Institute, which maintains a branch office in the state and is backed by the federal and state departments on aging. Another prominent paralegal source of assistance is your local ACTION office referred to earlier.

Wills

A will is nothing more than a legal document that states your wishes as to the disposition of your property when you die. If you die without leaving a will (this is called dying "intestate"), your property will be distributed according to California law. Not only may this distribution not be what you wished, but it may be expensive and create legal problems for your family.

The legal requirements for making a will are simple:

- You must be at least 18 years old.
- When you make your will, you must be of "sound mind." This means that you must know you are making a will and understand its provisions.
- You must intend that the document be your will.
- You must satisfy the state's legal requirements, depending on the type of will you are making.

Making Your Own Will You do not necessarily need an attorney to make a will — particularly if you do not own substantial property and are leaving what you have to a member of your family. The more complicated your property and your bequests, however, the more advisable it is to have legal assistance.

Senior Californians are fortunate (in most counties) in that senior legal assistance centers offer free help in making wills and also provide the necessary forms. This assistance is generally provided by paralegal persons with expertise in the field. Thus there is nothing to be gained by making your own will without any legal advice. By all means take advantage of this legal help when you make your will. Your heirs will be glad you did!

If you nevertheless want to make your own will, you must fulfill the following as well as the requirements already stated:

- You must state in the document that you intend it to be your will.
- Your will must express your intention to dispose of your property.
- You must sign the will, and tell at least two witnesses who are present that you are signing your will.
- At least two witnesses must sign the will in each others' presence.

It is permissible to make a will in your own handwriting. These are called "holographic wills," and they need no witnesses. Such a will must be free of any marks on the paper other than your writing (for example, the words of a letterhead) and must be signed and dated. But you are asking for trouble if you make a holograph will — *don't* unless you simply can't avoid it.

What Property You Can Leave Generally you can leave any property you own to whomever you choose. Remember, though, that if any of your property is in joint tenancy (such as your home), that property will not be disposed of under your will. Rather, the other joint tenant will be automatically entitled to it at your death.

Similarly, if you are part owner of community property (property owned by you and your wife, for example), you can only dispose of *your* interest in it. Again, consult with your legal assistance center on this question.

Note: You may, of course, disinherit any member of your family if you wish. But this is somewhat technical and should be done with legal help also.

Changing, Revoking, and Reviewing Your Will You may change any part of your will when you wish. This can be done by writing a new will or changing part of the old one. A change is called a "codicil." Obtain legal assistance when changing your will — always.

A will may be revoked (canceled) at any time, provided you are of sound mind. There are legal requirements, however, and you should always obtain legal assistance.

Cost of Private Attorney In the event that you wish to hire a private attorney to make your will, be prepared to pay $100 – $500, depending on the complexity of your will. If you already have an attorney, he or she may make your will free of charge or at a reduced rate in consideration of your established business.

Where to Keep Your Will If your will was prepared by an attorney, he or she will keep either the original or a copy, depending on your wishes. Keep your own document in a safe, fireproof place such as a safe deposit box. You may wish to send a copy of it to your executor or executrix (the person you direct to carry out your will) in the event that your death occurs away from home.

Sources of Help In addition to paralegal and legal assistance at senior centers, you may obtain general will and estate information from the trust department of many banks and other financial institutions.

Remember that financial institutions are not in the business of practicing law and do not draw up wills. However, their trust officers are willing to advise a potential trust customer and his or her attorney on the drawing up of a will at no cost or obligation.

Many banks have wide experience in acting as executors or co-executors of a will. (Executors carry out the wishes of the person making the will.) Executor's fees are set by law in California and are the same whether a bank or an individual is named as executor. Also, an established bank has the further advantage to you of never being ill, absent, or otherwise unavailable.

Trusts

Trusts generally fall into two categories — those providing for someone during his or her lifetime and those providing for his or her estate. The former are often called "living trusts," and the person setting up the trust (the trustor) may name himself or herself beneficiary. Living trusts are useful for property management, reduction of income taxes and estate taxes, and reduction of probate costs.

"Testamentary trusts," on the other hand, are trusts you create in your will. They go into effect when someone dies and their will is probated. These trusts are useful to conserve principal, manage estates, provide flexibility in meeting the needs of beneficiaries, and reduce taxes.

Your local bank or other financial institution will help you with further information on trusts and will act as a trustee if you desire.

The State Bar of California issues free of charge a pamphlet entitled "Do I Need Estate Planning?" (pointing out that planning your estate *is* necessary). Copies of this pamphlet, which is highly recommended, may be obtained free of charge by sending a stamped, self-addressed envelope to

The State Bar
Communications Division
555 Franklin Street
San Francisco, CA 94102

Reputable insurance companies also often have available excellent printed materials, free of charge, that offer advice on estate planning and wills.

Small Claims Courts

The purpose of Small Claims Courts is to settle disputes involving $750 or less without lawyers. Small Claims Courts are usually part of a Municipal Court (called "justice courts" in some counties).

The procedures involved in Small Claims Courts are simple and may be explained by the clerk of the court. Most Small Claims Courts also have instruction sheets that outline the procedure followed by the particular court. The fee for filing a small claims case is usually $3 – $5.

Typical of matters that are settled by Small Claims Courts are disputes over defective or inadequate services, automobile accidents, rental deposits, insurance policies, and the like.

If you need further information on Small Claims Courts, ask at your senior assistance law center or try your local Information and Referral telephone number (under "Senior Citizens' Organizations" in the yellow pages). The SALA organization in Palo Alto also publishes, free of charge, an excellent booklet entitled "Small Claims Courts in California." Write for a copy to

SALA
624 University Avenue
Palo Alto, CA 94301

or call (415) 321-0580.

Natural Death Act

Terminal Illness — Your Rights The Natural Death Act was passed by the state legislature in 1976. This law permits an adult person to decide whether or not life-sustaining procedures should be withheld or withdrawn in the case of his or her own terminal illness. It is felt that the prolongation of life for persons with a terminal condition may cause them to lose their dignity and suffer unnecessary pain and suffering, while providing nothing medically necessary or beneficial.

A decision by an adult, under the new law, is made by as directive to his or her physician as required by law. At all steps of the procedure the patient's rights are well protected. Furthermore, if a patient makes a directive such as this, his or her insurance is not affected; that is, the following death is not a suicide. And no health provider may require a person to sign a directive as a condition for being insured or for receiving health services.

The law is not to be construed as permitting mercy killings. Patients may, of course, revoke their directive.

You must follow very specific requirements in order for the provisions of this law to be honored. You cannot simply write your wishes on paper or indicate them to your family and be assured that they will be followed. For this reason contact your local senior assistance center, your physician, or the State Department of Health for information and assistance. If you are in a health care facility, call your local Information and Referral number and ask for the Ombudsman. He or she will assist you and explain the details of this fairly recent change in the law.

15
Housing

Mr. Miller (age 76) lives in a cheap hotel in San Francisco's Tenderloin district. He pays $150 a month for his small room with a hot plate. It is unsafe to walk the streets, and Mr. Miller's room has been burglarized when he has left it to sit in the lobby. The neighborhood is so dangerous that Meals-on-Wheels and other senior volunteers refuse to enter it. Mr. Miller's health is failing, partly due to a stroke and partly due to his enforced isolation.

The lack of adequate housing is a statewide disgrace. For many California seniors, it is a personal disaster. As housing costs rise beyond the means of persons with low fixed incomes, many seniors are forced into housing ghettos to survive as best they can. Many are in poor health, live alone, and are unable to move if an opportunity is presented.

Mrs. Johnson, a widow (age 76), lives alone in an older house in Redding. Her children are married and gone, and, since her husband's death, she has paid off most of the mortgage. The property tax has tripled since her husband's death, and she barely pays off the rest of the mortgage and property taxes with a small pension and Social Security benefits. The house is in general disrepair and poorly insulated. Mrs. Johnson is forced to use a great amount of heat and despairs as her utility rates keep climbing. She has considered selling the house and taking a small apartment. She cannot find a moderately priced apartment, however, and she is told by her Social Security service worker that her SSI benefits will stop or be reduced if she sells the house.

In general, of course, the problems of homeowners are similar throughout the country. Skyrocketing property taxes, overpriced and poor quality home repair, rising energy bills, occasional shortages of essential goods and services — all of these and more tend to give all homeowners the same types of headaches.

For seniors, however, such problems may cause an immediate crisis.

What can be done — what answers are there for the Mrs. Johnsons and the Mr. Millers? Fortunately the picture in this state has become somewhat brighter — due in large part to an increased public consciousness and an aroused senior population. This chapter outlines some of the answers and suggests others that may help you if you are a senior with an immediate housing problem.

Rental Housing

Seniors in this state seeking adequate rental housing at affordable prices are, of course, only part of a population that shares the same problem. Seniors have the disadvantage of being on a fixed income in competing for available rentals, but they also have certain important advantages. Among these are rental assistance, rental subsidies, and the increasing availability of restricted senior housing.

Locating Rentals – Getting Help To find rental housing, the first step is to call or visit your Area Agency on Aging and ask whether they have a housing specialist. If they do, this person should be of immediate assistance. If they do not, the next step is to contact your local senior citizens' centers and inquire whether they maintain housing services. In any event, be sure to ask the Information and Referral Service in your county about other possible official sources.

You should, of course, inform your friends, family, and associates of your needs. Also you should get your local newspapers as early in the day as possible and check in the categories that are feasible for you ("Furnished, Unfurnished," etc.).

Inspect and use bulletin boards in markets, laundromats, local colleges, churches, and the like. When you post a sign for "apartment wanted," give your phone number but not your name. Be sure to include all the information you feel a potential landlord may need.

If possible, drive around your city and look for "vacancy" signs or have someone do this for you. Check with reputable rental services and real estate offices as well as your local Chamber of Commerce.

In some counties, an apartment guide is published that lists apartment complexes by areas. Your Chamber of Commerce can tell you if there is such a guide in your county. If so, it will be free of charge.

Questions to Ask When Renting You should ask yourself the following questions about rentals you may be considering (assuming you are lucky enough to find a decent place at an affordable price):

- Are there deposits (breakage, cleaning, security, etc.) and are they refundable?
- Does the lease or rental agreement contain restrictions (such as no pets, children, etc.)?
- Are there security arrangements for your protection?
- Is transportation readily available?
- Is there basic shopping nearby?
- What is included in the monthly rent (such as utilities, garbage service, etc.)?
- Is the housing well-maintained? Electricity, water, etc. in good working order?
- Considering your needs, is the apartment safe for *you* (do you need handrails, a lowered tub, etc.)?

Obviously, if the rental market is tight you may need to compromise on some of these matters. Still, use caution when renting. You may be required to sign at least a six-month lease and, if so, you'll want to be as sure as possible that you'll be safe and comfortable for your money.

For information on the rights of renters, you can get an excellent pamphlet entitled "Landlord – Tenant," which discusses the questions most frequently asked by persons renting, free of charge from the

California Dept. of Consumer Affairs
P.O. Box 310
Sacramento, CA 95802

Another good publication on renters' rights is "Landlord – Tenant," published by the

Palo Alto Human Relations Commission
250 Hamilton Avenue
Palo Alto, CA 94301

The charge for this booklet is $1.00.

Housing Projects for Moderate- and Low-Income Seniors Throughout the state, HUD (Department of Housing and Urban Development) has assisted in building rental housing developments for persons with low and moderate incomes. These rents are lower than in the market place generally, and for some seniors these units are the answer to their housing problems.

Most of these housing units require that seniors be in relative good health and capable of independent living. Usually the age range is from 62 years and up, although exceptions are made on occasion if the applicant is handicapped. The upper age limit usually depends on health rather than on age per se.

In most of these low-income rental developments the apartments have full or pullman kitchens and necessary appliances. Most have emergency "call" buttons that can summon help. The apartments may be furnished or unfurnished.

Rents ordinarily include utilities and in some cases parking privileges. Community meal programs are available in many developments (dinner, with lunch being optional) at a reasonable monthly rate. Most complexes have meeting rooms, libraries, and so on.

The type of construction, the amount and kind of federal assistance, and the location of the units control the income limits (and in some instances the amount of rental). As a rule of thumb, however, the maximum allowable annual income of residents is about $13,000 for singles and somewhat more for a couple. Rent supplements for seniors with very low incomes may lower the rent even further. Partial subsidy of rent for seniors is available through your city or county Housing Authority, and is discussed later.

Most low-income rental units have waiting lists, so you may have to be patient. Seniors are generally preferred for the studio and one bedroom apartments. You should keep in touch with the unit manager every so often to determine your place on the waiting list. And, if you hear of plans to construct a complex in your area, ask to be put on its waiting list.

Further information on low- and moderate-income housing for seniors, including the range of rental charges, can be obtained from your local senior center, your Area Agency on Aging, or perhaps from your local legal assistance center. You might also try the housing authority in your city or county for further help.

Public Housing Projects Low-income seniors, as well as younger persons, can secure inexpensive housing in public housing projects. However, these projects are often plagued with crime problems, physically run-down, and lacking many of the amenities and services desired by seniors. If you have other housing choices, you are generally better off living elsewhere.

Rental Subsidies: "Section 8 Housing" Individual seniors or those with families may qualify for supplemental rent assistance. This program is called the "Section 8 Existing Housing Program" and is funded through HUD but implemented by local county housing authorities.

The rental subsidy program is designed to help qualifying people and their families pay no more than 25% of their income for rent. The landlord must be willing to participate to the extent that he or she accepts a given figure as a fair rental for the property. The tenant pays up to 25% of his or her income for rent, and the balance is paid directly to the landlord by the housing authority.

The yearly income limits are set at $13,100 for a single person; $15,000 for a couple; and $18,700 for more than three persons. If your income or that of your family is below these limits, you qualify for the program.

In most counties, there is a long waiting list for rental subsidies. Some counties give priority to low-income, employed families and those on welfare, whereas other counties give preference to seniors and disabled persons.

Although it may be discouraging to apply for these subsidies because of the waiting lists, why not put your name on the list if you are in need? You have nothing to lose.

Subsidies from Builders Recently (February 1981) in San Francisco, Ramada and Holiday Inn (the developers of two luxury hotels in the downtown area) agreed to pay certain community groups $400,000 during the next four years. The proposed hotels will displace many seniors, and the money will go for health care, senior counseling, nutrition, and the like for those seniors displaced by the project.

This is an example of what a community — and the seniors in it — can do if they pull together. Perhaps these types of agreements will become more common in the future in cases where their impact is particularly devastating on senior housing.

Renters' Assistance The state program called Renters' Assistance is similar to Renters' Subsidies, which is discussed earlier. In the Renters' Assistance program, the State of California reimburses the portion of the property taxes that is presumed to have been paid by the owner of the property from your rent.

Note: Both "Section 8" Rent Subsidies and Renter's Assistance are different from the Renter's Credit you can receive by filing a state tax return. You very well may be eligible for all three programs. Renter's Credit is discussed in Chapter Eighteen.

To be eligible for Renters' Assistance, you must show the following to qualify as a senior:

- You were 62 years of age or older on December 31 of the prior year (the year before you make a claim).
- You occupied a rented premise all or part of that year and paid at least $50 a month or more in rent.
- Your household income for that year was $12,000 or less.
- The rented premises were not tax-exempt (such as public housing or church-owned property).

To be eligible as a blind or disabled person, you must show the following:

- You were blind or disabled on December 31 of the prior year.
- You occupied a rented residence for all or part of the prior year and paid at least $50 a month or more in rent.
- Your household income for the prior year was $12,000 or less.

"Household," as used above, means you, your spouse, and all other persons who lived in your home as their main residence during the prior year, except minor children, students, other renters, and the owner of the premises.

The types of buildings that may qualify for Renters' Assistance include:

- apartments
- single-family dwellings
- boarding houses
- convalescent homes
- residential care homes
- hotel rooms
- mobile homes (on rented land)
- duplexes or flats

You will note that you must have paid at least $50 a month or more in rent. If your rent was lower in some months, you will receive no assistance for these months.

Life insurance proceeds are considered income if they are more than the expenses incurred for the terminal illness and funeral of the deceased spouse of the person making the claim.

If you are a senior filing for rental assistance for the first time since 1977, you must show the Franchise Tax Board proof of your age. This can be a copy of one of the following:

- birth certificate or hospital birth record
- church baptismal record showing your date of birth
- Medicare card issued before July 1, 1973
- Medi-Cal card with the third and fourth I.D. numbers 10-19
- a Social Security document showing your eligibility for benefits at age 62 or older
- any other acceptable document that proves you were 62 or older on December 31, 1979

Additional documents relating to capital gain or loss, business gain or loss, etc. are required where appropriate. The necessary forms are available at the Franchise Tax Board, where they will be explained to you.

If you are both a senior and blind or disabled, file as a senior. Blind or disabled persons must file proof of their blindness or disability yearly, but seniors need file proof of age only for the first year they claim assistance.

Rental Assistance payments range from $10 to about $240. What you receive depends both on your income and the number of months you qualify as a renter.

Note: If you receive Renters' Assistance and SSI or AFDC, the latter benefits will not be reduced because you receive Renters' Assistance.

You must file your claim for Renters' Assistance between May 16 and September 2 of the year in which you make the claim. If you have a good reason for a late filing (such as a disabling illness), you may be granted additional time but not beyond March 1 of the following year. If you need an extension of time, call the Franchise Tax Board, toll-free, at the following telephone numbers and ask for Form FTB 9102 (Request for Extension of Time to File) before the deadline (September 2):

From Area Codes	Call
209, 408, 415, 707, 916	(800) 852-7050
213, 714, 805	(800) 852-5711

Mail your claim to:
Franchise Tax Board
P.O. Box 1588
Sacramento, CA 95807

Renters' Assistance checks are mailed after June 30 and are usually received by the end of October.

Retirement Residences

Retirement residences for seniors may be a workable alternative to renting an apartment, depending of course on your income and needs. These facilities vary widely in their availability, cost, and nature. In some, for example, meals are included, facilities for overnight guests are available, health care is provided — at least on a limited basis — recreation facilities are provided, and limited hospital or convalescent care may even be offered. Others have some of the above features but not all.

The cost of these residences varies, of course, with what is offered and the principle of supply and demand. Rest assured that the more desirable residences will have a lengthy waiting list. Nevertheless, if you find one that appeals to you, join the waiting list — you have nothing to lose. Before you sign anything, though, be sure to check the provisions of occupancy, including the amount and refundability of deposits, the initial cost, the monthly charges, and what they include. If possible, of course, talk with the other residents first before you sign on the dotted line.

To locate a private retirement residence, you might try the local Information and Referral Service, Area Agency on Aging, any senior center, the Chamber of Commerce, and local churches and lodges (such as the B.P.O.E., Elks, etc.). And, of course, check in the yellow pages of your telephone book.

Generally, you should expect to pay $350 – $800 per month for a semi-private room or studio for singles, and about $800 – $1600 per month for couples (with meals).

Life Care Contracts

Life care contracts have been called a "gamble with the annuity tables." They are frequently offered by retirement homes and generally provide a guarantee of occupancy for life in specified quarters in the retirement home. Some of these contracts provide that in the event you suffer severe financial reverses over which you have no control you are entitled to remain at the facility for as long as you live. This provision is important and you should insist that it be included in the contract.

Costs Most life care contracts provide for an entry fee (usually from $700 to $1200) and the total cost (anywhere from $10,000 to $50,000 or more). The latter amount represents your rent paid in advance for the length of time called for by the contract. Note: Even though these agreements are called "life-care" contracts, they may provide for you to stay a given number of years or your lifetime.

The costs referred to above vary, of course, depending on the location, size, quality, etc. of your quarters, the food you desire, the medical services to be provided and — last but not least — how long you probably will live (as shown by actuarial life expectancy tables).

Ordinarily, the total cost is broken down into a monthly fee and covers the following:

- food
- linen service and, in some instances, maid service
- telephone and utilities
- use of a TV room and library
- program facilities
- cost of doctors' visits —usually by regular appointment

Items ordinarily excluded from total cost would include:

- prosthetic devices and fittings
- eyewear and hearing aids
- podiatric care
- laboratory tests

Necessity for Medical Examination Since your total cost is based largely on your life expectancy, most retirement homes offering life care contracts require applicants to have two physical examinations

— one by the applicant's own doctor and one by the home's doctor. If the retirement home rejects your application because of the results of the examinations, any deposit you have paid (usually around $1,000) is refunded, but they retain part of the deposit to cover their administrative costs (usually around $350).

Limited Trial Period Most retirement homes, when offering life care contracts, permit interested persons to contract for quarters on a limited time basis (three or four months, for example). If, at the end of this period, you decide that the retirement home is not your cup of tea, you are permitted to withdraw and receive back the balance of any entry fee you paid.

Types of Facilities – Sponsors Many retirement homes offering life care contracts are sponsored by church organizations and are conducted on a non-profit basis. The same is true of such facilities that are owned and operated by professional organizations, such as retirement homes for retired teachers. Generally, the contracts offered by such retirement homes may be worth the money — in many instances it would be impossible to duplicate such services and care for the same cost.

Other retirement homes (or communities of such homes) are financed by private commercial interests, and their life care contracts may be less attractive from a cost viewpoint. In any event, if you are interested in such a plan, after you find the facility in which you are interested take a copy of their contract to your lawyer, have him read it over and make any suggested changes he recommends. Be particularly careful if the contract calls for the sale of your home, or its transfer, in exchange for the life care offered. This is very tricky, and you'll need expert help in making any such decision.

Caution: Be advised that in the past several years a number of life care retirement homes have gone bankrupt — even reputable ones. If they do, your money goes down the drain with them.

American Association of Homes for the Aging

The American Association of Homes for the Aging is an association of non-profit voluntary and governmental homes, facilities, and housing for seniors. The association works with congressional and federal agencies to develop policies to the benefit of older Americans.

The AAHA has affiliated offices in most counties, many of which are church-connected homes for seniors. Generally, these homes provide residential, semi-independent care for persons 65 or over. Fees range from $300 – $700 or more a month. In most instances, the facilities are pleasant, well-maintained, and offer a central dining room area for the residents.

Many of these facilities have safeguards related to the needs of older persons, such as handrails inside and out, specially equipped bathrooms with tub rails, etc. If you are interested in finding out what might be available in your area, look in your telephone book under Association of Homes for the Aging. If you cannot find that listing, inquire at one of the larger local churches for information.

Alternative Housing Situations

Private Home Placement In a few counties (for example, San Francisco, Santa Clara, and San Bernardino), volunteer persons or organizations place seniors in private homes at reasonable rates. These persons and agencies keep a list of property owners and a list of seniors seeking private rentals and their financial abilities. Check for services such as this with your Information and Referral number or your Area Agency on Aging.

Shared Housing

Mr. Heise is 86 and in a wheelchair. He owns his home but can't afford the taxes and upkeep, nor can he hire the in-home help he needs.

Mr. Bolten is 90 and is deaf. He has been staying with his niece but must move. He has an average Social Security retirement income, which doesn't match his needs.

If Mr. Heise and Mr. Bolten live in a part of the state that has a shared housing program and both register for it, they may get together and live in Mr. Heise's house. Together their incomes might suffice for their needs, each could help the other with his handicap and, best of all, they will have companionship — provided they're compatible.

Mrs. Sargent bought her house when her family was six persons, including her late husband. She now lives in it alone and must pay all the costs. Mrs. Reed

lives in an apartment that is being converted into a condominium, and she cannot afford the purchase. Mrs. Edwards' husband recently died, and she has sold her home and is seeking companionship as well as a place to live.
All of these ladies are about the same age.

Here also, a shared housing arrangement might work to the advantage of all three of these senior ladies. Mrs. Sargent will share costs of her home with the other two ladies, both of whom need a place to live as well as the company of compatible persons who share mutual interests and needs.

Several years ago the California Department on Aging started a pilot project designed to promote shared housing arrangements for seniors. One of the first of these projects was called Project MATCH, Inc., located in Santa Clara County:

277 West Hedding Street
San Jose, CA 95110
Cāl (408) 287-7121

MATCH was an instant success, as was a similar project in Santa Monica:

Santa Monica/Westside Project
SHAS
Martha Fitzgerald, Director
Senior Multiservice Center
1235 5th St.
Santa Monica, CA 90406

Similar projects have been started in the counties of San Francisco, Alameda, Los Angeles, Ventura, Riverside, and San Bernardino. Shared housing has helped alleviate some of the critical housing problems faced by countless California seniors.

Shared housing is not a government benefit or program, even though government money helped start the concept. For it to succeed, the seniors in a given community need to participate, and a lot of work and time must be donated by volunteers. The way it generally works is that the group of persons interested obtains a list of seniors who are agreeable to sharing their homes with other seniors. These people register with the organization, indicating their age, financial ability, health, personal interests, and so on. The lists are matched and, if the seniors involved agree, the match is made.

There are no particular formalities involved other than the agreement the two (or more) seniors make with one another as to the details of the new arrangement. Should the arrangement not work out, it can simply be terminated by one of the persons involved.

If you are interested either in sharing your housing with another senior or in looking for a place to share with another, contact your local Area Agency on Aging or Information and Referral Service. Ask if they have a housing specialist who can help you. If they have little or no information, try your senior center or legal assistance office.

Condominium Conversion

One of the more recent problems facing many senior renters is that arising from a building owner's decision to convert the apartment or flat building to condominiums. Many seniors who live on the premises are unable to stay as renters and are unable to find alternative housing they can afford. The following illustrates the plight of many:

Mr. and Mrs. Jensen, both 73, have lived in their small one-bedroom apartment for many years, close to shopping, friends, and their doctor. They receive notice from the building owner that he is converting the building to a condominium and that they can buy their apartment for $85,000. The Jensens, shocked and bewildered, cannot buy their apartment, are forced to move into an apartment in a high-crime area in the city far from shopping centers or medical help. They are burglarized several times, unable to cope with the demands imposed by the change, and their health and mental outlook deteriorate rapidly.

The Jensens' problem is one that is becoming increasingly common among senior apartment renters. Those with an adequate income, can, of course, choose condominiums for retirement living. But generally seniors simply cannot afford to buy an apartment that frequently costs more than 150 times their monthly rent, excluding interest, maintenance fees, and taxes. Furthermore, seniors may find it difficult to obtain a mortgage.

The Jensens, in the example above, are lucky if they live in an area that has enacted stop-gap laws regulating the conversion of rented property to condominiums. Among such areas, for example, are San Francisco and the two nearby cities of Tiburon and San Jose. San Francisco ordinances specify that 35% of tenants must agree in writing to purchase their unit before the owner can convert the building.

The first step, if you have this problem, is to check with your lawyer or a senior legal assistance center in your area to find out if the building owner can convert the building.

In some counties, laws have been passed providing for relocation compensation for displaced tenants. Such compensation is little help, however, to a displaced senior — if anything, a mere token. In most instances, this compensation won't even pay the moving costs for the tenant. Nevertheless, you may want to check on this where you obtain legal services and advice.

Local laws have been passed or proposed that require a building owner to help displaced tenants find a comparable unit before the tenant is evicted. San Francisco, for example, has such a measure. Again, check with your legal assistance center to see if the area in which you live has such a law.

The federal government, though participating actively in several programs designed to alleviate the housing problems of seniors, to date has not taken many concrete measures in respect to condominium conversion. There is a federal law called the Uniform Relocation Assistance Act, designed to provide assistance to persons displaced because of federal or federally assisted programs. The trouble is that the law doesn't include persons displaced from condominium conversions. Several organizations for the elderly, however, are trying to get the law amended to include such persons, and they may be successful in the very near future.

Assistance for Senior Home Buyers

It may happen that an older person or couple needs to buy a home — frequently because they were forced to sell their prior home to maintain themselves. Several federal programs are designed to assist such persons.

Mortgage Insurance If you are what is called a "marginal" credit risk, but still want to purchase a home, you might be interested in the HUD program that insures lenders against loss on home mortgage loans to low- and moderate-income families. If so, contact your local HUD Area Office.

The U.S. Department of Housing and Urban Development (HUD) also insures mortgages that are made by private lenders for the purchase of individual family units in condominium housing. If you are interested in purchasing your apartment as a condominium and need help in financing it, contact your local HUD Area Office to see if you qualify for assistance in the purchase.

Under another federal legal provision, HUD provides mortgage insurance to purchase or rehabilitate housing in older, declining areas in cities. The government agency assures lenders against losses, but you must be an "acceptable risk" to qualify. Another qualification is that you must be a homeowner who is eligible for FHA mortgage insurance.

Federal Home Loans Under a federal law, the U.S. Department of Housing and Urban Development makes direct loans for housing for seniors and the handicapped. Under this program, long-term direct loans to eligible persons are made, and the current interest rate is based on a relatively low figure. To qualify for such a direct loan, there must be a household of one or more persons, the head of which is at least 62 years old or handicapped. If you are interested in trying to get such a loan, contact your local HUD Area Office in the white pages under "United States" or:

Assistant Secretary for Housing — Federal Housing Comr.
Department of Housing and Urban Development
Washington, D.C. 20410

All questions concerning any federal housing program or assistance may be addressed as follows:

Communications Services, Office of Public Affairs
Room 9245
HUD
451 7th Street, SW
Washington, D.C. 20410
Telephone: (202) 755-5284

Senior homeowners are entitled to certain state tax credit and deferment benefits. These are discussed in Chapter Eighteen. And senior homeowners in some counties receive home winterization credit and discounts on home maintenance and repair bills. These are outlined in Chapter Nineteen.

Disabled Persons Under HUD, the Office of Independent Living for the Disabled was established to promote awareness of the housing needs of people with disabilities. Any individual or organization seeking specific information about housing or programs for the disabled can apply to this office (OILD) for information. Furthermore, any disabled person who is a victim of housing discrimination in programs administered by HUD may also turn to this agency for assistance.

For more information or questions relating to this office, write:

Assistant Secretary for Housing — Federal Housing Comr.
Office of Independent Living for the Disabled
Department of Housing and Urban Development
Washington, D.C. 20410

Discrimination in Housing

Under the federal Civil Rights Act, it is illegal to discriminate against any person because of his or her age in:

- selling or renting housing or residential lots
- advertising the selling or renting of housing
- financing of housing
- providing real estate services

The federal government must act under this law, or you can go directly to court.

If you are a senior who has suffered this kind of discrimination, you can, within 180 days of the incident, call and file a complaint with the Department of Housing and Urban Development at:

(toll free) (800) 424-8590

If you prefer to file the complaint yourself, go to your nearest HUD office, and they will give you the form and help you prepare the complaint. You send this complaint to:

The Department of Housing and Urban Development
Fair Housing
Washington, D.C. 20410

In the complaint, you simply tell HUD what happened. They may:

- investigate the incident to see if the law has been broken
- contact the person responsible and persuade him or her to stop discriminating
- refer your complaint to a state or local Human Rights Commission for investigation

• recommend you go to court

Under the California Fair Employment and Housing Law, a senior who has been discriminated against in housing because of his or her age has a similar, effective remedy. This is discussed in detail in connection with age discrimination in employment; see Chapter Sixteen.

Home Repair and Maintenance

There are a number of ways in which seniors can make needed home repairs and reduce the costs. Some counties' Housing Redevelopment Agencies give grants for home repair, including plumbing, electrical, and roof repair. Such Agencies also render home repair emergency services. The grants are usually up to a maximum of $2500.

Weatherization of homes, with special priorities for seniors and the handicapped, is offered in some areas for low-income seniors. These services include ceiling insulation, weather stripping, caulking, and replacing broken windows. Your local Area Agency on Aging is the best place to start for obtaining further information on this. Ask for their housing specialist.

Your local senior employment agency is an excellent source of expert help for home repair at reduced rates. In most instances you will receive fast and dependable service from other retired seniors with backgrounds of technical help. Don't overlook this possibility if you need work done on your home or apartment. Such agencies also usually offer handiwork — gardening, hauling, carpentry, painting and more.

You may be able to obtain needed materials for home repair at a special discount rate for seniors. Be sure and check Chapter Nineteen for such discounts.

16
Employment

Employment is a necessity for many seniors. As inflation diminishes their retirement income and devalues their hard-earned savings, many seniors must work in order to maintain even a modest standard of living.

Seniors seeking employment have diverse needs. Many wish to work only part-time or only during certain months of the year. Others wish to earn only the maximum allowed by Social Security without penalty. Some want to explore a new line of work. Many want to pursue their lifetime occupation with continued gusto. And those who are desperate just want to pay their bills.

The problem of finding suitable employment at a decent wage is, of course, a problem that besets many people — not just seniors. For older workers, however, it is particularly difficult to find new employment for a number of reasons. Many older workers find it hard to travel as much as some jobs require or perform the manual labor that other jobs entail. Older women worker often lack the necessary credentials to compete for jobs, since many of them have spent their lives as homemakers and have acquired no special skills. And mandatory retirement, though now modified, forces many seniors into the job market completely unprepared to compete for jobs against the younger work force.

Perhaps, now that the voters of this country have chosen a senior as their chief executive, employers can be educated out of their prejudices against hiring seniors. Hiring older workers makes financial sense. Recent research has shown the following about older workers in general:

- Many seniors have higher production rates than do younger employees.

- Older worker tend to be more stable on the job in terms of attendance, health, safety, and turnover records.
- Most seniors have shown they are more flexible than younger workers and can shift occupation fields more easily.
- Most seniors have no physical handicap that affects job performance.
- Most seniors have a greater sense of responsibility than do younger workers.

Despite these facts seniors continue to experience problems in finding appropriate work and in maintaining employment. This chapter discusses strategies useful in finding the right job and in overcoming obstacles to employment such as mandatory retirement and age discrimination. Problems regarding pension rights from past work are also discussed.

Looking for Work

The basic techniques of searching for a job are pretty much the same no matter what your age. The primary thing to keep in mind is what you have to offer a prospective employer. Hopefully, what will count the most is your ability to do a competent job. The following suggestions may help you to prove that you have job skills and practical experience:

- Outline your work history, going backward from your most recent job.
- Describe your unique skills, training, and education.
- Assemble your Social Security records and military documents.
- Give updated, good references.
- Prepare a resume if you are seeking a professional, technical, or managerial job.

If necessary, consult with an agency that can give you professional guidance. These will be listed in the telephone directory yellow pages under "Employment Counseling." The state Employment Development Department can also be of assistance.

Senior Women Older women who are seeking employment should remember not only that they are seniors but that they are *women.* Thus they qualify for numerous programs designed to afford women equality in the job market, such as Affirmative Action and job re-entry training. Many senior women may be reluctant to join their younger sisters in the battle for equality in employment. They will find, however, that generally the personnel at women's centers and the like will welcome them with open arms and give them every assistance possible.

Don't Forget Your Continuing Benefits If you are an unemployed senior, don't forget to apply for Social Security and/or SSI benefits if you haven't already. See Chapter One for an outline of these benefits.

If you have been fired or retired from a job and are looking for work, you may be eligible for unemployment insurance. Important reminder: Unemployment insurance covers those persons who have been forcefully retired (mandatory retirement), as well as those persons who have been let go for other reasons. Apply as soon as possible at your nearest office of the state's Employment Development Department.

State Employment Development Department The state EDD (Employment Development Department) tries hard but simply is not very effective in finding suitable employment for seniors. Still, it pays to register for work with them and occasionally badger them for some action if you hear nothing for long periods. You will find them listed under "California, State of" in the white pages of your telephone directory.

Retirement Job Agencies One of the best sources of meaningful work for seniors is to be found in the relatively new private employment agencies that specialize in employment for retired seniors. Most of these agencies are staffed by volunteers with an active interest in this problem. Some receive help (funding) from the county or state; others pay their own way. By and large, they are competent, professional, and realistic when compared with many of the "make-work" programs for seniors operated by the government.

These agencies are of particular use to seniors who wish to find part-time or temporary employment. Seniors who wish to update their work record or make employment contacts also find these agencies a valuable resource.

In almost all these agencies, no fee is required — either from the senior looking for work or from the employer. They operate on a straightforward supply-and-demand basis, matching the experience and job skills of the senior applicant with the needs of the business community. Both the community and the seniors benefit greatly from putting to work men and women whose training and experience would otherwise be lost.

By and large, employers of seniors from these agencies receive dedicated, loyal workers who need not be taught the work ethic. Senior employees from these agencies have proven their worth in the competitive job market to the extent that many employers have promoted them to supervisory positions. Furthermore, many homeowners who need skilled services such as plumbing or electrical work find these seniors invaluable.

Mrs. Acevedo is 67 and until her retirement worked as a secretary. The secretary of a small business concern in her town has requested a three-month maternity leave. Her employer contacts a retirement job agency, and Mrs. Acevedo goes to work for three months at full pay. The employer, the secretary, and Mrs. Acevedo are all delighted.

Some of these agencies are listed under "Temporary Employment Agencies"; others under "Retirement Jobs" or similar names.

One of the largest of these agencies in the state is Retirement Jobs, Inc. This agency has had considerable success in placing unemployed, qualified seniors in rewarding work. Check in the yellow pages of your directory under "Employment Agencies" for the office nearest you.

Another agency is called SCORE (Service Corps of Retired Executives). This agency places retired executives with small business owners who need management expertise and help in solving the problems of an existing business or of a new business. You will find your nearest office in the yellow pages under "Employment Agencies."

The Retired Executives Volunteer Program recruits and places retired executives, managers, and professional persons in work as management consultants in non-profit and public service agencies. They will be listed in the yellow pages of your directory under their name.

Seasonal Employment Many companies — particularly department stores — employ seniors seasonally at Christmas and other holidays. The pay is adequate, and many seniors find that this kind of employment augments their income and provides an enjoyable break. The companies benefit because many of their other employees (such as students) are not available before the holidays or on weekdays. If you are interested, apply at your larger department stores well before the season arrives.

Day Care and Nursing Assistants Senior men and women are often in great demand by the community to act as foster parents or day-care workers, as well as to assist in caring for the elderly or mentally ill. Check with your local nursing and hospital employment agencies for these opportunities, as well as with various volunteer agencies such as the Red Cross and the Gray Panthers.

Check with Your Area Agency on Aging If none of the above works out for you and none of the government-sponsored programs mentioned below answers your needs, check with your local Area Agency on Aging listed in the Appendix. Also, if there is an ACTION office near you, look into the opportunities they may have listed. You have nothing to lose!

Federal Employment Programs

There are a number of federally funded programs designed to assist older workers in finding a full or part-time job. Some of these programs offer work on a volunteer basis, while others pay a stipend. Some of these positions, of course, are "make-work" jobs, but many offer real challenges and opportunities to older workers and are worth looking into, depending on one's background and interests. Many seniors use these programs to update their work records.

Senior Community Service Employment Program This program, referred to as the "Title IX program" (or SCSEP), is a federally funded program that provides work opportunities for low-income persons age 55 or older who have poor employment prospects. State and local governments and private, non-profit organizations may use Title IX employees to upgrade human services — particularly in rural areas.

These community service jobs pay an average of about $4.00 an hour and are not available in all areas of the state. The older persons in the program work in day-care centers, schools, hospitals, facilities for the handicapped, senior citizen centers, nutrition programs, and beautification, conservation, and restoration projects. In addition to wages, the workers receive yearly physical examinations, personal and job-related counseling, job training, and in some cases placement in regular unsubsidized jobs.

If you are interested in these programs, contact your local Information and Referral service or your Area Agency on Aging. Or you can write to:

Office of National Programs
Employment and Training Administration
Department of Labor
601 D Street, N.W.
Washington, D.C. 20210

Senior Environmental Employment Program The U.S. Environmental Protection Agency and the Administration on Aging have established the Senior Environmental Employment Program to demonstrate the effectiveness of older Americans in jobs relating to the protection of our natural resources.

The program is based on the idea that retired and unemployed older workers are talented, experienced, and a reliable source of qualified manpower, and that these resources are needed to meet the objectives of the state and federal government programs relating to the environment.

One of the benefits an older worker may receive from working in such a program is the opportunity to supplement his or her income, as well as to continue to use the skills he or she has in service to the community.

The older workers who participate in the program are trained and assigned to such projects as:

- public information
- air monitoring and emission testing
- pesticide inventory and control
- water quality sampling and monitoring

- technical libraries
- solid waste disposal survey
- clerical functions and writing up grants
- carcenogenic (cancer) survey and follow-up
- hazardous materials routing and surveys
- rural health screening
- noise abatement and control

Persons in the program also serve as assistant inspectors for water supply, pesticides, water quality, and solid waste.

If you wish to receive more information about this program, call or write the U.S. Environmental Protection Agency Manpower Offices in your vicinity (under United States Government in the white pages), your local Information and Referral Service, or write to:

California Department of Housing and Community
Development
Sacramento, CA 95814

State Employment Programs

As mentioned before, the state Employment Development Department attempts to find suitable employment for seniors but simply does not have the time or resources to be of much help in most cases. Nevertheless, be sure to stay listed with them and call occasionally to update your interest and availability.

Tutoring Migrant Workers The State Department of Education sponsors a program in four adult school districts (Tracy, Manteca, Salinas, and Santa Maria) in which seniors are employed 25 hours per week in teaching and tutoring migrant workers.

The program has been very successful to date, and the seniors employed are enthusiastic about their work and find it very rewarding. The tutoring consists chiefly of teaching English as a second language, together with basic math. If you are interested, contact the State Department of Education for further information.

State Educational Institutions If you are a retired teacher or have special skills that are appropriate for a teaching position, contact the State Board of Education and inquire about night or part-time employment as a counselor or teacher. This is an exceptionally good opportunity for qualified seniors, since educational institutions, of course, are bound by law not only to hire regardless of age but to implement Affirmative Action guidelines.

Foster Grandparents The state foster grandparent program is funded by the California Department of Disability in partnership with ACTION — a federal agency. The positions are part-time, and involve a one-on-one relationship with children in schools or other institutions. About 20 hours a week are required, and the wage is an hourly stipend. This has been a very successful program, and you should inquire further if you feel you are qualified and interested (men and women). For further information and details on this program contact the ACTION office nearest you. It will be listed under "U.S. Government" in the directory white pages.

Age Discrimination

The information in this section is for the older worker who is (or might be) having difficulties with age discrimination in employment. The discussion is not a legal treatise on the subject of age discrimination in employment. It is intended, however, to make seniors more aware of their rights in employment practices and to help them avoid some of the pitfalls that often cause their cases to be thrown out of court. If readers have a specific age discrimination problem in employment, they are advised, of course, to seek legal help. (See Chapter Thirteen.)

How Effective Are the Laws? The enforcement of federal and state laws prohibiting discrimination in employment because of age leaves much to be desired. The main federal law, called the Federal Age Discrimination in Employment Act of 1967, bars employers from denying jobs or dismissing employees 40 to 70 years old solely because of their age. California has a law that is worded similarly.

It is commonly recognized, however, that these laws — state and federal alike — are not well known and have not been enforced vigorously. Perhaps this is the result of older workers being less aggressive in exercising complaint procedures and bringing lawsuits than other groups of discriminated workers.

What Is Age Discrimination? That seems like a pretty silly question to ask seniors who find themselves looking for jobs — they *know* what age discrimination is! Older job applicants find positions closed to them that would have been open several years earlier. Some of the reasons given (and methods used) to close these doors are subtle and some are not so subtle.

For older persons on the job, age discrimination may be equally devastating. Many of these workers find themselves passed over for promotion or training opportunities (or laterally "transferred"), or asked to take early retirement.

Proving that you have been discriminated against because of your age in seeking or holding employment is difficult — as lawyers working on such cases will tell you. Proving such discrimination would be simple, of course, if your employer or prospective employer, an employment agency, or even a union told you right out that you were being turned down or let go because you "were too old." But, of course, they don't say that outright.

In most instances, age discrimination is practiced more subtly, and it will be up to you (and your lawyer) to piece together the whole picture keeping in mind one basic issue: Would you have been treated the same way, given your work record and qualifications, if you were younger? If your answer to this issue is no — and you can prove it — you may be in business.

Facts Tending to Show Discrimination Listed below are some facts and situations you should look for if you suspect you are a victim of age discrimination. Some are preliminary facts that have nothing to do with age discrimination but must be proved as a matter of course, such as the existence of a job that is open.

These facts and circumstances, standing alone, do not prove discrimination nor are they necessarily illegal. But together they can be evidence of age discrimination when they form a pattern. You can greatly help your lawyer, if you decide to take legal action, by noting and recording these facts.

The following facts and circumstances may help to prove age discrimination practiced on an older person seeking employment:

- The existence of the job and your application for it.
- Your qualifications for the job — was there a job description or a list of qualifications? If so, and you still have it, keep it!
- Your interview — was there any mention of age? Did there seem to be an emphasis on youth?
- Reasons given by the employer why you were not hired — was your age mentioned? If the reasons are not clear, keep asking. If an employment test was given, ask to see the results and how they were scored. If you were interviewed orally, insist on being given the reasons why you were not hired — what it was that you lacked.
- Who *did* get the job? Was it a younger person? If so, was he or she as qualified as you?
- How many older workers does the employer have?
- Find out, if you can't remember, whether there was a notice posted telling persons about the federal and state Age Discrimination in Employment Acts.
- Were you told you were overqualified, that you might not like working with younger people, or that the job might be too much for you?
- Did the advertisement for the job refer to age or recent school graduation?
- Did the application ask your age? This question is not illegal, but the employer must give you some clear indication the answer will not be used against you.

The following facts and circumstances may prove a pattern of age discrimination against an older person who is presently employed but being let go.

- Are there very few or no older workers on the job?
- Have workers been asked to leave or retire early as they become older without any other apparent reason?
- Have some workers been fired before their pensions vest (become effective)?
- Was your job changed to one that was more strenuous?
- Were you passed over for promotion when your qualifications were as good as those promoted?
- After many years of good job performance ratings, did you begin to receive bad annual evaluations?
- If you were asked to retire early, or fired, were you replaced by

a younger worker? If so, were his or her qualifications as good as yours?

Preserving Facts Needless to say, your word and memory alone may not be good enough to win a lawsuit. You should write down your entire experience as soon as possible — especially dates and names. Write down what was said in the job interview, or other conversations, and who said it. Keep copies of any documents involved — get names of other personnel who may be sympathetic to your cause or who also have been fired or refused a job for the same apparent reasons. In short, keep as complete a record as you can of the whole experience.

Caution: Employers may have legitimate reasons for letting an older employee go. For example, a company may decide that a shakeup in management is essential or that overhead is excessive and some high-priced executives should be fired. Furthermore, the state and federal laws permit dismissal where a certain age level is a valid occupational qualification (for example, if public safety is at stake, as might be the case with bus drivers). The point is that a good age discrimination case cannot be made out of every firing of an older employee.

Obtaining Help Most discrimination in employment cases based on age go to the state or federal Equal Employment Opportunity Commission. Although the procedure to redress these grievances is not overly complicated, nevertheless you will always need legal representation. Age discrimination cases invariably involve facts that are susceptible to various interpretations and usually require a good legal presentation to a jury.

Your local Legal Assistance for Seniors office is probably your most immediate source of help. In most instances they have handled such cases, are familiar with the procedures, and will either represent you or refer you to an experienced attorney who will.

The Gray Panthers is a national group working to eliminate age discrimination practiced against seniors. Call your local office for assistance, or write:

Gray Panthers
944 Market Street
San Francisco, CA 94102

Gray Panthers
833 Blackburn Avenue
Los Angeles, CA 90048

Gray Panthers
601 Market Street
San Diego, CA 92102

Check your telephone directory for other Gray Panther office addresses.

Mandatory Retirement — Your Rights

Largely as a result of the efforts of older workers and organizations representing them, in 1978 the Federal Age Discrimination in Employment Act was amended to prohibit mandatory retirement of employees under age 70 for reasons of age. The exceptions to this are persons who, for two or more years prior to retirement, held executive or high level policy-making jobs and who are entitled to a pension of at least $27,000 a year.

This law went into effect January 1, 1979 for most persons, but does not go into effect until July 1, 1982 for college professors.

California has a similar law. This means that in many instances seniors are able to enforce their rights in both state and federal courts.

Effect on Job Benefits The new law has raised a number of questions regarding the entitlement to fringe benefits by employees who would ordinarily be retired at 65 years of age. These employees have participated, for example, in qualified retirement, profit-sharing, or other employee benefit plans. If these plans at present depend on a normal retirement age of 65, questions arise as to what adjustments must or can be made in order for the plans to remain valid under the new law.

First, the changes in the federal law make it unlawful for an employer to mandatorily retire a worker at 65 and cut off his or her rights to health and life insurance and other benefit plans. On the other hand, Congress has realized that the cost of providing certain fringe benefits to older workers is substantially higher than that of providing them to younger workers.

A few things are clear under the change in the federal law. An employer maintaining a retirement plan is not required to give credit, for purposes of benefit accrual (time required for entitlement to benefits), for those working years after the employee has reached the normal retirement age under the plan.

Pete works under a retirement plan funded solely by his employer. The plan provides that a worker must have at least ten years employment by age 65 to be entitled to pension benefits. Pete is 65 and has worked eight years. If he stays on, the years after he is 65 will not count toward the ten-year requirement.

Furthermore, an employer is not required to pay the actuarial equivalent (years of life expectancy) of normal retirement benefits to employees who work beyond the normal retirement age.

Pete again, but this time he is entitled to pension benefits. If Pete works on past 65, his employer will not be required to adjust upward the size of any periodic payments made to him for the additional years worked, when he retires.

It is also clear under the federal law that an employer is not required to provide for accrual (earned) benefits under a retirement plan during any years of service by an employee after normal retirement age (age 65).

Pete starts working for the same employer when he is 65. His employer is not required to set up a plan in which Pete is a beneficiary during the years he worked after age 65.

Various congressional committees and the U.S. Department of Labor are studying the above problems, in detail, as well as many others that will arise under the new federal law. If you are over 65, still working, and are entitled to benefits from an employee benefit plan, be sure to check with your lawyer or legal aid group from time to time and find out whether new regulations on these problems have been passed.

Other Effects of the Law Caution: The Age Discrimination in Employment Act does not change the age eligibility requirements for collecting Social Security benefits, railroad retirement, or military retirement benefits. Nor does the law require persons to work until age 70 — it just gives most employees the option of working until age 70.

Other important accomplishments of the new law:

- It abolishes mandatory retirement at any age for most federal employees (exceptions to this include law enforcement officers, CIA officials, air traffic controllers, and firefighters).
- It gives persons suing under the law a right to a jury trial on

some of the issues that may be involved.

- It requires persons suing under the law to file a charge (complaint) with the Secretary of Labor instead of presenting a formal notice of intent to sue (as is required in most employment discrimination lawsuits).

Note: The provisions of the new law do not apply to employees of a firm with 20 or fewer employees.

Information If you have questions about the new mandatory retirement law, you may write the Secretary of Labor or the Department of Labor — Wage and Hour Division (look in the directory white pages under "United States"). Or, you may contact

NRTA Age Discrimination Project
1909 K Street, N.W.
Washington, D.C. 20049

For information on the state law, contact the Labor Commissioner, listed under Industrial Relations Department, "California, State of" in the white pages of the telephone directory.

Private Pension Problems

In the past, and to some extent at present, a great many older persons who planned their retirement carefully suddenly have found that their pension funds are insolvent or have gone broke. One study estimates that over half of all pensioners enrolled in private pension programs fail to receive benefits. Fortunately for many of us, new laws have been passed that help correct such abuses.

ERISA – Pension Reform Act In 1974, Congress enacted the Employee Retirement Income Security Act, referred to as ERISA or the Pension Reform Act. Since that time, the law has been amended to tighten up loopholes that cost retiring persons millions of dollars. These laws are intended to halt and prevent pension fund abuse and arbitrary termination of pension rights by employers and other organizations such as unions.

ERISA has proven to be fairly effective. However, the law is complicated, is subject to different interpretations by courts and lawyers, and, if you have a problem with pension fund abuse, you probably will need expert legal assistance to enforce your rights.

In general, ERISA provides for fixed standards of eligibility, the duties and responsibilities of persons who control pension funds, the vesting of benefits, fairer tax treatment for pensioners, and provisions protecting workers who change jobs.

The requirements that ERISA imposes on all new pension plans are as follows:

- Participation and coverage requirements must be based on age and service.
- Accrued (earned) benefits must vest (cannot be taken away) according to a specified time schedule.
- There are funding requirements for earned benefits.
- Plans providing for an annuity payout must provide for a joint and survivor annuity (be payable to one's spouse or survivor).
- Distribution of plan benefits must begin by a specified time.
- Social Security wage base or benefit increases cannot reduce plan benefits of retired or separated employees.
- Employees who have a right to 50% or more of their accrued (earned) benefits cannot forfeit their benefits just because they withdraw their voluntary contributions.
- Employees in the plan cannot sell or transfer their benefits.
- If the plan merges with another plan or transfers its assets, each employee must have the same or greater benefits thereafter.

Contributory and Noncontributory Pension Plans — Your Rights

Courts and lawyers have argued for years over the issue of whether a pension plan to which the employee made no cash contributions is an enforceable contract between the employer and employee. If it is, of course, and the employer breaks this contract, the employee may sue him and collect the benefits or damages. If such a plan is not a contract, the employee probably has no recourse when he receives no benefits from it.

If the wording of the plan itself states that it does constitute a contract between employer and employee, then of course there is no question — employees have a vested (earned) right to benefits which cannot be taken away from them. And where a pension plan is reached as a result of *collective bargaining* (such as many plans that result from union negotiations with employers), the plan is considered a contract and may be enforced according to its provisions.

Although there may be exceptions in some instances, the law generally will enforce employees' rights to benefits under a pension or retirement plan if such rights are *vested* — even where the employees contributed nothing to the plan. Vested, in this sense, means that the employees have met all of the conditions of the plan and are now eligible for benefits. In other words, they have earned these benefits.

For example, if you were justifiably fired from a job some years before you would have been entitled to pension benefits, your right to benefits did *not* vest, you probably are not going to win if you sue your former employer in court. The same is true, for example, if you accept an early retirement voluntarily and that fact leaves you ineligible for benefits under the plan.

On the other hand, if your employer, for example, terminates you a few weeks before your retirement age on a technicality, the courts are very apt to conclude that he did so in bad faith and award you your benefits or damages.

In short, your right to benefits under a pension plan to which you contributed nothing in cash depends, to a very large extent, on the provisions of the plan itself and the circumstances of your termination. Again, don't attempt to analyze the situation yourself. Consult with your lawyer!

In almost all instances, you may recover at least your contributions to a pension plan even though you are terminated.

Wrongful Termination of Retirement Benefits The provisions of ERISA provide remedies for cases in which an employer wrongfully terminates the retirement or pension rights of eligible employees. But suppose you are an older employee who has earned pension rights, are deprived of them by your employer, and your case does not come under the provisions of ERISA?

Generally, you are entitled to sue your employer and seek one of two remedies: all of your accumulated unpaid benefits and a court order requiring that your employer must pay future benefits as due; or damages in a lump sum which would be the present value (when you sue) of the money benefits you would have received over your life expectancy. And, in either case, you may seek court costs and your lawyer's fees as well.

17
Consumer Protection

All consumers need protection, of course, but protection is particularly important to seniors. First, many live on fixed, low incomes. Second, seniors frequently live alone and are particularly susceptible to the fraudulent devices of dishonest salesmen, especially door-to-door salesmen.

Areas of particular concern for seniors are those involving hearing aids, eye glasses, dentures, prescription drugs, prosthetic devices, retirement villages, funeral arrangements and costs, home repairs, land sales, credit, work-at-home schemes, and so-called "cures" for diseases such as arthritis and cancer.

Department of Consumer Affairs

State Office The State of California maintains a Department of Consumer Affairs in Sacramento with branches in most large California cities.

A main function of the department is to license and enforce the state law as it applies to various professions and vocations. For example, the department oversees legal complaints against contractors, accountants, barbers, and so on.

If you have a typical complaint against a seller or manufacturer of goods (for example, for defective merchandise or over-pricing), you will probably not get much satisfaction from the personnel at the state office. But they will refer you to the proper local agency to make your complaint. However, if you have a complaint that involves licensing problems, such as faulty work done by an unlicensed contractor, they will assist you.

You will find the correct office, board, or bureau in the telephone directory under "California, State of." For example, a complaint regarding an auto repair garage would be directed to the Bureau of Automotive Repair.

Local Offices Consumer complaint and protection coordinators are listed in the white pages under that name. There you can register a complaint that you have been unable to resolve with a business or a complaint that is outside the limited scope of the state offices described above. You can also use the local agencies as a resource to obtain information about a business or establishment.

You will note that almost every profession and vocation is listed under this heading in the white pages, from "accountants" to "warranties."

These agencies basically use their powers of persuasion to help resolve your dispute, but, if they are unsuccessful, they will refer you to Small Claims Court or wherever may be appropriate. They have no power to sue the person or business against whom you have the complaint, but they can make life difficult for them.

These local consumer complaint agencies are usually quite effective. If you have a complaint, be sure to contact them. They'll take it from there.

Automobiles and Mobile Homes If you take your automobile or mobile home in for repair, you are entitled to a *written* estimate of the repairs. Furthermore, the garage or repairman cannot charge you more than the estimate without your knowledge and permission in advance. Remember, however, that no law regulates automobile repair prices.

Warranty problems regarding motor vehicles should be referred to your local consumer complaint and protection agency mentioned above.

If your problem involves the owner of a mobile home park, call the local building department to see if they can help. If they can't, contact the Department of Consumer Affairs in Sacramento at (800) 445-0135.

Complaints against Medical Practitioners The State Board of Medical Quality Assurance handles complaints against doctors and other kinds of medical practitioners in this state.

If you have a dispute with your physician and are unable to resolve it with him or her, contact the board's regional office nearest you. Someone at the office will look into your complaint and determine whether that office or another is best able to resolve the problem.

If the board's office accepts the complaint, it will investigate and, if appropriate, submit the complaint to the proper state authorities.

The matters handled by the board include:

- gross negligence (extreme carelessness)
- repeated similar careless acts
- incompetence
- dishonesty in practice or criminal acts
- misuse of drugs or alcohol
- prescribing dangerous drugs without a medical examination first
- mental illness

Note that the board does not handle fee disputes. For resolution of these, contact your local county medical society. If the complaint involves Medi-Cal, contact the

State Department of Health
Surveillance and Utilization Review
714 P Street
Sacramento, CA 95814

For a complaint form, write or call the office nearest you:

Sacramento	701 Howe Ave., Suite 59 Sacramento, CA 95825 Telephone (916) 920-6013
Santa Ana	34 Brookhollow Drive Santa Ana, CA 92705 Telephone (714) 558-4452
San Mateo	155 Bovet Road, Suite 660 San Mateo, CA 94402 Telephone (415) 574-8363
Los Angeles	8939 South Sepulveda Blvd., Suite 520 Los Angeles, CA 90045 Telephone (213) 641-8110

You may also make complaints to the board against acupuncturists, audiologists, hearing aid dispensers, physical therapists, physician's assistants, podiatrists, psychologists, and speech pathologists.

Hearing Aid Problems

One of the most common problems facing senior consumers is that of hearing aids. Many of the people who have hearing defects are elderly; and unethical conduct by hearing aid salesmen and companies has a particularly adverse effect on the aged. Unfortunately, the practice of selling and fitting hearing aids readily lends itself to abuse.

Need for Prior Medical Examination It has been estimated that more than five million persons 65 years old or older have hearing impairments. There are, of course, many causes for the loss of hearing, including birth defects, ear infections, eardrum rupture, and adverse drug reactions. One of the most common causes, however, is simply the aging process.

Many older persons who have a hearing loss do not take the precaution of obtaining a preliminary medical examination from an ear, nose, and throat specialist. In fact, about 40% of persons 65 years old or older go to a hearing aid dealer before they consult a physician or other specialist.

A hearing aid dealer may, of course, provide an older person with efficient, effective service. On the other hand, many of them lack adequate training and the facilities to evaluate properly an older person's need for a hearing aid. For example, many older people are sold the wrong type of hearing aid, are improperly fitted, or are sold a hearing aid that offers no chance of restoring their hearing. Consequently, many older persons suffer unnecessary financial losses, since hearing aids generally cost from $400 to $600.

What a Hearing Aid Can and Cannot Do It has been repeatedly pointed out that it is crucially important for consumers to understand what a hearing aid can and cannot do. Essentially, the hearing aid is a miniature sound amplifier. As such, it cannot restore inadequate hearing to normal hearing, nor can it stop the progression of hearing loss.

In fact, a hearing aid will rarely reduce, and may increase, the distortion and reception of speech experienced by some seniors with a hearing loss. And it will not help people with a hearing loss to understand conversation better in noisy situations, or to understand group conversations better. Nevertheless, despite these limitations many people with a hearing loss do benefit from using hearing aids.

Federal Requirements and Regulations To protect consumers generally, but particularly seniors, the federal Food and Drug Administration has issued regulations on how hearing aids must be labeled and sold. The regulations require hearing aid sellers to keep records for three years after the sale, including the required medical statement.

Under these regulations, the purchaser must have had a medical evaluation at least six months before he or she purchases a hearing aid. Furthermore, a statement from the examining physician that a hearing aid may help the purchaser is necessary in order to purchase the device.

A purchaser may "waive" (give up) the medical evaluation and necessity for the physician's written statement by signing a statement that the purchaser knows that a medical examination is advisable. Note: The regulations forbid a hearing aid seller from encouraging prospective purchasers to waive the medical examination.

Under the regulations, manufacturers of hearing aids must give consumers detailed brochures informing the consumer what hearing aids can do, how they work, and how to use them. And they must permit a consumer to read the entire brochure before the sale is completed.

The required brochure warns hearing aid sellers and dispensers to advise prospective purchasers to consult immediately with an ear specialist or other physician if any one of eight ear or hearing problems apparently exists. These problems include diseases, ear deformity, pain or fluid drainage, rapid onset of hearing loss, or a foreign body in the ear.

The Food and Drug Administration advises older consumers who are considering buying a hearing aid to seek out a seller who will let them rent one on a trial basis, to ensure that the device will actually improve their hearing and that they will feel comfortable with it.

Complaints — Whom to Contact In 1977, the Federal Trade Commission (FTC) filed legal complaints against six major hearing aid manufacturers and charged them with false advertising, supplying false advertising materials to dealers and dispensers, and other unfair and deceptive acts. If you feel that you have been a victim of one of these acts, consult your lawyer or your legal assistance center immediately. (See Chapter Fourteen.) You may also wish to contact the Consumers Complaint Commission (see "Hearing Aid Dispensers").

Another group you may wish to contact if you feel you have been victimized by a hearing aid dispenser is called "Retired Professional Action Group," which is referred to as RPAG. If this organization has an office in your county, it will be listed under that name in the white pages.

In addition, if you have a complaint regarding a hearing aid in which you feel you have been a victim of fraud, unfair trade practices or advertising, etc., you should write the U.S. Department of Health and Human Services, Public Health Service, Food and Drug Administration, Office of Public Affairs. This office will be listed under "United States" in the white pages of your telephone directory.

Eyewear

The Federal Trade Commission has now enacted regulations permitting dispensers of eyewear products to advertise prices of prescription eyeglasses and contact lenses. This makes it easier for the consumer to compare prices charged by various dispensers.

Funeral Costs and Swindles

A simple, traditional funeral and burial that is arranged by an honest mortuary often costs $3,000 or more. Some alternatives to be considered are:

- low cost funerals (See Chapter Nineteen)
- cremation, which eliminates the need for embalming and burial expenses
- making a gift of the person's body to science, which reduces funeral expenses and increases scientific knowledge

- immediate burial or cremation, which will eliminate the need for costly embalming

Some common swindles after funerals are:

- collection of non-existent debts owed by the deceased
- delivery of merchandise that was never ordered by the deceased
- collection of final payments on a non-existent life insurance policy

Financing Funerals Here are some of the methods that may be useful in financing a funeral for an older person:

- use of the government death benefits that are available, including a $255 Social Security benefit for the survivor of a worker, and $250 for the survivor of a veteran with an honorable discharge
- life insurance, which can be designated to pay for funeral and burial expenses (shop around for the best deal)
- preplanning, which might save worry and money (however, before you sign a preplanned funeral contract, be sure to seek legal advice and get what you pay for)
- memorial societies — consumer groups that help people plan low cost funerals

These are discussed in Chapter Nineteen. Also, if you are interested, write:

Continental Association of Funeral & Memorial Societies
1828 L Street, N.W., Suite 1100
Washington, D.C. 20036

Where to Send Complaints If you have any complaints about a funeral home or cemetery, contact your local consumer protection agency. You will find it in the white pages under "Consumer Complaint and Protection Coordination, Funeral Directors and Embalmers." If you want to file a complaint with the U.S. Government, write:

Bureau of Consumer Protection
Federal Trade Commission
Washington, D.C. 20580

Veterans' Funerals The Veterans Administration reminds former servicemen and women that their families should be made aware of the VA burial allowances available to eligible veterans.

The Veterans Administration provides $250 toward the burial expenses of eligible veterans, and an additional $150 is available as a plot or interment allowance, if burial is not in a national cemetery or other government cemetery. These payments will be reduced or eliminated if the veteran's employer or state agency has made such payments.

Note: In cases where the veteran's death is service-connected, the Veterans Administration will pay an amount not exceeding $800 in lieu of the usual burial allowance.

With the exception of Arlington National Cemetery, burial is available to eligible veterans at all national cemeteries that have space, and burial may also be authorized for an eligible veteran's wife or husband, minor children, and under certain circumstances, unmarried adult children.

If you want to obtain the eligibility requirements for burial at Arlington National Cemetery, write to:

Superintendent
Arlington National Cemetery
Arlington, VA 22211

Otherwise, with respect to eligibility, veterans eligible for burial in a national cemetery are those discharged under conditions other than dishonorable, those who served in the Spanish-American war, Mexican Border war, World Wars I and II, the Korean war, or the Viet Nam war. Also eligible are all peace-time veterans with other than dishonorable discharges.

If you want additional information on any of the above, contact your nearest Veterans Administration Regional Office listed in the white pages of your telephone directory.

Bill Collectors — What They Can and Can't Do

Seniors are frequently easy prey for bill collectors. Often they are under emotional pressure from a general financial shortage, and they may suffer physical and emotional damage from the harassing tactics of an unscrupulous bill collector. Fortunately, there are remedies, some of which are outlined below.

"Reasonable" Means of Collection Laws (both state and federal) have been enacted to protect you from bill collectors who use unreasonable and harassing tactics. Some of these laws are very specific as to what "unreasonable" means, while others are more general.

Bill collectors may use all legal means to collect whatever debts may be owed them. For example, they may threaten debtors with proper legal procedures in order to collect. If their methods are unreasonable, they are liable to you for damages.

It is frequently difficult to pin down what is meant by "reasonable." However, both courts and lawyers consider the following acts of a bill collector to be unreasonable:

- use of a loud, harsh voice
- a nasty, obnoxious manner
- insulting language that may or may not include cursing and derogatory remarks
- publishing lists of debtors other than as permitted by law
- threatening prosecution by persuading people to give them post-dated checks that bounce
- not crediting the account specified by the person when the person makes a payment and owes more than one creditor

If a bill collector has done any of the above, call your lawyer or legal assistance center immediately. You may well have a good court case, and you may be able to stop such harassing tactics immediately.

Fair Debt Collection Practices Act Under a federal law that has teeth in it, if bill collectors do something that the law prohibits, you can sue them and, if you win, collect all the damages you suffered from their illegal tactics, plus attorney's fees and court costs. And if other seniors you know were victims of the same illegal methods, you can all join in the same suit and save costs.

This law is called the "Fair Debt Collection Practices Act" and prohibits:

(1) harassing or abusing a person by —

- using obscene or profane language
- using or threatening violence to people, their reputation, or property
- advertising people's debts for sale in order to make them pay it, or telling them that such a sale would cut off their rights

- telephoning people continuously to harass them or anyone else, or phoning without identifying themselves as collectors
- threatening to arrest people for nonpayment

(2) making false or misleading statements, such as —

- telling people that they have been sued when this is not true
- misrepresenting their "professional status," for example, by representing that they are lawyers when they are not
- deceiving people into believing that bill collectors represent a state, local, or governmental agency
- using documents that appear to be issued by a court when in fact they have not been and have no legal status
- deceiving people into believing that the debt has been turned over to an independent collection agency when it is the creditor who is actually trying to collect

(3) causing undue embarrassment or humiliation, such as by —

- contacting the people before 9:00 a.m. or after 9:00 p.m. unless the bill collector has reason to believe that other hours are more convenient for the person
- using postcards to tell people that their debts have been assigned for collection (only notices in envelopes may be used)
- listing their business names, as collection agencies, as their return address on any envelope they send the person
- failing to contact the person's attorney when they know the person has one
- contacting people at their jobs when the bill collector knows or should know that it is against the employer's rule
- threats, including a threat to blacklist the debtor with retail credit associations
- any acts that cause debtors to lose their jobs, to have their reputations tarnished, or to be arrested
- calling debtors "deadbeats" and accusing them of lying

If you are a senior and your creditor has done any of the above, contact your senior legal assistance center or the state Collection and Investigative Services Bureau. Look in the white pages under "California, State of."

Are You "Judgment Proof"? Many older persons are what lawyers call "judgment proof." This means that the debtor does not have enough assets to satisfy a judgment, even if the creditor goes ahead and sues in court and gets a judgment. This is partly because the assets of older people, such as pension checks, Social Security benefit checks, public assistance checks, etc., cannot be attached or garnished by creditors; that is, these benefits cannot be seized by creditors to satisfy debts — they are exempt (see below).

Since the assets of many seniors consist primarily of these benefits, most creditors will think at least twice before starting a lawsuit, because they know they will collect little, if anything. This does not mean, of course, that older people, because of their unique position, should avoid honest debts. It does mean, however, that if they find themselves unable to fully satisfy a debt, they should protect themselves as best they can.

What property you may keep, even if your creditor gets a court judgment against you, is one of the most important things for you to learn and remember. This kind of property, including cash, is called "exempt" property by courts and lawyers, and it is up to you to take the necessary steps to protect your exempt property. You will need to do this, for example, if your automobile, bank account, or other personal property is being seized by your creditor, if you file papers for bankruptcy, and if you have protected your home by filing homestead papers.

The following property, or a part of it, is exempt from your creditor's court judgment and cannot be taken from you:

- your home, if it is homesteaded
- your household and kitchen furniture and appliances
- the tools of your trade or profession
- your family automobile
- current wages for personal services
- workmen's compensation benefits
- veteran's benefits and soldier's savings
- pension payments, such as those from firemen's and policemen's pensions
- retirement funds of teachers and state and city employees
- government benefit checks
- part of a savings account or checking account

Any legal aid office can tell you more about how to make a claim of exemption and how to homestead your dwelling place if you have not yet done so.

Right to Cancel Credit Sales Contracts

One of the most important rights consumers have in general is the right to cancel, without obligation, certain credit agreements they have signed. The lawyers call this the right to rescind, which means the right to cancel. If you see any boldface lettering on an agreement sheet you signed that includes the word "rescind," be sure to read it. The creditor with whom you signed the agreement may not charge you a service charge, finance charge, etc., when you cancel an agreement properly. But in each case you must be careful to cancel within the time and manner that is required, or your cancelation will not be effective.

Cancelation of most credit agreements is very simple, since the law requires the seller to give consumers the form to be used if they decide to cancel. This form has all the legal requirements in it. Furthermore, the seller must tell you about your right to cancel the agreement by giving you a completed receipt or copy of the agreement that alerts you to this right by displaying, in big black type, the words "Notice of Cancelation."

All you have to do to cancel the agreement is to sign the "Notice of Cancelation" form where indicated and send the notice, or a copy of it, back to the seller in time.

In most sales, you must cancel by midnight of the third business day following the transaction.

Credit Discrimination

Under federal and state law, a creditor may not ask credit applicants their age for the purpose of discriminating against them. A creditor can ask you your age, of course, to find out if you are old enough to make a contract the creditor can enforce.

Mr. Walker, age 70, makes a credit application for an automobile purchase and is refused, the credit manager telling him that the company's files show that "older men just aren't responsible with credit and we have nothing but trouble with them." Mr. Walker should call his lawyer, assuming, of course, that he is a good credit risk otherwise.

Furthermore, you may not be discriminated against, in applying for credit, if your income is all or partially from welfare. However, the creditor may ask you whether any or all of your income is from a public assistance program if the creditor's only purpose is to find out the amount of your income and the probability that it will continue as it has been.

Credit Reporting Agencies

All "credit reporting agencies" (which include collection agencies, credit bureaus, and even private detective agencies) must be very careful that any information they gather about consumers and pass on to others is complete and accurate. This is particularly true of those kinds of credit agencies that use computers in processing this information. Remember that under the Fair Credit Reporting Act, credit reporting agencies also may not discriminate in credit transactions against a person because of his or her age. For example, such agencies may not issue negative credit reports based on a person's age. If you are so discriminated against, contact your lawyer or legal assistance center immediately.

Disclosure Laws: Truth in Lending

Important federal and state laws apply to all credit transactions for personal, family, household, or agricultural purposes. These laws apply to all types of credit transactions, including cash loans, credit sales, revolving charges, credit extensions, and any other credit transaction in which the consumer is obligated to pay in at least four installments.

The state and federal laws generally work together to require any seller of goods on credit to disclose to you certain important information concerning those goods and the cost of them. You may find out more about these important laws, as well as any violation of them by a creditor, by calling Consumer Credit Practices, listed under Consumer Complaint and Protection in the white pages. Alternatively, you may write:

Division of Consumer Credit
Federal Trade Commission
Washington, D.C. 20580

Violation by Creditor If your creditor has violated the state or federal Truth in Lending laws that require disclosure of credit cost information, you may sue regardless of his or her motives. If you win, you may recover, as damages, twice the amount of the finance charge, with a minimum of $100 and a maximum of $1,000, plus reasonable attorney's fees and court costs. Your creditor may also be criminally liable if these laws were violated intentionally.

Advertising of Credit Terms Under the Truth in Lending laws, and others, the advertising of credit terms is regulated. The law provides, among other things, that if a business is going to mention one feature of credit in its advertising, such as the amount of down-payment, it must also mention all other important terms, such as the number, amount, and period of payments that follow. For example, if an advertisement states "Only $2 down," the advertisement must also state, for example, that a person has to pay $10 a week for the next two years. The intent of this law is to provide you with full information so that you can make informed decisions.

Help for the Consumer

There are a number of organizations that may be of assistance to you, depending on the specific type of complaint that you have. Some of these "consumer" organizations are basically for information only, while others will help you if your problem is within their field of interest. Occasionally, a state or national organization can put pressure on creditors practicing unfair or illegal tactics by threatening adverse publicity, economic boycotting, or even legal action on behalf of the credit consumer.

National Organizations Some of the national groups listed below deal specifically with the problems and financial practices of creditors, while others deal with these problems as a small area of consumer problems generally. But it never hurts to try!

Clearing House for
Professional Responsibility
P.O. Box 486
Washington, D.C. 20044

American Council on
Consumer Interests
238 Stanley Hall
University of Missouri
Columbia, MO 65201
(314) 882-7836

Consumer Alliance
P.O. Box 11773
Palo Alto, CA 94306
(415) 328-7771

Consumer Federation of America
1012 14th St., N.W., Suite 901
Washington, D.C. 20005
(202) 737-3732

Consumers Education and Protective Association
6048 Ogontz Ave.
Philadelphia, PA 19141
(215) 244-1441

Consumers Union
256 Washington Street
Mount Vernon, NY 10550
(914) 664-6400

National Consumer Finance Association
701 Solar Building
1000 6th St., N.W.
Washington, D.C. 20036
(202) 638-1340

National Consumers League
1785 Massachusetts Ave., N.W.
Washington, D.C. 20036
(202) 797-7600

Federal Government Offices Federal government offices that may be of assistance in credit consumer problems involving older people include:

Consumer Information Center
General Services Administration
Washington, D.C. 20407
(202) 343-6171

Office of Consumer Affairs
Washington, D.C. 20201
(202) 245-6164

Bureau of Consumer Protection
Federal Trade Commission
Pennsylvania Ave., 6th Street
Washington, D.C. 20850
(202) 962-0151

Consumer Affairs Coordinator
Housing & Urban Development Department
Washington, D.C. 20410
(202) 755-7976

Office of the Director
Department of Health & Human Services
Washington, D.C. 20201
(202) 245-6164

The federal government maintains information centers throughout the state. These centers offer information to consumers or their lawyers regarding which federal agency is most likely to be of service to the consumer. These centers also provide, free of charge, government consumer bulletins.

You may get in touch with the center nearest you by telephone, by mail, or in person. Telephone numbers for the Federal Information Centers are: Fresno – (209) 487-5016; Los Angeles – (213) 688-3800; Sacramento – (916) 440-3344; San Diego – (714) 293-6030; and San Francisco – (415) 556-6600. In other areas, check the white pages of your telephone directory under "United States Government."

Better Business Bureau California's Better Business Bureau (BBB) is an independent branch of a national organization that has been assisting consumers generally for many years. One of their more effective functions is supplying reports to consumers about businesses and firms upon the consumer's request.

If you have a complaint against your creditor, BBB will generally try to straighten out your problem with the creditor after contacting him or her. The bureau does not necessarily act on your behalf only but acts as a sort of arbitrator on a case-by-case basis. If creditors or bill collectors refuse to correct unfair or illegal practices, the BBB may pressure them to stop by means of adverse publicity within the business community, together with other tactics.

Contact your local BBB about any unfair or illegal practices by your creditors. They are listed in your telephone directory white pages.

The bureau will send you, on your request, any or all of the following information booklets, which might be of great help to you:

- tips on sales contracts
- facts you should know about schemes
- consumer tips on "bait and switch"
- consumer tips on buying on time

18
Taxes

Many California seniors pay more federal and state income taxes than are legally due. One reason for this is that many seniors are overwhelmed by the complexities of the U.S. and California tax laws. Another is that many are unaware of the deductions that can save them precious dollars. Yet another is that the tax laws change rapidly and often require the services of a tax specialist to update exemptions and deductions. Many seniors cannot afford these experts.

Some tax benefits for older Californians are well-publicized, and most seniors are aware of, for example, the annual homeowners' exemption. Others such as the renter's credit receive less attention and are frequently ignored by taxpayers. The purpose of this chapter is to outline the federal and state tax benefits available specifically to seniors, and to advise them where to seek help when preparing their tax returns.

Where to Get Help

NRTA/AARP If you need assistance in preparing your taxes, check with the tax aide program of the National Retired Teachers' Association/American Association of Retired Persons. Membership dues are $4.00 per year, and the association provides free of charge a tax aide program. The program is run by member volunteers trained by the IRS in federal, state, and local tax preparation. For more information, check the white pages of your directory for the office nearest you, or write to

NRTA/AARP
1909 K Street, N.W.
Washington, D.C. 20049

Federal and State Government You can obtain, upon request, an annual federal publication called "Tax Benefits for Older Americans." It is published by the Department of the Treasury, Internal Revenue Service, Pub. 554 (the current one was revised in November 1980, for use in 1981). Ask at your local IRS office or write for one to the

Superintendent of Documents
U.S. Government Printing Office
Washington, D.C. 20402

Your local senior center may also have this publication.

For general information from the federal government with regard to tax relief for older citizens, write:

Advisory Commission On Intergovernmental Relations
726 Jackson Place, N.W.
Washington, D.C. 20006
(202) 382-4947

The Internal Revenue Service is usually helpful to seniors who need assistance with their federal tax returns. And the State Franchise Tax Board will help seniors with state tax problems and forms. The telephone numbers of these offices are listed later in the chapter.

Local Senior Assistance Centers Many counties maintain senior assistance centers that offer tax services. And many privately sponsored senior centers have this kind of help available. Ask your Information and Referral worker or your local Area Agency on Aging for further information.

Public Libraries Public libraries all have state tax forms and schedules, which are available on request. Many also have other printed materials that are of assistance in understanding the state tax laws.

State Programs for Tax Relief

Three California programs offer property tax relief for seniors in this state: the property tax exemption, homeowner's assistance, and the property tax postponement. Renter's credit on taxes and capital gains exclusions for sale of your residence are also discussed in this section.

Each program has its own eligibility requirements and filing period. Particular attention must be paid to the filing period dates, since you will be penalized in most cases if you file your claim late.

Homeowner's Property Tax Exemption If you are a California senior (62 years of age or older) and own your own home in the state, you may qualify for a state property tax exemption, provided:

- You owned your home and occupied it as your principal place of residence as of 12:01 A.M., March 1.
- You have not claimed a veterans' tax exemption on the same property.

To obtain this exemption, you must file a claim with your county assessor's office by April 15. That office will provide the necessary forms and help you, if necessary, in filling them out. If you continue to own and occupy the same dwelling as of March 1 of the following year or years, you need not re-file again each year.

If you are late in filing your claim, you may still obtain 80% of the allowed exemption, provided you owned and occupied your home as of March 1 and file your claim by December 1.

The property tax exemption or reduction is $1,750 of the assessed value (see your tax bill) or $7,000 of the market value of your home on March 1 of the year for which you file the claim. That is, you will not be charged property tax on these amounts, which are generally exactly the same.

If you file your claim late, as discussed above, you are only entitled to 80% of the exempt amounts ($1,400 of the assessed value or $5,600 of the market value).

If you have any questions about the homeowner's exemption, contact your county assessor. Also, your local legal assistance center will be able to help you.

Homeowner Assistance California seniors may also be eligible for a refund of part of their property taxes paid on homes. The eligibility requirements are:

- You must have been 62 years of age or blind or disabled* on December 31 of the year prior to which you make your claim.
- You must have owned and occupied your own home as of December 31, in the year prior to which you make your claim.
- Your household income for the prior year must have been $12,000 or less.

Only one claim for homeowner's assistance may be filed for each household. But note that you are eligible even though you received SSI or other public assistance the year before and even though you claim the veteran's or homeowner's exemptions. However, if you own a mobile home on land owned by you and have claimed the homeowner's exemption, you are not entitled to this assistance.

Under homeowner's assistance, you will receive a refund on the state property taxes you paid the prior year on the first $8,500 of the net assessed value of your home, after deducting any homeowner's exemption discussed above. The size of the refund depends on your net household income from the prior year.

For further information and assistance on this benefit, call the Franchise Tax Board toll free — Northern California: (800) 852-7050; Southern California: (800) 852-5711.

Property Tax Postponement If you were 62 years of age or older on December 31 of the prior year, lived in your own home, and had household income of less than $26,800, you may postpone part or all of your state property taxes.

You must file a claim for postponement between May 6 and December 31, and you will be issued a certificate if you meet the eligibility requirements. This certificate must be kept by you or by your estate for use when the property passes to another.

For claim forms and further information, contact the State Controller's Office in the white pages under "California, State of," or contact your local legal assistance organization, or call toll free (800) 952-5661.

---

*"Disabled," for the purposes of these benefits, means that you are unable to engage in any substantial activity (earn more than $300 a month) and the disability may be expected to last for at least one year.

Renters' Tax Credit California seniors (as well as others) may be entitled to a tax refund for rent paid in the prior taxable year. Here are the qualifications:

- You must have been a California resident and renting premises on March 1 of the taxable year.
- Your apartment or house must not have been tax-exempt property, such as church-owned property.
- You must not have received the homeowners' property tax exemption discussed above.
- You must not have lived with another person who claimed you as a dependent for income tax purposes.

You may be eligible for renters' credit even though you lived (during the above period) in a convalescent home, mobile home, boarding house, hotel room, apartment, etc., provided the owners of the property paid property taxes. Furthermore, you may be eligible for this credit even though you received SSI, Medi-Cal, food stamps, and other general welfare benefits.

You may file for renters' credit any time after January 1. You may even file for four back years in which you qualified for the credit. But note that eligibility requirements differed in previous years; also, until 1979 the credit was only $37 per renter.

Obtain Renter Credit Schedule H at the Franchise Tax Board office. File Schedule H with your state tax return (if you had income, Schedule 540; if no income, Schedule 540A). Note that you may receive a credit even though you had no taxable state income for the prior year.

The credit is in the form of a refund of $137 for a married couple filing a joint claim and the same amount for the head of a household; $60 for a single person.

For further information and help on renters' credit, call the State Franchise Tax Board — Northern California: (800) 852-7050; Southern California: (800) 852-5711 — toll free.

The state program of Renters' Assistance and the federal program of Section 8 Rent Subsidy are discussed in Chapter Fifteen.

Sale of Personal Residence If you are over age 65 and sell your personal residence you may exclude the first $100,000 profit ($50,000 if you are married and filing separately) from your income for that year. You must have lived in your residence for a total of three years out of the last five in order to claim the exclusion. You may do this only once in your lifetime.

Remember, this applies to your state taxes only. Federal tax laws have a similar provision but allow you to claim the exclusion at age 55 rather than 65. (Discussed later in this chapter.)

Federal Tax Benefits

Four specific federal income tax benefits are available to seniors, in addition to the benefits that are available to American taxpayers generally. Two of these specific benefits are available to all persons aged 65 or over. The other two are available only to those who qualify. Note: For federal income tax purposes, you are considered to be 65 on the day before your 65th birthday.

Tax laws change rapidly. After reading the following material, be sure to check with the IRS or your tax advisor to see whether any laws have been changed since this was written.

Who Must File a Federal Tax Return

Filing status	Required to file a tax return if gross income is at least —
Single (age 65 or older)	$4,300
Married couple (1 spouse 65 or older) filing jointly	$6,400
Married couple (both spouses 65 or older) filing jointly	$7,400
Married filing separately	$1,000

Additional Personal Exemption for Age Besides the regular $1,000 exemption allowed a taxpayer, a husband and wife who are 65 or older on the last day of the taxable year are each entitled to an additional exemption of $1,000 because of age. As mentioned previously, you are considered 65 on the day before your 65th birthday. Thus, if your 65th birthday is on January 1, 1981, you will be entitled to the additional $1,000 personal exemption because of age for your 1980 federal income tax return.

"Zero Bracket Amount" (Standard Deduction) The former standard deduction has been replaced by a flat amount the law calls "zero bracket amount." This amount depends on your filing status. It is no longer a separate deduction as such; instead, the equivalent amount is built into the new simplified tax tables and tax rate schedules. Therefore taxpayers who itemize deductions will need to make an adjustment. However, itemizers will not experience any change in their tax liability, and the tax computation will be simplified for many of them.

New Tax Tables New simplified tax tables have been developed to make it easier for you to find your tax if your income is under certain levels. Now, even if you itemize deductions, you may be able to use the tax tables to find your tax more easily. In addition, you no longer need to deduct $1,000 for each exemption or figure your general tax credit, because these amounts are also built into the tax table for you.

General Tax Credit The general tax credit has been revised to take into consideration the exemptions for age and blindness. Married taxpayers filing separate returns are limited to a credit based on $35 per exemption.

Multiple Support Agreements In general, a person may be claimed as a dependent of another taxpayer, provided five tests are met: (1) support, (2) gross income, (3) member of household or relationship, (4) citizenship, and (5) separate return. But there are cases in which two or more individuals provide support for another individual, and no one has contributed more than half that person's support. However, it still may be possible for one of the individuals to be entitled to a $1,000 dependency deduction if the following requirements are met for multiple support:

- Two or more persons — any one of whom could claim the person as a dependent if it were not for the support test — together contribute more than half of the dependent's support.
- Any one of those who individually contribute more than 10% of the mutual dependent's support, but only one of them, may claim the dependency deduction.
- Each of the others must file a written statement that he or she will not claim the dependency deduction for that year. The statement must be filed with the income tax return of the person

who claims the dependency deduction. Form 2120 (Multiple Support Declaration) may be used for this purpose.

Note: If you are a senior and are claimed as a deduction by one of your family who contributes half or more of your support, he or she need not take into account contributions to you and your welfare by Medicare or Medi-Cal. That is, such amounts are no longer included in your total support amount.

Sale of Residence by Senior Taxpayer A senior taxpayer (over 55 years of age) may elect to exclude from gross income $100,000 of gain ($50,000 if you are married and filing separately) on the sale or exchange of his or her home after July 26, 1978, provided:

- the senior was 55 years of age or older before the date of the sale or exchange, and
- he or she owned and lived in the property as his or her principal residence for at least five years of the eight years preceding the sale or exchange (This rule applies only to sales or exchanges after July 26, 1981.)
- the senior taxpayer or his spouse have not claimed the exclusion before

California tax laws allow a similar exclusion from your state taxes. However, this state only allows the exclusion for persons over age 65. (See section on state programs, above.)

Additionally, taxpayers may choose to defer reporting the gain on the sale of their personal residence if, within 18 months before or 18 months after the sale, they buy and occupy another residence, the cost of which equals or exceeds the adjusted sales price of the old residence. Additional time is allowed if (1) you construct the new residence or (2) you were on active duty in the U.S. Armed Forces. Publication 523 (Tax Information on Selling Your Home) may also be helpful.

Alimony Paid Payments for alimony are now adjustments to income. You no longer have to itemize deductions to claim a deduction for alimony you paid.

Credit for Seniors An expanded and simplified credit for seniors has replaced the former more complex retirement income credit.

A taxpayer may be able to claim this credit and reduce taxes by more than \$375 (if single), or \$562.50 (if married filing jointly), if the taxpayer is:

- age 65 or older, or
- under age 65 and retired under a public retirement system

To be eligible for this credit, taxpayers no longer must meet the income requirement of having received over \$600 of earned income during each of any 10 years before this year.

Credit for Child and Dependent Care Expenses Certain payments made for child and dependent care may be claimed as a credit against tax.

Taxpayers who maintain households that included a child under age 15 or a dependent or spouse incapable of self-care may be allowed a 20% credit for employment-related expenses. These expenses must have been paid during the taxable year in order to enable the taxpayer to work either full or part-time.

For detailed information, see the instructions on Form 2441.

Earned Income Credit Taxpayers who maintain households for a child who is under age 19, or are students, or are disabled dependents, may be entitled to a special payment or credit of up to \$500. This is called the earned income credit. It may come as a refund check or be applied against any taxes owed. Generally, taxpayers who report earned income and have adjusted gross income (line 31, Form 1040) of less than \$10,000 may be able to claim the credit.

"Earned income" means wages, salaries, tips, other employee compensation, and net earnings from self-employment (generally the amount shown on Schedule SE [Form 1040] line 13). A married couple must file a joint return to be eligible for the credit. Certain married persons living apart with a dependent child may also be eligible to claim the credit.

For more information, see instructions for Form 1040 or 1040A.

Checklist of Itemized Deductions for Schedule A (Form 1040)

The checklist below follows the information contained in "Tax Benefits for Older Americans" (Internal Revenue Service Pub. No. 554 — revised November, 1980). It is intended for the vast majority of seniors, to make sure that they claim all the deductions, credits, and exemptions to which they are entitled. Furthermore, the checklist can help you determine whether it would be more advantageous to itemize deductible expenses or claim the standard deduction.

You may discover, on reading the checklist, that you failed to claim allowable deductions on tax returns you filed in the past. You can obtain a refund for proper deductible expenditures you have overlooked by filing an amended return for the year in question. The form you use for this amended return is Form 1040X. However, you must file this form within three years after the original return was due or filed, or within two years from the time you paid the tax — whichever is latest.

Medical and Dental Expenses Medical and dental expenses (unreimbursed by insurance or otherwise) are deductible to the extent that they exceed 3% of a taxpayer's adjusted gross income (line 31, Form 1040).

Insurance Premiums One-half of medical, hospital, or health insurance premiums are deductible (up to $150) without regard to the 3% limitation for other medical expenses. The remainder of these premiums can be deducted but is subject to the 3% rule.

Drugs and Medicines These are included in medical expenses (subject to the 3% rule) but only to the extent that they exceed 1% of adjusted gross income (line 31, Form 1040).

Other Medical Expenses Other allowable medical and dental expenses (subject to the 3% limitation) are:

- abdominal supports (prescribed by a doctor)
- acupuncture services
- ambulance hire
- anesthetist
- arch supports (prescribed by a doctor)
- artificial limbs and teeth
- back supports (prescribed by a doctor)
- braces

Capital expenditures for medical purposes (e.g., elevators for persons with heart ailments) are deductible to the extent that the cost of the capital expenditure exceeds the increase in value to your home because of the capital expenditure. Taxpayers should have an independent appraisal made to reflect clearly the increase in value.

- cardiographs
- chiropodist
- chiropractor
- Christian Science practitioner, authorized
- convalescent home (for medical treatment only)
- crutches
- dental services (e.g., cleaning, X-ray, filling teeth)
- dentures
- dermatologist
- eyeglasses
- food or beverages specially prescribed by a physician (for treatment of illness, and in addition to, not as substitute for, regular diet; physician's statement needed)
- gynecologist
- hearing aids and batteries
- home health services
- hospital expenses
- insulin treatment
- invalid chair
- lab tests
- lipreading lessons (designed to overcome a handicap)
- neurologist
- nursing services (for medical care, including nurse's board paid by you)
- occupational therapist
- ophthalmologist
- optician
- optometrist
- oral surgery
- osteopath, licensed
- pediatrician
- physical examinations
- physical therapist
- physician
- podiatrist
- psychiatrist

- psychoanalyst
- psychologist
- psychotherapy
- radium therapy
- sacroiliac belt (prescribed by a doctor)
- seeing-eye dog and maintenance
- speech therapist
- splints
- supplementary medical insurance (Part B) under Medicare
- surgeon
- telephone/teletype special communications equipment for the deaf
- transportation expenses for medical purposes (9¢ per mile plus parking and tolls or actual fares for taxi, buses, etc.)
- vaccines
- vitamins prescribed by a doctor (but not taken as a food supplement or to preserve general health)
- wheelchairs
- whirlpool baths for medical purposes
- x-rays

Taxes

- real estate
- state and local gasoline
- general sales
- state and local income
- personal property

If you use sales tax tables to arrive at your deduction, you may add to the amount shown in the tax tables only the sales tax paid on the purchase of five classes of items: automobiles, airplanes, boats, mobile homes, and materials used to build a new home if you are your own contractor.

When using the sales tax tables, add to your adjusted gross income any nontaxable income (e.g., Social Security, Veterans' pensions or compensation payments, railroad retirement annuities, workmen's compensation, untaxed portion of long-term capital gains, recovery of pension costs, dividends untaxed under the dividend exclusion, interest on municipal bonds, unemployment compensation, and public assistance payments).

Contributions In general, contributions may be deducted up to 50% of your adjusted gross income (line 31, Form 1040). However, contributions to certain private nonprofit foundations, veterans organizations, or fraternal societies are limited to 20% of your adjusted gross income.

Cash contributions to qualified organizations are deductible for (1) religious, charitable, scientific, literary, or educational purposes, (2) prevention of cruelty to children or animals, or (3) federal, state, or local governmental units (tuition for children attending parochial schools is not deductible). Fair market value of property (e.g., clothing, books, equipment, furniture) for charitable purposes is also deductible. (For gifts of appreciated property, special rules apply. Contact your local IRS office.)

You may also deduct:

- travel expenses (actual or 9¢ per mile plus parking and tolls) for charitable purposes (you may not deduct insurance or depreciation in either case)
- cost and upkeep of uniforms used in charitable activities (e.g., scoutmaster)
- purchase of goods or tickets from charitable organizations (excess of amount paid over the fair market value on the goods or services)
- out-of-pocket expenses (e.g., postage, stationery, phone calls) while rendering services for charitable organizations
- care of an unrelated student in your home under a written agreement with a qualifying organization (deduction is limited to $50 per month)

Interest You may deduct most interest payments. This includes the interest on your home mortgage, auto loan, installment purchases, bank credit cards, and revolving charge accounts. However, you cannot deduct the cost of service charges, loan fees, credit investigation fees, or similar charges.

Mortgage points are deductible as interest by the buyer where the financing agreement provides that they are to be paid for the use of the lender's money. They are not deductible if the points represent charges for services rendered by the lending institution (for example, VA loan points). Furthermore, they are not deductible if they are paid by the seller. However, the penalty you might be required to pay for prepayment of a mortgage is deductible, and will be treated by the IRS as interest.

The "finance charge" from revolving charge accounts can be deducted as interest if this charge is based on your unpaid balance and computed monthly. Other charge accounts for installment purchases are handled somewhat differently. You may deduct the lesser of the following: six percent of your average unpaid balance or the total fee or service charge for the year.

Casualty or Theft Losses You may deduct your losses to nonbusiness property from theft and casualty (tornado, flood, fire, auto accident, and the like). Generally, you can deduct the lesser of either the loss to the extent of the fair market value *or* the value of your interest in the property. Insurance payments or any other type of recovery you make will reduce your deduction. Furthermore, the maximum deduction for property held for personal use is $100. You may use Form 4684 for computing your personal casualty loss.

Note: You cannot make a deduction if your loss was the result of your intentional act or your willful negligence.

Miscellaneous You may deduct:

- appraisal fees for casualty loss or to determine the fair market value of charitable contributions
- union dues
- cost of preparation of income tax return
- cost of tools for employee (depreciated over the useful life of the tools)
- dues for Chamber of Commerce (if as a business expense)
- rental cost of safe-deposit box for income-producing property
- fees paid to investment counselors
- subscriptions to business publications
- telephone and postage in connection with investments
- uniforms required for employment and not generally wearable off the job
- maintenance of uniforms required for employment
- special safety apparel (e.g., steel toe safety shoes or helmets worn by construction workers, special masks worn by welders)
- business entertainment expenses
- business gift expenses not exceeding $25 per recipient

- employment agency fees, under certain circumstances
- cost of a periodic physical examination if required by employer
- cost of installation and maintenance of a telephone required by the taxpayer's employment (deduction based on business use)
- cost of bond if required for employment
- expenses of an office in your home if employment requires it
- payments made by a teacher to a substitute
- educational expenses required by your employer to maintain your position or for maintaining or sharpening your skills for your employment

Political Campaign Contributions Taxpayers may now claim either a deduction (line 32, Schedule A, Form 1040) or a credit (line 38, Form 1040) for campaign contributions to an individual who is a candidate for nomination or election to any federal, state, or local office in any primary, general, or special election. The deduction or credit is also applicable for any committee supporting a candidate for federal, state, or local elective public office, national committee of a national political party, state committee of a national political party, or local committee of a national political party. The amount of the tax credit is one-half of the political contribution, with a $50 ceiling ($100 for couples filing jointly).

Additionally, taxpayers may voluntarily earmark $1 of their taxes ($2 on joint returns) for the presidential election campaign fund.

Additional Information For any questions concerning any of these items, contact your local IRS office. You may also obtain helpful publications and additional forms by contacting your local IRS office. Look under "United States" in the white pages of the telephone directory.

19
Community Benefits and Programs

Far too many Californians grow older with little or no preparation for handling the stresses and strains of their later years, such as reduced income, loneliness, and loss of meaning in their lives. This chapter describes the local services and benefits that can help seniors deal with these problems and enjoy the years ahead.

Most local senior programs are partially funded but require donations and volunteer help. The support of other seniors and of the community at large produces a remarkable amount of friendliness and enthusiasm in local programs. New seniors are amazed by the vitality these programs have to offer and find that by offering their own services they bring enrichment and new friendships into their lives.

Older Americans Act

The Older Americans Act of 1965 (and its amendments) are the underpinning of local programs for seniors. The act provides funding for the Area Agencies on Aging, which sponsor senior programs in nutrition, health services, transportation, legal assistance, homemaker services, and employment.

Mrs. Lee, a widow aged 70, felt desperately lonely in her new neighborhood and needed help. Her Social Security checks barely covered her expenses. She was referred to her local senior center by her pastor, and since then her life has changed. At the center she has her main meal, attends classes, receives a periodic health screening, and has made friends. She now stretches her income with shopping discounts, part-time work, and tax benefits she had never applied for before. Now she is saving for a trip to see her grandchildren.

Many of the benefits Mrs. Lee received, such as her meals, health checks, and part-time job, stem from the Older Americans Act. Her center was probably funded by federal, state, county, and private sources. The tax help was given by a volunteer. Her senior discounts came from the help of private businesses and volunteers.

Diversity of Local Programs

California is a large and varied state, and senior programs vary accordingly. A senior living in an isolated mountain town may desperately need transportation for medical help; another senior, living in an urban high crime area, may require housing help and protective assistance.

Good programs exist in communities with a history of active volunteers and community support. The famous Little House in Menlo Park, started 31 years ago by volunteers, is an internationally recognized model center for seniors. On the other hand, there are also centers that operate out of store-fronts in blighted urban areas where community support and interest are just now developing.

Obviously, if you plan to move, it would be wise to check out the senior centers in the area before you do so.

Political Support Local political support largely determines how adequate local senior programs are. The county supervisors must approve the funding, and they can either help or undermine the work and interest of volunteers. In one county in California, for example, senior benefits are few and far between. Yet that same county has the highest percentage of people 60 and over in the United States — and the lowest per capita income in the state.

Information and Referral

As a starting point to learn about senior services in your area, contact Information and Referral — also called I & R. For the telephone number, look in the yellow pages of the directory under "Senior Citizens' Organizations and Services." Information and Referral is a telephone network service with offices either in senior centers or in downtown locations. This service is very valuable, since the programs are often called by different names in different areas and are sponsored by a variety of organizations.

The following list covers some of the senior services that may be available in your locality and to which Information and Referral can refer you:

- consumer affairs
- counseling programs
- discounts
- education and recreation
- employment
- financial aid
- food and home-delivered meals
- health care — general and special
- housing and household repairs
- legal aid
- Medicare and Medi-Cal assistance
- residential care and nursing homes
- Social Security
- taxes
- transportation and escort services
- volunteer opportunities

Information and Referral offices are staffed with trained volunteers and usually at least one paid professional person who is knowledgeable in the field. Many offices have a program of need-assessment interviews at the time of initial inquiry. Other offices have plans for such a service. So don't hesitate to ask for an interview.

Follow-Up Services Some Information and Referral offices offer follow-up services, if such help is indicated at the time of the initial assessment interview. People can easily become discouraged or confused and fail to follow through with the steps necessary to get needed help. The follow-up services can include home calls, help in filling out forms correctly, contacting relatives, and above all in making sure that the needed assistance is received. Unfortunately, follow-up service is not widely available.

Community-Sponsored Senior Centers

Throughout the state, senior centers provide people who are 60 years of age and older with a wide variety of programs and services.

Since most centers receive some public funding, their services are available to all seniors. This includes centers sponsored by religious and ethnic groups.

Most of these centers are warm, enthusiastic places that are busy using the facilities they have and planning on how to expand them. If you walk into one, the chances are you will be greeted warmly, given a newsletter, and informed of the various programs.

Multi-Purpose Senior Centers Currently, planners are calling for the development of centers that are centrally located and provide many services under one roof. These are meant to provide greater coordination of programs and better information for seniors about their benefits and the available services. Seniors are also spared the inconvenience and irritation of traveling from office to office.

The following is a list of the services that might be available in a *model* center (which probably doesn't exist). But keep in mind that many of these services, though not all, are available in smaller centers. Some of the specific services will be discussed later in the chapter.

- central dining room
- recreation programs
- educational programs
- health screening
- legal assistance (See Chapter 14)
- Information and Referral
- social events
- senior transportation
- senior discount programs
- tax preparation assistance
- preparation of Medicare and other insurance claims
- job placement and counseling (See Chapter 16)
- Retirement Senior Volunteer Program (RSVP)
- newsletter and information bulletin board
- Social Security representation in disputes
- mobile library service
- group sessions for emotional support
- excursions and trips
- centers' own special programs

Programs Special to Area Unique programs stem from the needs of seniors in each particular area and from the interests of volunteers and staff. Check out what might be available in your area.

Mr. Fred Ferris, age 72, had just retired, sold his successful travel agency, and moved to California to be near his daughter. Fred was bored, uneasy with his daughter's friends, and lonely for his old golf buddies. He wandered into a center and found golf partners — in fact, he organized a golf tournament. Now, as a volunteer, he runs a senior travel discount service at the center and conducts trips for a day or several weeks. His service offers the best senior travel bargains in the area and is open to all seniors in the county. Fred is no longer bored.

The following are examples of senior center programs developed to meet the special needs of the area:

- special services to Indians and retired farmworkers
- legal assistance to aliens
- bilingual programs and English classes
- cultural and nutritional classes for ethnic groups
- investment and tax shelter counseling
- alcohol and drug abuse programs
- travel excursions and social and cultural events

Senior Programs at Churches and Non-Profit Agencies

Your church is a source of support that should not be overlooked. Although many churches do not have formal senior programs, the members of the congregation often provide their senior members with temporary and permanent volunteer transportation, shopping, household help, assistance while ill, telephone calls, and visits. Moreover, a church's congregation can provide a reliable pool from which you can hire someone to help you at home.

Some churches have programs for seniors, senior clubs, retirement residences, and other activities that are sponsored under church auspices. A few churches have responded to the problems of both isolated seniors and isolated younger families by bringing these groups together and forming multi-generational church families. These groups can share their holidays together and give support in times of need.

Catholic Social Service, Jewish Community Centers, and others offer community-wide help, including counseling, to all seniors regardless of faith. Don't hesitate to visit these centers; you will be very welcome.

Community Emergency Help for Seniors

This is offered by such groups as the Salvation Army, FISH (Friends in Service to Humanity), St. Vincent de Paul Society, and the welfare departments. In emergencies, first contact Information and Referral for the best source of help in your community.

Transportation and Escort Services

Most of your community benefits will mean little to you without safe, reliable transportation. Fortunate seniors are able to use their own vehicles for transportation, despite the expense. However, many others must rely on public transportation or be helped to get from one place to the next.

Obviously, your friends and family can be of great help. However, most areas have some form of transit assistance for seniors and handicapped persons. Your community may have one or more of the following: escort services, discounted senior public transit, coupons for discount taxi services, volunteer or community-supported drivers, and prescheduled van service for handicapped persons.

Taxi Service In some areas, seniors are able to purchase taxi coupons that entitle them to use private taxis for a fraction of the usual cost. These taxis are generally only for use within the community in which you live. Contact Information and Referral or your City Hall for information.

Public Transit Most areas that have public transit offer seniors a discount fare. Proof of age (usually 65 or older) is required. A state senior gold card (issued by the State Department of Consumer Affairs) is a convenient proof. There can be some disadvantages to public transit; for example, most of the routes may be designed for commuters and may be too far away from hospitals, senior centers, senior housing complexes, and other facilities. And senior discounts are sometimes only honored at non-peak commuter hours. The amount of discount varies — some transportation services are free at non-peak hours, others charge 10¢ for the first zone, then 5¢ for each additional zone, and others charge more.

The San Francisco Bay Area Rapid Transit (BART) system offers a unique type of discount. A ticket worth $6 can be purchased for only 60 cents from a bank near each stop. Telephone (415) 788-2278 for the name of the bank near you if you live in the Bay Area.

Public Door-to-Door Transit Los Angeles has a plan called Senior Ride for seniors 60 and over that provides free door-to-door rides in four areas within the city limits. This service requires 24-hour advance notice. Inquire through Information and Referral or a senior center for the boundaries of your area and for the telephone number if you live in Los Angeles. If this doesn't work out, then call (213) 485-4402 for the Aging Division of the Community Development Department.

Other counties and cities have similar programs called such names as "Senior Ride" or "Dial-a-Ride." These services may make wide use of volunteers, though generally they are contracted out to a non-profit provider or are a part of a municipal transit system, particularly when specially equipped mini-buses are used. Services are almost always available to handicapped people, many of whom are seniors.

In metropolitan areas, there is often van group transportation scheduled at certain hours for travel to and from centers and dining rooms.

Private Agencies Many social services, such as the American Red Cross, the Cancer Society, Catholic Family Services, and many others, contribute a great deal to the necessary transportation of seniors and the handicapped. Their programs and funding vary. Some operate their own vehicles, including vans and mini-buses, some are equipped with chair lifts and are generally driven by volunteers. Some volunteers use their own cars. The uniqueness of each county's and city's plans makes the centralized and coordinated Information and Referral Service important. This is where you should go for information.

Rural Areas If you live in the country and don't drive, transportation is a real problem for you. Hopefully you will have family nearby or friends to help you. In some counties there are scheduled minibus services on certain days of the week to and from the nearest central city, where services are centralized. Some county hospitals offer direct transportation on scheduled dates for non-emergency visits. In other rural areas your bus fare into town may be subsidized.

Distance Transportation Discounts AMTRAK now offers a rate reduction for people aged 65 and older. For fares of $40 or more, there is a reduction of 25% for travel in one direction only. For a round-trip visit you must pay full fare for the return trip. Proof of age is required. Greyhound Bus Lines offer a 13% discount for persons aged 65 or over. Again, proof of age is required. Ask about discounts for other bus lines.

Most major airlines offer a senior citizen discount for those aged 65 and over with proof of age. However, this is no bonanza, since special excursion rates for coach travel are generally much lower. The advantage of the senior discount is for fares bought during the last 24 hours before departure, since these are less than the standard coach fare. For travel between San Francisco and Los Angeles, the commuter coach fare is less than the senior discount fare. However, the fare between these cities and Seattle, for example, is often a bargain to seniors.

Escort Service This senior benefit can be utilized in two ways: to help the frail or handicapped keep necessary appointments, and to assist seniors with protected transportation in high crime areas. The police are often very active in sponsoring this service, although the escorts are usually volunteers.

The record of escort services in preventing criminal assaults on seniors in dangerous areas is excellent. Unfortunately, the need for the service is greater than its availability. One answer to this is group-escorted trips that are scheduled in advance, and many California communities have adopted such a modification.

Escort services do not exist in many rural communities, but they are generally found in urban areas. If you are interested, make inquiries of your local Information and Referral Service or Area Agency on Aging, and be persistent.

Discounts for Merchandise and Services

These are truly local programs usually initiated by seniors. The success of a discount program depends on the enthusiasm and push of community support, hard leg work, and persistence.

Merced County has just proudly issued an excellent directory of discounts for merchandise and services offered by local businesses to help seniors stretch their limited budgets. The park and recreation department joined with the seniors in organizing the drive, and the board of supervisors helped with the printing costs. The directory spoke of the "show of strength when older Americans work together for a common good."

The San Francisco Bay Area has many such local programs, as does San Diego. The key to their success is a handy directory widely distributed to seniors. Merchants are also asked to put discount stickers on their windows.

If your community does not have such a program, you can start organizing one. From January 1981 through December 1982 the Department of Consumer Affairs is authorized to give technical help and how-to information to seniors setting up discount programs in their communities. Check with your Area Agency about your plans. If this doesn't work out, write or call the

Department of Consumer Affairs
Development and Resource Unit
Senior Programs
1020 North R St., Room 591
Sacramento, CA 95814

or call (916) 323-7237. Good luck!

Discounts on merchandise and services range from pharmacies to hot tubs, from barber and beauty shops to automobile repair, from restaurants to free notary service, and from hearing aids to cleaners. Your pet may also receive a discount at veterinarians and pet shops. Local grocery stores usually offer discounts on a scheduled Tuesday or Thursday.

In some communities there are discounts but no directory is published. Look for signs advertising these discounts outside as well as inside places of business and amusement. And don't hesitate to ask if you're in doubt.

Proof of Age Proof of age is always expected. Some discount programs are available to seniors 60 or older, some to persons 62 or older, and some to persons 65 or older.

The State Department of Consumer Affairs issues state senior citizens' discount gold cards, which are accepted as proof. These cards can be obtained at Information and Referral offices or at senior centers. A gold card sticker can also be added to a local discount card.

The state Department of Motor Vehicles issues an identification card for non-drivers that costs $3. You will need other proof of age to obtain this card.

Bank and Savings & Loan Benefits If you have reached 62 years of age, many banks and savings and loans offer you special services. These services might include:

- unlimited check writing privileges with no service charge and no minimum balance required
- special, personalized checks at no charge
- travelers' checks issued without commission charges
- direct deposit of Social Security benefits and other recurring federal payments (see Chapter One)
- check guarantee cards, if you qualify

Health Related Discounts Discounts may be found at pharmacies and at businesses selling optical products, hearing aids, and prosthetic assistive devices, such as crutches, wheelchairs, and other devices to equip homes for invalids. Be sure that these devices and pieces of equipment are recommended by a health care professional and that this professional examines what you buy and teaches you how to use it correctly.

Discount dental care and health screenings are discussed in Chapter Ten.

Telephone Aids for the Deaf In January 1981, the state Public Utilities Commission voted to provide free telecommunication devices to allow deaf people to receive printed messages over their telephones. These telephone users can only transmit to a similar telephone. Your telephone company is probably the best source of further information. It will be a while before these aids are actually in use.

Utilities At the present time there seems to be no rate discount for seniors in northern California. But for Los Angeles city residents there is a senior citizen utility tax exemption program available for financially qualified seniors. In Los Angeles, call (213) 485-3972 for further information.

There are lifeline rates for gas, electricity, and telephone available to the community as a whole. If you stay below a certain lifeline rate of consumption, you are charged at the lowest rate.

Fish and Game Licenses Licenses are free to persons 62 and over with a minimal income — $420 monthly if single and $773 if married.

National Park Facilities The national parks offer persons 62 or older "Golden Age Passport" cards free of charge. These cards entitle the holder to admission to and use of national park facilities all year without admission or use fees. Cards can be obtained at the entrance to any national park.

Funerals A simple traditional funeral, which includes embalming, hearse, and a simple casket but not a cemetery plot, will cost somewhere around $1,700 – $1,900. This is what a reputable mortuary must charge for overhead, merchandise, and profit.

Local funeral societies offer an alternative. These are non-profit groups that usually charge a membership fee of about $15. For this, members receive funeral information and low-cost rates for funerals. The society asks various mortuaries in the area to bid on contracts to provide simple traditional funerals and cremations for all group members. Group buying power can lower the cost of a traditional funeral to $750 – $900.

Another alternative to costly funerals is provided by the Teleophase Society in southern California — (714) 299-0805 — and the Memorial Society in northern California — (415) 493-2335. These non-profit organizations will record a person's wishes regarding a funeral and then, after his or her death, carry out those wishes. For around $400 they will do all of the following: transport remains, arrange for cremation, scatter or do as requested with ashes, and handle Social Security and Veteran's benefits paperwork. Families of recently deceased persons can also use these services. The Neptune Society also provides similar low-cost disposal of remains throughout California.

All of the above organizations can be located by calling your local Information and Referral or by looking in the white pages of your telephone directory.

Library and Book Services Libraries offer special help to seniors, in addition to the services provided to the public generally. For example, upon request, books can be delivered to seniors at their homes by volunteers. The same service may provide phonograph records and paintings. In some areas, this service is provided by RSVP (Retired Seniors Volunteer Program).

Book mobiles stop at locations where there are a number of seniors, such as senior centers and senior residence areas.

Usually libraries have available books printed in large type for the visually impaired. These may include best sellers in paperback as well as the classics.

Education

Community colleges and the adult high school education program offer a wide variety of classes that are open to seniors as well as the rest of the public. Private and state colleges and universities are open to persons of all ages, but everyone must meet the scholastic and admission requirements.

Community colleges are far more flexible, requiring only that you be age 18 or above and live in a designated area. Furthermore, they charge no tuition fees. If you don't want to compete, you may take some classes for no credit or grade. Remember also that you may find that you can compete very well with other students.

The staff at community colleges (an some state universities) teach at senior centers by means of out-reach programs. Some of the more successful of these programs include four weekly classes on an academic subject or adaptive physical education classes.

Seniors are generally as eligible for educational financial aid as anyone else. This aid includes student loans, grants, and student work-study programs. Most student aid is exempt from SSI requirements and partially exempt from the earnings maximum of Social Security benefits.

For further information on financial aid, contact the financial aid office at the educational institution you have chosen. Remember that student loan programs have deadlines, usually the first of February for the coming academic year.

Nutritional and Food Programs

In many cities, there are central dining rooms that offer free or reduced cost hot meals to seniors — usually at midday. Often you will be requested to make a donation of 50 cents or 75 cents in a sealed envelope. There is generally a van service to and from these dining rooms. Often these dining rooms are located in large senior centers in order to afford the seniors who come there to eat access to other senior services. For seniors who are homebound, meals are delivered, usually by volunteers.

For more information about local food and nutritional programs call Information and Referral or your Area Agency on Aging. Congregate senior meals, home delivered meals, and Food Stamps are discussed in detail in Chapter Ten.

Produce Distribution and Community Gardens The diets of many seniors, especially those of low income, are too often inadequate nutritionally and especially lacking in fresh produce. Throughout the state there are programs, sometimes called Food Banks, where fresh produce is collected and distributed through a senior center brown bag program and delivered to homebound seniors.

The produce can be surplus from a community garden, or purchased in large discounted quantities through a grower, or donated.

Often there is a canning facility connected with a community garden, and classes are given in canning procedures. Seniors who are interested in gardening can be allotted their own plot in the community garden and are free to use the produce themselves.

Food Cooperatives In food cooperatives people join together to buy food at a discount rate. In some areas — San Diego, for example — these cooperatives receive some government help. Generally cooperatives are started by private groups made up of people of all ages. Seniors are encouraged to join, often at a reduced membership fee. These co-ops have been so successful that they are spreading throughout the state. Buying produce and other foodstuffs in large quantities can mean sizeable savings. Seniors, friends, and neighbors can join together informally and buy food in quantity at considerable savings from a co-op, market, or from a farmer who trucks in his produce.

Trends

The change in the national administration has left us all wondering about the future of senior programs. The most widespread guess is that the basic structure will remain intact, but there will be budget slashes in some programs. Now more than ever it is important that seniors remain informed and be heard loudly and clearly when help for basic necessities is threatened. Probably local programs will remain, though future funding for new facilities will be difficult.

Volunteer and new innovative services will be more important than ever, and the need for seniors to help other seniors will increase. Older adults are creative, and their abilities and persistence do pay off.

The trend now is for businesses, banks, and local merchants (the private sector, in other words) to work together with senior agencies and volunteers to create new services and extend existing ones. For example, the *Sacramento Bee* printed a directory of senior citizens programs as a Sunday supplement. This was done in connection with the Area Agency, senior centers, and the park and recreation department. This directory is available throughout the year, and the advertisers, including church groups, get continued exposure. Everyone comes out a winner.

Use your talents, volunteer, and get involved. We hope your life will be richer for the experience.

Appendix

Area Agencies on Aging

County/Counties Served	Agency, Address, & Telephone
Del Norte, Humboldt	Area 1 Agency on Aging Humboldt Senior Citizens Council 3300 Glenwood Street Eureka, CA 95501 (707) 442-3763
Lassen, Modoc, Shasta, Siskiyou, Trinity	PSA 2 Area Agency on Aging P.O. Box 1400 Yreka, CA 96097 (916) 842-1687
Butte, Colusa, Glenn, Plumas, Tehama	PSA 3 Area Agency on Aging University Foundation California State University — Chico Second and Normal Streets Chico, CA 95929 (916) 895-5961
Nevada, Placer, Sacramento, Sierra, Sutter, Yolo, Yuba	Area 4 Agency on Aging 1820 J Street Sacramento, CA 95814 (916) 447-7063
Marin	Marin County Area Agency on Aging Marin County Civic Center Room 279 San Rafael, CA 94903 (415) 499-7396

San Francisco	San Francisco City & County Commission on Aging 1095 Market Street, #700 San Francisco, CA 94103 (415) 558-2126
Contra Costa	Contra Costa Office on Aging 2425 Bisso Lane, Suite 110 Concord, CA 94520 (415) 671-4233
San Mateo	San Mateo Area Agency on Aging 617 Hamilton Street Redwood City, CA 94063 (415) 364-5600 ext. 4511
Alameda	Alameda County Area Agency on Aging 1755 Broadway, 5th Floor Oakland, CA 94612 (415) 874-7233
Santa Clara	Council on Aging of Santa Clara County, Inc. 277 W. Hedding Street San Jose, CA 95110 (408) 287-7111
San Joaquin	San Joaquin County Area Agency on Aging 222 E. Weber Avenue Stockton, CA 95202 (209) 944-2202
Alpine, Amador, Calaveras, Mariposa, Tuolumne	Central Sierra Area Agency on Aging 56 North Washington Street Sonora, CA 95370 (209) 532-6272
San Benito, Santa Cruz	Seniors Council of Santa Cruz and San Benito Counties, Inc. 234 Santa Cruz Avenue Aptos, CA 95003 (408) 688-0400
Fresno, Madera	Fresno-Madera Area Agency on Aging 2014 Tulare Street, Suite 611 Fresno, CA 93721 (209) 488-1584
Kings, Tulare	Kings-Tulare Area Agency on Aging 1821 W. Meadow Lane Avenue, Suite F Visalia, CA 93277 (209) 733-1079

Inyo, Mono	Inyo-Mono Area Agency on Aging P.O. Box 1799 Bishop, CA 93514 (714) 873-5240
San Luis Obispo, Santa Barbara	Central Coast Commission for Senior Citizens Area Agency on Aging 301 S. Miller Street Santa Maria, CA 93454 (805) 925-9554
Ventura	Ventura County Area Agency on Aging 800 S. Victoria Road Lower Plaza Ventura, CA 93003 (805) 654-3660
Los Angeles County	Los Angeles County Department of Senior Citizens Affairs 601 South Kingsley Drive Los Angeles, CA 90005 (213) 738-3281
San Bernardino	Office on Aging 602 S. Tippecanoe, Bldg. #3, Room 1320 San Bernardino, CA 92415 (714) 383-3861
Riverside	County of Riverside Office on Aging 647 N. Main Street, Bldg. 3 Riverside, CA 92501 (714) 683-7780
Orange	Orange County Area Agency on Aging 801-C North Broadway Santa Ana, CA 92701 (714) 834-6017
San Diego	San Diego County Area Agency on Aging 8665 Gibbs Drive San Diego, CA 92123 (714) 560-2427
Imperial	Imperial County Area Agency on Aging 654 Main Street El Centro, CA 92243 (714) 352-8521

Los Angeles City	Los Angeles City Area Agency on Aging Community Development Department Aging Division 215 W. Sixth Street, 6th Floor Los Angeles, CA 90014 (213) 485-4402
Lake, Mendocino	Northcoast Opportunities, Inc. Area Agency on Aging 101 W. Church Street Ukiah, CA 95482 (707) 462-1954
Sonoma	Sonoma County Area Agency on Aging 2230 Professional Drive Santa Rosa, CA 95401 (707) 527-3153
Napa, Solano	Solano-Napa Agency on Aging 1814 Capitol Street Vallejo, CA 94590 (707) 644-6612
El Dorado	El Dorado County Area Agency on Aging 330 Fair Lane Placerville, CA 95667 (916) 626-2149
Stanislaus	Stanislaus County Area Agency on Aging 1024 J Street, Room 416 Modesto, CA 95354 (209) 526-6700
Merced	Merced County Area Agency for Aging Programs 2150 M Street, Suite 3 Merced, CA 95340 (209) 726-7550
Monterey	Department of Social Services Area Agency on Aging Division 1322 Natividad Road P.O. Box 299 Salinas, CA 93902 (408) 757-2911
Kern	Kern County Office on Aging 1100 26th Street Bakersfield, CA 93301 (805) 861-2445

Index

Update Supplement Information

To place your name on the publisher's mailing list for information on update supplements to this book, send your name and mailing address (including ZIP code) to:

Cragmont Publications
SPC Supplements
P.O. Box 77072
San Francisco, CA 94107

Registering your name does not obligate you to purchase anything.